A HISTORY OF THE JEWISH PEOPLE DURING PERSIAN, AND GREEK PERIODS • CHARLES FOSTER KENT

Publisher's Note

The book descriptions we ask booksellers to display prominently warn that this is an historic book with numerous typos or missing text; it is not indexed or illustrated.

The book was created using optical character recognition software. The software is 99 percent accurate if the book is in good condition. However, we do understand that even one percent can be an annoying number of typos! And sometimes all or part of a page may be missing from our copy of the book. Or the paper may be so discolored from age that it is difficult to read. We apologize and gratefully acknowledge Google's assistance.

After we re-typeset and design a book, the page numbers change so the old index and table of contents no longer work. Therefore, we often remove them; otherwise, please ignore them.

We carefully proof read any book that will sell enough copies to pay for the proof reader; unfortunately, many don't. For those we try to let customers download a free copy of the original typo-free book. Simply enter the barcode number from the back cover of the paperback in the Free Book form at www.RareBooksClub.com. You may also qualify for a free trial membership in our book club to download up to four books for free. Simply enter the barcode number from the back cover onto the membership form on our home page. The book club entitles you to select from more than a million books at no additional charge. Simply enter the title or subject onto the search form to find the books.

If you have any questions, could you please be so kind as to consult our Frequently Asked Questions page at www. RareBooksClub.com/faqs.cfm? You are also welcome to contact us there.

General Books LLC™, Memphis, USA, 2012. ISBN: 9781150535468.

-⚬- -⚬- -⚬- -⚬- -⚬- -⚬- -⚬- -⚬-

Edited by Professor CHARLES F. KENT, Ph.D., of Brown University, and Professor FRANK K. SANDERS, Ph.D., of Yale University.

IN response to a widespread demand for non-technical yet scholarly and reliable guides to the study of the history, literature, and teaching of the Old and New Testaments, and of the contemporary history and literature, this series aims to present in concise and attractive form the results of investigation and exploration in these broad fields. Based upon thoroughly critical scholarship, it will emphasize assured and positive rather than transitional positions. The series as a whole is intended to present a complete and connected picture of the social, political, and religious life of the men and peoples who figure most prominently in the biblical records. Each volume will be complete in itself, treating comprehensively a given subject or period. It will also refer freely to the biblical and monumental sources, and to the standard authorities. Convenience of size, clearness of presentation, and helpfulness to the student, will make the series particularly well adapted for (i) practical text-books for college, seminary, and university classes; (2) handbooks for the use of Bible classes, clubs, and guilds; (3) guides for individual study; and (4) books for general reference.

HISTORY OF THE HEBREW PEOPLE.
I. The United Kingdom. Fifth edition. Charles F. Kent, Ph.D., Professor of Biblical Literature and History, Brown /. The Divided Kingdom. Fifth edi-University.

HISTORY OF THE JEWISH PEOPLE. 3. The Babylonian, Persian, and Greek Charles F. Kent, Ph.D., Professor of Periods. Biblical Literature and History, Brown University.
4. The Maccabean and Roman Period

James S. Riggs, D.D., Professor of Bib- (including New Testament Times). lical Criticism, Auburn Theological Sem inary. CONTEMPORARY OLD TESTAMENT HISTORY. 5. History of the Egyptians. James H. Breasted, Ph.D., Assistant Professor of Semitic Languages and Egyptology, The University of Chicago. 6. History of the Babylonians and As- George S. Goodspeed, Ph.D., Professor Syrians. of Ancient History, The University of Chicago.

NEW TESTAMENT HISTORIES. 7. The Life of Jesus. Rush Rhees, Professor of New Testament Interpretation, Newton Theological Seminary.
8. The Apostolic Age. George T. Purves, Ph.D., D.D., Pro fessor of New Testament Literature and Exegesis, Princeton Theological Seminary.

OUTLINES FOR THE STUDY OF BIBLICAL HISTORY AND LITERATURE.
g. From Earliest Times to the Cap- Frank K. Sanders, Ph.D., Professor tivity. of Biblical Literature, Yale University. 10. From the Exile to 200 A.D. urt »url «. II.

I-.M-. 111. Oc hy- PREFACE

The destruction of Jerusalem in 586 B. c. by the army of Nebuchadrezzar marks a radical turning-point in the life of the people of Jehovah, for then the history of the Hebrew state and monarchy ends, and Jewish history, the record of the experiences, not of a nation but of the scattered, oppressed remnants of the Jewish race, begins. Henceforth, not Judeans and Israelites, but Jews and Samaritans are the chief actors in the great drama which the biblical writings record. This sharp distinction between Hebrew and Jewish history is also based upon the fundamental difference in the life, thought, and religion of the chosen people before and after the great catastrophe of 586 B. c. The transformation was as complete as it was sudden.

There was really little in common between the careless, self-confident Hebrews to whom Amos and Isaiah preached, and the despondent, sin-oppressed Jews to whom Bzekiel and Haggai addressed their stirring appeals.

Until within comparatively recent times the four centuries which followed the destruction of Jerusalem have ordinarily been regarded as the least important and the most uninteresting of those which constitute the background of the Bible. The results of modern critical study, however, have revealed their supreme importance. To the student of the Old Testament they are of the deepest interest, for they witnessed for the first time the popular acceptance of the principles enunciated by the pre-exilic prophets, and the remarkable expansion and application of the ceremonial law. It is now generally accepted that more than half of the literature of the Old Testament comes from this period, when the leaders of the Jewish race meditated and wrote rather than acted; while probably every book of that ancient library was either written then, or else edited and revised. The most perplexing problems of Bible study — the date of the Psalms, of the Book of Job, and of Isaiah xl. to lxvi., and the composition of the Hexateuch — all belong to this age, so that a familiarity with it is absolutely essential to an understanding of the literature of the Old Testament.

It was also the age which selected certain writings from the common literary heritage of the race and declared that they were sacred and authoritative, so that before 165 B. c. the canon of the law and of the prophets was practically closed.

For the New Testament scholar these centuries possess equally. great attractions, since in them the life gradually developed, and the parties arose and the ideas gained acceptance, which furnish the setting and the atmosphere of the New Testament history and teaching. To the student of Christianity they are of the greatest interest, for then many of the religious rites and usages developed, which, adopted with but slight modifications, have become the institutions of the Christian Church.

PREFACE. Vii

The age also possesses an unequalled importance for the study of comparative religions, since then Jehovah-ism came into intimate contact with and was more or less influenced by the four great representative religions of the past, — the Assyro-Babylonian, the Egyptian, the Persian, and the Greek. It will also never cease to fascinate and hold the attention of the general student of ancient and modern history, because then was born and developed that marvel of all succeeding ages — Judaism.

Modern biblical research has placed a wealth of new and varied materials at the disposal of the historian. The task of reconstruction is peculiarly difficult, but for that, as well as for the other reasons which have been suggested, exceedingly fascinating. The testimony of the new sources and a more careful study of the old have made necessary the revision of many conclusions long regarded as established. Fortunately most of the changes only involve questions of historical fact, so that they are assured of a dispassionate and fair consideration. That the reader may be in possession of the data, so as to form an independent judgment, full references to the sources have been inserted in the text. References to sections, preceded by the Roman numerals I. and II., refer respectively to the first and second volumes of this history, which treat the period before the exile.

It is well that in these latter days we are learning to be content at times with a mere probability, or even with leaving a doubtful question open, since our historical sources often do not furnish us with the basis for an absolute certainty. If " probably " seems a mannerism in the present volume, the reason is obvious.

While many of the conclusions suggested will doubtless be modified by later study, it has been a constant source of encouragement to find that other investigators in this and foreign countries, working independently, have arrived at the same results. The debt which I owe to them is partially indicated in the list of books of reference given in Appendix III.

It has also been my privilege to profit by the valuable critical suggestions of Professors Frank K. Sanders, Ph.D., and George S. Goodspeed, Ph.D., and by the constant collaboration of my wife and sister.

C. P. K.

Brown University, *March* 21, 1899.

THE HISTORICAL SOURCES AND LITERATURE OF THE PERIOD 1. During the dark half century, which followed the destruction of Jerusalem in 586 B. c., and which is known as the period of the Babylonian exile, Jewish historians found but one political event which they deemed worthy of recording. The second Book of Kings closes pathetically with a short note telling of the release of the Jewish king Jehoiakin from his long confinement in Babylonian prisons. Their silence is all the more significant because the period was by no means one of literary inactivity. It emphasizes the fact that the real history of this important epoch is not the record of external events, but of the mighty struggles and transformations going on within the souls of the Jewish exiles, who were scattered throughout the great Babylonian empire. That record is found in no connected narrative, but must be reconstructed from the sermons of prophets and the songs of poets. These, however, represent the testimony of earnest, inspired men who themselves saw and felt that of which they spoke, so that during the Babylonian exile the inner life of the Jewish people is revealed as at no other epoch in their history. 2. During the fateful years which intervene between the first and second deportation, Jeremiah describes, in the twenty-fourth chapter of his prophecy, the character of the first group of exiles who were carried away with Jehoiakin, while chapter xxix. contains a pastoral letter which he wrote to them in their new home. Chapter xliv. introduces us, through the stern preaching of the aged prophet, to the exiles in Egypt, among whom he spent his last days. The section, I. 2 to li. 58, which treats of the destruction of Babylon, clearly reflects an age subsequent to that in which Jeremiah lived and labored and is therefore an important source for the period under consideration. The exiles in Babylon to whom it is addressed are not urged to " build houses and dwell in them," as they were by the great prophet in his pastoral letter (xxix.); but instead they are earnestly exhorted to flee with all possible haste from the doomed city (1. 8; li. 6, 45). The long years of exile predicted by Jeremiah are nearing a close. Babylon's destroyers are already upon the northern horizon (I. 3, 9, 41); in fact, the author of the section calls them by name; they are the Medes (li. 11), and at their head is Jehovah's agent of destruction. This leader can be no other than Cyrus, who in 549 B. c., after becoming master of the Median empire (sect. 63), entered upon that career of conquest which ended a decade later, as the prophet predicts, in the capture of Babylon. The evident exultation with which the impending overthrow of the mighty city is proclaimed, also reflects the experiences of one who had himself felt the pains of the Babylonian exile, rather than the experiences of Jeremiah, who at the final destruction of Jerusalem was liberated by the conquerors (xxxix.), and who in his latest breath continued to declare that the Babylonian king was carry- THE PROPHECIES OF EZEKIEL 5 ing out Jehovah's will among the nations (xliv. 30). The many passages which reveal familiarity with exilic prophets, and the style, which is more diffuse than that of Jeremiah, furnish additional evidence which indicates that the author was some unknown prophet, perhaps a disciple of Jeremiah, writing during the period following 549 and preceding 539 B. c. The notice in li. 59-64 of a prophecy written by Jeremiah concerning the evil that would come upon Babylon, probably gave the suggestion to the later editor which led him to place these chapters in their present setting. 3. Bzekiel, naturally a man of method, and writing in the calm of the exile, carefully dated most of his prophecies. His work began in the year 592 and his latest prophecy is dated 570 B. c. (i. 2; xxix. 17). During the six

years which immediately preceded the final destruction of Jerusalem, his energies were chiefly devoted to the consideration of the grave moral and political dangers which imperilled the existence of the Judean kingdom. Chapters i. to xxiv. record this activity and contain only chance suggestions concerning the thought and conditions of the exiles who shared the captivity with him. Chapters xxv. to xxxii. consist of foreign prophecies, written for the most part contemporaneously with the fall of Jerusalem. As soon as the Jewish sanctuary lay in ruins, Bzekiel turned his entire attention to the exiles in Babylon, in whom he recognized the preservers of the best religious life of his race. The remainder of his book (xxxiii. to xlviii.), written between the years 585 and 572 B. c., is the monument of his devotion to them. Chapters xxxiii. to xxxix. constitute the best extant historical source for the earlier half of the exile; while xl. to xlviii. contain Ezekiel's program for the restored Jewish state, which he predicted would ultimately be reestablished in the land of Canaan with Jerusalem as its centre. 4. Certain chapters of the Book of Isaiah reflect, not the problems and storms of Assyrian invasion which agitated the people of Judah, to whom Isaiah, the son of Amoz, addressed his stirring sermons, but instead the totally changed conditions amidst which, two centuries later, the Jewish exiles in Babylon moved. When one recalls the tendency, so strong in later circles, to assign all anonymous pieces of literature to some earlier writer, who figured as the chief representative of the department of thought to which he belonged, the inference that the Book of Isaiah contains prophecies from other and later hands, causes no surprise. The same habits of editorship, which, in an age when the modern historical and literary methods of determining date and authorship were unknown, assigned all ancient Hebrew proverbs and many very late books, like Ecclesiastes and the Wisdom of Solomon, to Solomon, the majority of the Psalms to David, many apocalyptic writings to Enoch, and all the laws to Moses, most naturally in-

fluenced later editors to attribute certain anonymous prophecies to the prince of prophets. The author of the Gospel of Mark, in the opening of his narrative (i. 2), illustrates the same tendency when he introduces a quotation, the first part of which comes from the Book of Malachi (iii.), with the words " even as it is written in Isaiah, the prophet." No thoughtful student can fail to recognize a providential influence in this harm- EXILIC SECTIONS IN THE BOOK OF ISAIAH 7 less custom, which preserved many a priceless literary treasure from the oblivion which otherwise threatened to engulf it; for the succeeding ages were prone to give more attention to the name associated with a given writing than to the eternal message which it contained. 5. Even a cursory reading of the section, Isaiah xiii. 2 to xiv. 23, furnishes conclusive evidence that its historical background is the Babylonian exile. Already Babylon, which in the days of Isaiah was, like Judah, a vassal state subject to Nineveh, has passed the zenith of its power and is declining. The author bids his fellow exiles unite in a song of exultation over the impending destruction of this harsh taskmaster, who has so long oppressed them (xiv. 3-23); for his fall means for them restoration to their native land and the rebuilding of their destroyed temple. The agents of Babylon's overthrow, as in Jeremiah li. 11, are mentioned: the Medes, who in the days of Isaiah, the son of Amoz, were known only as a mountain people whose territory furnished a favorite field for Assyrian conquest. The language and religious ideas of the passage also present far more affinities with the writings of exilic prophets than with those of Isaiah. Thus the evidence becomes cumulative that the author was some unknown prophet living not long before the capture of Babylon. The absence of a distinct reference to Cyrus suggests that the section was written either a short time before or not long after 549 B. c., when the Median empire merged into the Persian. 6. The same age and general conditions constitute the background of the sublime message of comfort anS inspiration contained in chapters xl. to lv. of the Book of Isaiah. To the stirring political movements which characterized the closing years of Babylonian rule, there are clear and repeated references. The deliverer, who in Jehovah's providence is to restore the Jewish exiles to their desolate land and city, is not a distant people, but the advancing conqueror Cyrus, Jehovah's anointed, toward whom the eyes of the captives were eagerly turning (xli. 2; xliv. 28; xlv. 1). The energies of the prophet are not devoted, as were those of Isaiah ben Amoz two centuries before, to directing the policy of Judah in right channels, nor to correcting moral or social wrongs; but instead his aim is to encourage and inspire the halting exiles to return, and to offer themselves and their interests in Babylon to the noble service of rebuilding their city and temple, when once the opportunity comes, which he sees fast approaching. The Messianic ideals are also very different. The condensed, stately, and abrupt diction of the earlier prophet, characteri/ed by its peculiar phrases, is exchanged for the flowing, highly developed, closely connected, and often impassioned style which is begotten by quiet meditation and study rather than by public preaching. Many expressions peculiar to chapters xl. to lv., as for example "seize his right hand," "call by name" (xlv. 1, 3, 4; compare Cyrus Cyl. 12), are at once recognized by the student of Assyrian and Babylonian literature as characteristic of the court language of Babylon. These water marks, as well as the vivid historical allusions, confirm the conclusion that the prophet was personally acquainted with the political life of the doomed city. His new conception of Jehovah and of the divine will DATE AND AUTHORSHIP OF ISAIAH XL. TO LV. 9 reveals the development of thought during the two revolutionizing centuries which intervene between Isaiah and the great prophet, who proclaims to the exiles in Babylon the new and glorious message which Jehovah has revealed to his waiting heart. 7. Since the remaining chapters of the Book of Isaiah present striking variations in style, thought, and

especially in the historical background which they reflect, they are reserved for later consideration; but, notwithstanding the occasional evidence of the work of later editors, which sometimes obscures the original thought, no one can seriously question the unity of the sections xl. to lv. These chapters as a whole are illuminated by the same fervid spirit, the same powerful figures, the same dramatic power, and the same breadth of vision, elements which were united to such a remarkable degree in the productions of no other Old Testament writer. The one theme also is restoration; and running through all is the new and marvellous conception of service, which makes the section unique. The same themes are repeatedly treated, and certain passages, as for example those which describe the servant of Jehovah, constitute distinct units, independent of each other, and only loosely connected with the general context. These facts suggest that the whole, like the Book of Jeremiah, is made up of smaller tracts written at different times and finally combined by the prophet himself, or possibly by one of his disciples. 8. In the collection contained in chapters xl. to xlviii., Cyrus is the central figure, and the fall of Babylon is predicted as something still anticipated in the future. The critical period between 549 and 539 B. c. is, therefore, established as the background of the section. In chapters xlix. to lv. attention is focused more and more on Jerusalem, suggesting that the hour was near at hand, if it had not already arrived, when the conquest of Babylon by Cyrus made it possible for the Jews to turn their faces toward the sacred city. Certain references might be regarded as evidence that when the author wrote he already stood on the soil of Canaan; but the language as a whole is best satisfied by the hypothesis that he was still in Babylon, urging his reluctant countrymen to improve the opportunity which opened to them and, by devoting themselves loyally and unreservedly to the arduous task of rebuilding their capital city, to reap the blessings which Jehovah was ready to bestow. This clarion call to duty may, it

is true, have been issued at any time during the following century, while the struggling community in Canaan longed and prayed for a general return of their race; but the superlative exaltation of its language and thought proclaims it to be from the same inspired spirit who speaks to the exiles in the preceding chapters, and the stirring days which witnessed the conquest of Babylon by Cyrus furnish the only entirely satisfactory background. 9. The pitiful group of Jews who were permitted by the Babylonians to remain in Judah were not left without spokesmen to voice their grief. The shortest and saddest of the prophetic books — Obadiah — fixes our attention upon conditions in Palestine. Its theme is the denunciation of the conduct of Judah's hereditary foes, the Edomites, in the hour of Jerusalem's humiliation. The hostility between these rival Semitic peoples extended through many centuries, and its de- AUTHOK-SIilP OF THE BOOK OF LAMENTATIONS 11 tails are frequently veiled in such obscurity that it is impossible to determine with certainty what are the exact events to which the prophet alludes. The close parallel in language as well as thought, between Jeremiah xlix. 7-22, and Obadiah 1-7, indicates that one is quoted from the other, or both from a common source. The prophecy may have been finally edited daring the Persian period, but on the whole the testimony of the varied evidence is that the author of the Book of Obadiah incorporated the words of an earlier prophet, and wrote during the opening years of the exile, referring to wrongs which perhaps he himself witnessed. 10. Another remarkably vivid picture of the scenes attendant upon the destruction of Jerusalem, and of the feelings with which the scattered exiles regarded those events, is preserved in the Book of Lamentations. From the third or fourth century B. c. comes a tradition, adopted by the translators of the Septuagint, that Jeremiah wrote these elegies. The element of prophecy which runs through the book, the elegiac tone and certain expressions which characterize it, recall many passages in the sermons of that prophet.

That he survived the destruction of Jerusalem is well known, and, therefore, no one can assert absolutely that there is not a basis for the tradition that Jeremiah was the author. On the other hand, the alphabetical arrangement of the verses in chapters i. to iv., according to which in the Hebrew each succeeding verse (or, as in the case of chapter iii., each group of three verses) begins with a succeeding letter of the alphabet, reveals an artificiality which is the antithesis of Jeremiah's ordinary style. Many surprising expressions, foreign to his prophecies, also occur. Frequently the point of view is not that of the Jeremiah whom we know, but of the people whose errors he combated (i. 21, 22; ii. 9; iv. 17, 20). In the light of Jeremiah xxxi. 29, 30, the statement (v. 7) that " our fathers have sinned and are not; and we have borne their iniquities " would be a direct contradiction to one of the prophet's most positive doctrines. Certain striking analogies with Ezekiel's sermons suggest familiarity with his utterances (compare ii. 14, with Ezek. xiii. and xxii. 28; ii. 4 with Ezek. xxiv. 16, 21, 25). In chapter v. the different point of view, as well as the absence of the alphabetical arrangement, raises the additional question whether one or several authors are represented in the book. Certainly in the closing chapter the strong hope of speedy restoration, repeatedly expressed in the preceding chapter, is supplanted by the wail, " Wherefore dost thou forsake us forever?" (v. 20"). On the whole the conclusion most in accord with all the facts is that the book consists of two or more originally independent sections, and comes from certain disciples of Jeremiah or Ezekiel, familiar with conditions in Palestine during the period of their nation's humiliation. The testimony of the book, therefore, like that of most of the sources for the period, is of the highest value, because it is practically contemporaneous with the events and conditions which it records. Several psalms, as, for example, the forty-second and forty-third, also voice the lamentations of faithful souls deprived of the enjoyment of their land and sanctuary. It is not impossible that they come from the period of the exile; but the absence of any clear historical allusions and the difficulty in establishing their date APOCRYPHAL WRITINGS 13 with certainty preclude their use as definite historical sources. 11. Certain other biblical and apocryphal writings, although not possessing the value of contemporary documents, preserve the impressions and dim memories of succeeding generations respecting the period under consideration. Of this character is Psalm cxxxvii., which recalls the feelings of the Jewish exiles beside the canals of Babylon. While the Book of Daniel is commonly recognized as a literary product of the post-exilic period (see sect. 261), the stories preserved in chapters i.-vi. are suggestive of the opportunities and experiences which came to gifted Jews in the lands of the exile. In the Greek version of the Book of Daniel are also incorporated two late Jewish tales which shed some reflected light upon the conditions of the Jews in the dispersion. At the beginning of the book is introduced the " History of Susanna," which relates how a beautiful Jewess of Babylon, betrayed by two elders of her people, was rescued from an unjust death by the inspired wisdom of the youthful Daniel. At the close is found in the Septuagint the fantastic story of Bel and the Dragon, which tells how Daniel exposed the deceptions of the priests of Bel and slew a great dragon which had become an object of popular worship. With the name of Baruch, Jeremiah's faithful scribe, was also associated in later time a group of prayers, confessions of national sin, and messages of consolation for the exiles, which are preserved in the apocryphal Book of Baruch. The work is clearly of composite authorship, but the section preserved in chapters i. 15 to iii. 8 may well come from the latter part of the Persian or the beginning of the Greek period, and reflects the attitude of the Jews of Palestine and of the dispersion toward the long series of national woes which was inaugurated by the disaster of 586 B. c. 12. At several points the writings of Josephus, the Jewish historian, supplement the biblical sources. Born in Jerusalem about 37 A. D., possessed of a good education, identified with his nation's history, and subsequently patronized by the Roman emperors Vespasian and Titus, he received a rare preparation for the literary work which he undertook. Unfortunately he wrote as a partisan Jew and not as an impartial historian, and, therefore, it is necessary to make constant allowance for his personal point of view and for his tendency to exaggerate or to omit facts uncomplimentary to his race. In his three great works, " The Antiquities of the Jews," " The Jewish War," and " Against Apion," he has preserved, however, a mass of valuable facts, no longer accessible elsewhere. For the earlier Hebrew history his one source was the biblical narratives, which are obscured rather than elucidated by his treatment. Respecting the period of the exile, he cites, in his treatise " Against Apion," from earlier extra-biblical historians. Chief among these authorities was the Babylonian priest Berosus, who lived in the time of Alexander the Great, and who translated a history of Babylonia into Greek. As a rule the statements of Berosus have been substantiated by later discoveries. The same cannot be said of the Halicarnassan historian, Herodotus, at least when he treats of Oriental history, nor of his rival, the Persian historian Ctesias. Their petty jealousy of rival historians, their credulity and its kindred fault, lack of accuracy, make it necessary constantly to test their statements. Notwith BABYLONIAN HISTORICAL INSCRIPTIONS 15 standing these grave faults, they furnish a wealth of valuable facts for the reconstruction of Babylonian and Persian history. 13. Fortunately we are no longer wholly dependent for our information respecting the contemporary history upon the traditions retailed by Inter writers. The kings who were the chief actors in the events of the period, now speak to us directly through their inscriptions. A large collection has been discovered, dating from the long reign of Nebuchadrezzar. With almost no exception, they all tell of his great building enterprises; while he describes these in great detail, he makes only general reference to his conquests. The most important literary monument of his reign is the so-called " East India Inscription," consisting of ten columns, which introduces us to the inner religious life and motives of the great ruler, as well as to his more important achievements. Several short building inscriptions have also been found, dating from the reign of Neriglissar, which in spirit and character closely resemble those of Nebuchadrezzar. The reign of Nabonidus, the last king of Babylon, is illumined by five or six important inscriptions, which revolutionize our conception of the period. In connection with the descriptions of his archsological excavations and temple repairs, are found not a few incidental historical references of the greatest value. His coronation inscription, discovered and published only recently, throws much light upon the events preceding and connected with his accession. The so-called " Nabonidus-Cyrus Annals" also give a condensed account of the conquests of Cyrus and the final capture of Babylon. The great conqueror himself now speaks to us, through a historical inscription which bears his name, and tells of the different steps which led to his gaining possession of the powerful city, and of the principles which guided him in his treatment of the conquered. With the aid of these varied sources of information, it is possible to reconstruct a definite picture of the conditions which constituted the background of the life and thought of the Jews during the half century when their intellectual and religious life centred in Babylon. THE DISPERSION OF THE JEWS 14. Viewed as an event in the world's history, the exile was a mere incident in the execution of the policy which the Assyrians and their successors, the Babylonians, adopted in their treatment of all nations who refused to submit to their rule. While the vassal states paid regular tribute, they were allowed to retain their own integrity and political organization. If, however, they repeatedly revolted, their permanent submission was insured by ex-

tinguishing all traces of independent national life. Deportation of the inhabitants, and recolonization of the territory by subjects transported from other parts of their empire, was the drastic method which the conquerors universally employed. Judah's annihilation was the more complete, because not once, but three times, it incurred their dire displeasure. By the first deportation, which occurred in 597 B. c., the young King Jehoiakin, his immediate family, the nobles, warriors, and skilled artisans of the kingdom were transported to Babylon. According to the account in II. Kings xxiv. 14-16, the total was ten thousand, of which seven thousand were warriors, one thousand artisans, and presumably the remaining two thousand nobles and officials (compare Jer. xxix. 2). The estimate, of course, is general, and makes no mention of the women and children who were allowed to accompany their husbands and fathers, and who may well have increased the numbers to thirty or forty thousand. 15. Eleven years later, in 586 B. c., another unsuccessful revolt of the Judeans led the Babylonians to institute still more extreme measures. Not even the common mob in Jerusalem, or those who early in the siege had fled to the camp of the conqueror, escaped deportation. The record in II. Kings xxv. 8-11, gives no detailed statistics, but suggests that a large proportion of those captured were deported. The author of Jeremiah lii. 28, 29, estimates the numbers carried away at this time (reading the seventeenth for the seventh year, which is probably a scribal error) from the villages of Judah, at three thousand and twenty-three; while those deported from Jerusalem, which was captured during the following year, number eight hundred and thirty-two, giving a total of three thousand eight hundred and fifty-five. As is always the case, unless distinctly stated, these numbers, which appear to be derived from an exact census, refer only to the men, suggesting that the total number carried away to Babylon in the second deportation was between twelve and fifteen thousand. From the narrative in II. Kings and from Jeremiah xl. to xli-

ii., we learn that the Babylonians left behind a few of the ruling class who had remained loyal, and the poorer inhabitants that they might till the soil and prevent the land from becoming a complete desolation. At their head was placed a trusty governor, Gedaliah. For a period all went well. Then through the treachery of a neighboring prince he, with his immediate followers, was slain. THE NUMBER OF JEWS DEPORTED 19 The rest of the Jewish community fled to Egypt. It was probably to avenge this deed that the Babylonians again, in 581 u. c., took occasion (as recorded in Jeremiah Hi. 30), to deport seven hundred and forty-five more men, or in all about two thousand five hundred souls. Accepting these figures as a basis, the total number carried into Babylon in connection with the three deportations was about fifty thousand. Compared with the twenty-seven thousand two hundred and ninety deported according to the Assyrian inscriptions from the city of Samaria at the time of its final fall in 722 B. c., this estimate seems reasonable. Furthermore, the sources from which the data are derived were probably written within a generation or two after the different deportations took place, and, therefore, may with good reason be regarded as reliable. The natural tendency on the part of a patriotic historian would be to minimize rather than to exaggerate numbers in a narrative so distasteful to him. The large number of Jews, found in Babylon and the East during the succeeding centuries, also confirms this estimate. 16. The Jews deported to Babylon represented, however, only a fraction of the former population of Judah, and certainly only a part of those who were driven into exile by the repeated disasters which overtook their nation. The numbers who quickly rallied about the standard of Gedaliah after the deportation in 580 B. c., indicate that a large proportion, if not a majority of the Jewish people remained in and about Judah. " We are many" was the testimony of " those who inhabited the waste places iu the land of Israel" at this time (Ezek. xxxiii. 24). The caves to the south and east of

Judah, which had proved secure hiding places during lesser crises in the history of the Hebrew race, doubtless shielded not a few fugitives until the Babylonian soldiers withdrew. From Jeremiah xl. 11, it appears that some found a temporary asylum in Moab, Ammon, Edom, and the other lands encircling Canaan, from whence they returned as soon as a favorable opportunity offered. The fact that the Babylonians did not deem it necessary to introduce colonists from other parts of their empire is in itself evidence that great numbers of the Judeans continued to develop the resources of their native land. 17. In view of the close political and commercial relations which had long existed between Egypt and Judah, it was most natural that the majority of those who fled from before the Babylonians, should take refuge in the land of the Nile. Hosea's references to Egypt as one of the lands of the exile (ix. 6; xi. 11) indicate that the Israelites, a century and a half before, when their nation was destroyed by Assyria, set the example which their southern kinsmen followed in very similar circumstances. Even after the first Jewish deportation, Jeremiah addressed his prophecy to them " that remain in this land (Judah) and to them that dwell in the land of Egypt" (xxiv. 8). If, as this reference plainly indicates, in 597 B. c., an important part of the Jewish race, as well as many descendants of the Northern Israelites, were already found in Egypt, their numbers must have been later greatly increased. When it became evident that Judah was doomed, patriots who believed the words of the true prophets recognized that they could serve their country better by going for a time into voluntary exile in Egypt than by remaining to fall into the hands of the Babylonians. THE JEWISH REFUGEES IN EGYPT 21

The strength of this tendency to seek refuge in Egypt was clearly illustrated at a subsequent date, when, after the murder of Gedaliah, his followers emigrated *en masse* to the land of the Nile. At Tahpanhes, on the eastern border of Egypt, they established themselves. Other centres of Jewish colonization were Mig-

dol, also a border town (as its name " watch tower" indicates), about twelve miles from Pelusium, Noph, which is identified with the ancient city of Memphis (compare Ezek. xxx. 13), and the country of Pathros, which is probably a designation of the territory of southern Egypt (Jer. xlvi. 1; Ezek. xxx. 13-18). Thus while many Jews remained on the borders of Judah, others found homes in the southernmost province of the new land of their adoption. The reference in Ezekiel xxx. 6 implies that they were found as far south as Syene, on the island Elephantine, in the Nile.

18. Unfortunately there are no definite data from which to determine how many Jews were to be found in Egypt at the beginning of the exile. Jeremiah xliv. 15 speaks of them as constituting a " great assembly." When one recalls how accessible from Jerusalem was the land of the Nile, and that it alone offered to the refugees a friendly asylum beyond the pale of Babylonian influence, the conviction deepens that about the year 580 B. c. a very large proportion, if not a majority, of the former inhabitants of Judah were found in Egypt. For more than a decade the current of Jewish population had been setting in that direction, powerfully accelerated as it was by the disintegrating blows dealt to Judah by Babylon. If Jeremiah had not deemed it more important to cast his fortunes with his countrymen who remained behind, than with the stronger type who were deported to Babylon, a most important chapter in the history of the Jewish race would have been unrecorded. As it was, after he died the Jews in Egypt had no Ezekiel or prophet like the Babylonian Isaiah, so that we are dependent partially upon inference in reconstructing the probable course of events; but it is obvious that the exiles in Egypt were a factor which can no longer be ignored in the study of the history of the Jewish race during the Babylonian exile, and especially during the succeeding period of reconstruction. 19, Ancient Semitic history presents many examples of the deportation of nations, but no instance of such a complete and widespread dispersion as that which

was the sad lot of the race of shepherds and agriculturists who inhabited the uplands of Canaan. Ezekiel and all the other writers of the period declare that "they were scattered upon all the face of the earth" (Ezck. xxxiv. 6; xxxvi. 19). Throughout at least the world dominated by Nebuchadrezzar, from the desert of Sahara to the uplands at the east of the Tigris, were to be found colonies of Jews. Three centres of Jewish population, however, may be distinguished: the first was Palestine itself, the second was Egypt, and the third Babylon. The character of the colonists in the three centres and the conditions under which they lived were so radically different that each must be studied independently. THE CHARACTER AXD CONDITION OP THE JEWS IN PALESTINE AND EGYPT 20. The destructive wrath of Babylon, like that of Rome six and a half centuries later, was visited chiefly upon Jerusalem, the political and religious centre of the Jewish race. As a result it became a complete desolation, "the haunt of jackals" (Lam. v. 18). There is no evidence that the smaller towns of Judah were subjected to the same drastic treatment. The Jews deported to Babylon in the first and largest deportation were all taken from Jerusalem. Not only did the comparative insignificance of the towns protect them, but they also saved themselves by surrendering to the conquerors at a much earlier stage of the war. According to the largest possible estimate, less than five thousand men were deported from the villages outside Jerusalem. The references in Jeremiah xl. indicate that many of them, like Mizpah and Netophah, survived, although, of course, their population was decimated by the ravages of war and of deportation. To leave behind a part of the native population was in perfect harmony with the wise constructive rule and humane spirit of Nebuchadrezzar. His ambitions, which already contemplated the conquest of Egypt, prompted him to develop, at any cost, the resources of Palestine, that his army might have the necessary base of supplies in case of a western campaign. This fact explains his attempt to revive the Jewish state under Gedaliah, even after Jerusalem had been laid in ruins. Contemporary writers, as well as the facts of subsequent history, testify that only the poorer and more ignorant were left behind in Palestine. In the East the peasants are always the ones who survive repeated waves of conquest. They also would be the last to revolt, and could best conserve the interests of Babylon. After the murder of Gedaliah, the conquerors took care that there should be no leaders among the remnant in the land. Gradually, however, as the years went by, prominent exiles undoubtedly found their way back to Judah from the immediately adjacent countries, like Edom, Moab, Ammon, and Egypt, where they had found a temporary place of refuge, just as earlier they rallied about Gedaliah (Jer. xl. 7-12).

21. The condition of those who clung to their beloved hills was anything but desirable. The loose rule of the Babylonians in Palestine was in itself galling. The poet of the remnant laments that:

Servants rule over us:

There is none to deliver us out of their hand.

The usual wrongs of an Oriental provincial government, injustice and extortion, were not lacking (Lam. v. 4). Since all independent political organization was denied the Jews in Palestine, they were the easy prey of the robber tribes who encircled them. The pent-up hatred of generations was visited upon their heads. Such wails as: Lam. v. 8.

HOSTILE ATTITUDE OF THE PEOPLES OF CANAAN 25

We get our bread at the peril of our lives,

Because of the sword of the wilderness.

Our skin is hot like an oven.

Because of the burning heat of famine;

They, who are mine enemies without cause,

Have chased me sore like a bird,

tell the story of wrong and helpless suffering. Others:

They have cut off my life in the dungeon,

And have cast a stone upon me;

The young men bare the mill,

And the children stumble under the

wood suggest the slavery which was the fate of many at the hands of their pitiless foes.

22. These conditions, which continued with little interruption for many generations, alone explain the bitter imprecations which appear on almost every page of the prophecies and poems of the period. Ezekiel devoted not a little time and energy to denouncing and to pronouncing woes upon the hostile nations, who at this time took base advantage of Judah's humiliation and weakness. Inasmuch as the Ammonites said, " Aha, against Jehovah's sanctuary, when it was profaned; and against the land of Israel, when it was made desolate; and against the house of Judah, when they went into captivity," Jehovah will visit upon them all the horrors of conquest (xxv. 3-7). Against Moab, Philistia, and Tyre, he directs similar predictions of coming vengeance. There is no suggestion in the exilic prophecies of any hostility between the Judeans and Samaritans; in fact, as in the passage just quoted, the interests of the descendants of the ancient Israelites and of the Judeans are regarded as the same, and the hope of a union of the two branches of the Hebrew race, who were then united in a common suffering, finds frequent expression. Of all their foes the Edomites are reckoned as the most grievous offenders (Ezek. xxv. 13). They were the people who called forth the bitter diatribe associated with the name of Obadiah. Their treachery at the time of Judah's downfall, their deeds of robbery, and their " delivery into slavery of those of his who remain in the day of distress," are the crimes for which they shall be judged (Ob. 11-14). Ezekiel's words in xxxv. 10 indicate that immediately after the destruction of the Jewish state, that northward movement of the Edomites began which is referred to in the closing verses of the prophecy of Obadiah, and which ended in their being expelled from their original home by the Arabs, and in their seizing the territory of southern Judah (Mai. i. 5). By the end of the Babylonian exile, they appear to have gained possession of the south country, including Hebron

and the lowlands to the west (Zech. vii. 7). During the succeeding centuries, they continued to hold the Jewish territory thus acquired, until they themselves were conquered by John Hyrcanus about 130 B. c. It is not strange, therefore, that these hated intruders always figure in the Jewish mind as a type of the foes of Jehovah, and as the enemies of all truth. This northern movement of the Edomites in turn crowded out the clans of the Calebites and Jcrahrneelites, who had from the very earliest times intermarried and Lam. v. 9, 10. Lam. iii. 53. Lam. iii. 52. Lam. v. 13. RELIGIOUS LIFE OF THE PALESTINIAN JEWS 27 united with the tribe of Judah (I. sect. 40). Driven from Hebron and the south country, they in time found homes in and about Bethlehem and Kirjath-jearim (compare I. Chrs. ii. 42-49 with ii. 50-55). As before the exile, they continued to affiliate with the Jews, and during the Persian period constituted an important part of the revived community (Neh. iii. 9). In time they were classified as regular clans of the tribe of Judah (I. Chrs. ii.; iv.; Ex. xxxi. 2; xxxv. 30). 23. In the light of their character and conditions, it is obvious that the religious life of the Jews who remained in Palestine was neither vigorous nor of an exalted type. In a prophecy, dated the twelfth year of the captivity (585 B. c.), and directed to those " who inhabit the waste places in the land of Israel," Ezekiel accuses them of deeds of lust and bloodshed, and of returning to that idolatry which always possessed such an attraction for the weak and ignorant inhabitants of Judah (xxxiii. 25-27). A chance reference in Jeremiah (xli. 5) indicates that certain of the externals of the worship of Jehovah were still kept up in connection with the site of the ruined sanctuary at Jerusalem. Not only from Judah, but also from the old Israelitish cities of Shechem, Shiloh, and Samaria, came bands of faithful pilgrims to lament over the fallen temple and to present meat offerings and incense on the rude altar which they raised there at least as early as the fifth year after the destruction of Jerusalem. If this was permitted so soon after the overthrow of the temple, we may believe that the sacred site became, in succeeding years, more and more the centre of the religious life of the Palestinian Jews. The most prominent priests of the temple were carried into exile, but some were doubtless left behind; and of the descendants of those who ministered at the old shrines abolished by Josiah, there must have been still more. For the most part, ignorant, disorganized, bereft of leaders, some of them robbers and outlaws within the land of their fathers, constantly attacked by merciless foes, it is not probable that the Jews in Palestine made much progress in the knowledge of Jehovah and of his will; instead, the doubts and despair voiced by one of their poets, constantly oppressed them (Lam. v. 19-22). The real development of this period must be sought among their kinsmen in the distant exile. Trom them came the religious impulses which were destined to determine the character of their history. The Jews in Judah, however, were an important element in the problem of the future of the Jewish race; for they were to furnish, to a large extent, the members of that community which was again to become the objective centre of Judaism. 24. Intellectually, those who fled to Egypt were superior to those who remained in Judah. In many ways also their environment was more agreeable. Although the motives guiding the Egyptian kings in their relations with the Judeans had been thoroughly selfish, they were the allies and patrons of the fallen people, and, therefore, under obligations to give them a friendly reception and to concede to them certain privileges. Egyptians, as well as Judeans, were trembling in the presence of the dread foe, Nebuchadrezzar. In the circumstances, the reigning Pharaohs, who depended for the protection of their state more upon foreign mercenaries than native warriors, must have THE JEWISH COLONY AT TAHPANHES 29 gladly welcomed, as valuable allies, the Jewish refugees who sought a home on their exposed eastern frontier. The majority of the exiles preferred these positions of danger because here they were

nearest to their native land, and because they regarded their sojourn in Egypt as transient (Jer. xliv. 28). For these reasons they took up their residence in the frontier towns of Migdol, Tahpanhes, and in the city of Memphis, which was not far distant from the borders of Judah. Since these places were on the direct line of the caravan route to Palestine and the East, they would be in constant communication with their kinsmen, and would be in a position to return whenever conditions were favorable. 25. The excavations of the Egypt Exploration Fund at Defenneh, the site of the Daphnae of Herodotus and of the Tahpanhes, where the refugees with Jeremiah settled, have thrown much light upon the environment of the Jews in Egypt (see Memoirs, 1886; Tanis, Part II., pages 47-96). The town was located on a sandy desert at the south of a marshy lake, a few miles from the cultivated Delta on the west, and the Suez Canal on the east. Past it ran the main highway to Syria, which it was intended to guard. The ruins of a fort built by Psamtik I., the founder of the town, still remain. Herodotus states that this monarch stationed guards here (ii. 30), and that, until late in the Persian period, it was manned by garrisons whose duty it was to repel Arabian invasions. The character of the remains confirms the testimony of Herodotus that from the first the majority of the population were Greeks. In this frontier territory Psamtik L., about 6G4 B. c., assigned homes to the Ionian and Carian mercenaries who had helped him to the throne. Jeremiah ii. 16 indicates that, in the days of Necho, Tahpanhes and Noph were important military centres of the Egyptians, and also suggests that Josiah met and was defeated on the plain of Megiddo by Greek mercenaries in the employ of Necho. Herodotus declares that Daphnas became at an early date a base of communication between Egypt and the Greek world (ii. 154). By virtue of its location, it was also a meeting place for eastern and western civilizations. Here Phosnicians, Greeks, Jews, and Egyptians met on common ground. Like Port Said of to-day, its life was in the highest

degree cosmopolitan. Its atmosphere was, therefore, most congenial to the Jewish colonists. There they lived together in a community by themselves. 26. No archaeological remains have been found to recall the residence of the Jews at Tahpanhes, but the marked absence of art treasures coming from the reigns of Psamtik II. and Hophra (594-564 B. c.) is in itself indirect evidence that the Greek population was largely supplanted by Jewish; for the Jewish civilization of this period was not of a character to leave behind permanent monuments. Strangely enough, however, eastern tradition has preserved a distant memory of Jewish occupancy in the name which is still given to the ruins of the fort, *Kasr el Bint el Yehudi*, " The Palace of the Jew's Daughter." The excavations, as well as the testimony of Herodotus, explain the significance of the unusual designation " palace," for the fort was also used on rare occasions as a royal residence. Many wine jars with the seal-ings of Psamtik II., Hophra, and Amasis (Aahmes) THE RELIGIOUS LIFE OF THE JEWS IN EGYPT 31 have been found. Conspicuous among the ruins, at the northwest of this military residence of the Pharaohs, was the great open-air platform of brickwork referred to in Jeremiah xliii. 8-10. It corresponded to the " mastaba " found in connection with every Egyptian house, and was the common place for social meeting and recreation. Hophra's successor, Amasis, represented the Egyptian party which was antagonistic to foreign civilization. The Greek colonists and trade were limited to Naukratis, and the Greek garrison was deported from Daphnae. Indeed, this city suffered most from these reactionary measures. It was left desolate and the fort garrisoned by Egyptians (Herod, ii. 154, 179). Thus, at least, by 560 B. c., if they had not already returned to Judah, the Jewish colonists must have been forced to seek homes elsewhere. To the Jewish colonists located, not only at Tahpanhes, but also in other cities, the changed attitude of the Egyptian court toward foreigners must have proved an added incentive to venture a return. 27. While

Jeremiah recognized the intense loyalty of the Jews in Egypt to their native land, he found in their religious life little to commend and much to attack. There is no evidence that they paid homage to the gods of Egypt, or that they completely abandoned the worship of Jehovah; but under the influence of the polytheistic atmosphere in which they found themselves, many of them reverted to the earlier idolatry of their ancestors. As in the days of Manassch, incense rose from many Jewish altars to other gods than Jehovah. The worship of an old Semitic goddess, the Queen of heaven, whom the Jerusalemites venerated even before the fall of their city (Jer. vii. 18), was especially popular with the women. Herodotus states (i. 131) that the Persians derived the worship of the Queen of heaven from the Assyrians and Arabs. He identifies her with the Greek goddess of love, Aphrodite. This identification is confirmed by the fact that the Assyro-Babylonian goddess of love, Ishtar, is called in the Babylonian prayers, " the Ruler of heaven." The reaction of the Jews against the reformation of Josiah and the law of Jehovah, in favor of an ancient Semitic goddess, was because they naively interpreted the misfortunes which had overtaken them as evidence of Jehovah's inferiority to the old gods of Canaan. In reply to Jeremiah's impassioned remonstrances, they stubbornly asserted that prosperity had come to their fathers in Judah, when they had served the goddess of heaven, and misfortune when they had ceased. Jeremiah could only meet this seemingly plausible but false philosophy of history by a counter-assertion: " Your apostasy to Jehovah made this national judgment, which has overtaken you, an absolute necessity. If you persist in neglecting him, only a few of you will realize the fond hope of your life and survive to return to Judah. Time will prove the truth of my words. When you see the reigning Pharaoh, Hophra, fall into the power of his rival, Nebuchadrezzar, recall my warnings " (Jer. xliv. 15-30). 28. Whether in his closing years the untiring ministrations of Jeremiah extended the ranks of the faithful few who

listened to him, is not stated. Bzekiel, in his latest prophecy, which is dated in April, 570 B. c., fixes his eyes, not on the Jews about him, but upon those in Egypt. Like Jeremiah, he asserts that Hophra is soon to fall before Nebuchadrezzar; but THE LOYAL JEWS IN EGYPT 33 his view concerning the future of his countrymen in Egypt is much more hopeful: " Egypt's downfall shall be the prelude to the exaltation of the Jews. Then will Jehovah vindicate his promises of restoration, and all shall recognize him as the supreme ruler of the universe" (Ezek. xxix. 17-21). It is a noticeable fact that the more intimately the old Hebrew prophets knew their audiences, the more they found to denounce. The majority of the exiles, whether in Babylon or Egypt, were far from realizing the ideals of their inspired teachers. The weak, the ignorant, and the indifferent were sadly in the majority. Not in large numbers, nor all at once, as the prophets seem sometimes to have hoped and taught, were the Jews destined to realize the divine plan, but gradually, as the few were found who were ready, by fidelity and sacrifice, to co-operate with the Eternal. Jeremiah, in his most despondent moments, never doubted that from the Jews in Egypt a few such immortals would come forth and participate in the revival of their national life (Jer. xliv. 14, 28). IV THE JEWISH EXILES IN BABYLON 29. All the Jewish writers of the period emphasize the fact that the best elements in their race were to be found in Babylon. Jeremiah, in contrasting those who were deported in 597 B. c. with those who were left behind, likens the former to good figs, while the latter are only vile and worthless. Ezekiel found many imperfections among his countrymen in Babylon, but he never denied their superiority to the remnant in the West. This superiority was a result of the policy of the Babylonians, who carefully removed all the more energetic and gifted leaders of the nation, that none might be left behind to head an insurrection. The ten thousand men deported in 597 B. c. represented in number two-thirds of all the Jewish exiles in Babylon, and

certainly more than that proportion of the total intelligence and moral culture. They included the leading princes, officials, prophets, priests, warriors, and artisans of the kingdom (II. Kings xxiv. 14-16; Jcr. xxix. 1). With them went their families and servants. As Ezekiel states, the kernel of the nation was thus transferred from Judah to Babylon (xvii. 3-6, 12-14). The prophet's words (see especially verse 5) imply that this kernel was not divided and planted in three or four widely separated spots, as in the case of THE HOME OF THE JEWISH EXILES IN BABYLON 35 the deportation of the people of Samaria in 722 B. C. (II. 104); but that all were permitted to settle in the same locality. 30. Babylon is always indicated as the goal of the deportation; but unfortunately it is not clear whether the city or the province, lying between the two great rivers, is intended, since both bore the same name. A variety of evidence, however, throws light upon this important question. Ezekiel describes the site as " a laud of traffic, a city of merchants, a fruitful soil, and beside many waters," where the colony like a willow was transplanted (xvii. 5). Psalm cxxxvii. 1, refers to the days when the exiles sat by the rivers or canals of Babylon. Ezekiel states that he lived among the exiles by the river or canal Chebar (i. 3). All these references point to the rich fruitful land, intersected by canals and plentifully watered, which lies to the south and east of the city of Babylon, between the Euphrates and the Tigris. We are not surprised, therefore, that the excavations of the University of Pennsylvania Expedition at Nippur (Series A: Cuneiform Texts, vol. ix. 28, 33) have recently uncovered two tablets, dated in the reign of Artaxerxes I. (464-424 B. c.), which refer to the large navigable canal Chebar (Kabaru) not far from Nippur. To the east of the great city of Babylon, in a territory closely connected with it by canals, Nebuchadrezzar established the community which he had transferred from the barren uplands of Judah. 31. The purpose, which actuated that great monarch in all his public acts, was not to destroy, but to construct. His inscriptions reflect nothing of the barbarous love of war which is so prominent in those of the Assyrian kings. Repeatedly he declares, in all genuineness, that his aim in his conquests was to glorify the name of his gods, and to secure the means wherewith he might rebuild and adorn their temples (East India Inscription ii. 11-29). Building was his master passion. In all his enterprises he succeeded. Out of the crumbling remnants of the Assyrian Empire he created a powerful well-organized state. The city of Babylon, which for generations under the rule of its rivals, the Assyrians, had been allowed to fall into political decay, he rebuilt on a scale far surpassing any other city of antiquity. The old town on the west bank of the Euphrates was enlarged and adorned with new palaces and temples; on the east side of the river a new quarter was added, connected with the old by strong bridges. The whole city, which, like Damascus of to-day, included parks and fields as well as the suburbs of the former town, was encircled by a huge wall many miles in circumference and of incredible height and strength. To facilitate the vast commerce, which was the chief industry of the Babylonians, Nebuchadrezzar built commodious quays on both sides of the Euphrates, and restored and extended the great system of canals which intersected the low, flat territory of southern Babylonia. As in Holland to-day, these waterways were also utilized for irrigation, so that the productiveness of the naturally fertile land about Babylon was marvellously increased. Large reservoirs were constructed, in which the waters of the Euphrates were stored for use in time of need. Into the territory thus developed, colonists from all parts of the empire were introduced; for the vast building enterprises of Nebuchadrezzar called for armies of workmen, and by these forcible means alone was he able in a generation THE CONDITION OF THE JEWISH EXILES 37 to make the dismantled city the metropolis of the world. The recently discovered coronation inscription of Nabonidus, in a passage which clearly refers to Nebuchadrezzar, declares

that " the god called him to repopulate his ruined city," Babylon (iii. 1). Such a huge population as centred about Babylon, demanded a correspondingly large food supply, and the Babylonians themselves had become a nation of traders rather than agriculturists; hence it is easy to appreciate the motives which prompted the great organizer, when a good opportunity offered, to deport large bodies of agriculturists to the newly developed lands near his capital. 32. Economic as well as political reasons undoubtedly operated in determining the fall of the Jewish people. The fact that their deportation was not merely a judgment explains why their material conditions were on the whole so favorable. The term "captivity " does not describe their lot. Two of their kings, and, perhaps, some of the leaders in their rebellions against Babylon, were kept in confinement, but the great majority of those who were first deported were almost as free as in Canaan. During the first ten years of the exile, at least, they continued in close communication with their kinsmen in Judah. In a pastoral letter written from Jerusalem, Jeremiah advised them to build houses and dwell in them, to plant gardens, and eat the fruit of them, to take wives and rear up families, that their numbers might increase rather than decrease in the land of their forced adoption (xxix. 5, 6). He further urged them to avoid all movements toward insurrection, and instead to identify themselves with the city whither they had been carried, for its prosperity and their own were inseparable. By one so well informed respecting the life of the exiles as was Jeremiah, such advice would not have been offered unless it was possible for his readers to have followed it. A homesickness, which frequently found expression (read, for example, Pss. xlii.-xliii.; cxxxvii.), filled the hearts of the Jews living on the level plains of Babylonia, as they thought of their rolling hills, their picturesque valleys, their rockbuilt capital, and above all their sacred temple; but those alluvial plains afforded them opportunities for the enjoyment of wealth and material prosperity un-

dreamed of in Judah. During the earlier part of the Babylonian exile, most of the Jews followed the advice of Jeremiah and "planted gardens, and ate the fruit of them." Nebuchadrezzar's object in carrying away the artisans to Babylon, was doubtless not merely to deprive the Judeans of resources for revolt, but also that they might be added to his great army of workmen. Certainly in their new homes they found ample opportunity to practise their various crafts. The old Hebrew aversion to traffic, which finds expression in the writings of certain prophets of this period, probably for a time deterred some of the exiles from becoming merchants; but the opportunities and advantages offered in their new home to those who engaged in commerce were too great to be spurned for a long time. The peculiar genius for trade, which the Jews have manifested ever since, was probably first developed amidst the favoring conditions which surrounded them in the land of the two rivers. In contract tablets recently found at Nippur, and dating from the earlier part of the Persian period, many familiar Old THE OCCUPATIONS OF THE JEWISH EXILES 39 Testament names occur, showing that by that time the Jews had been drawn into the streams of trade which flowed so strongly to and from Babylon. Since they were settled, not in a remote province of the empire, but under the very shadow of the Babylonian throne, it is reasonable to conclude that some of the abler men among the exiles found employment in the great army of officials required to attend to public affairs. Nehemiah later attained to a position of influence in the Persian court, and it is probable that other Jews did the same among the Babylonians with whom they were related by blood, language, and ideas. The references to the liberation and exaltation of Jehoiakin seem to indicate that they were placed on an equality with other conquered peoples which had been transported to Babylon. Although the familiar stories associated with the name of Daniel, in their present form, are much later, they at least favor the conclusion that certain public positions were then open to the Jews.

33. Respecting the fate of the later groups of exiles, there is no direct evidence. Their offences were so much more heinous in the eyes of the conquerors than those of the Jews deported in 597 B. c., that their leaders were put to death (II. Kings xxv. 19-21). Prom this fact it may be inferred that slavery was the price with which many of the survivors redeemed their lives. Bzekiel, commenting in 585 B. c. upon the fate of the scattered people, declares that the day is coming when Jehovah will break the bars of their yoke and deliver them out of the hand of those who have made bondsmen of them (xxxiv. 27). It is significant that while the references to forced labor and persecution are rare in the literature of the first part, they become very common in that of the latter part of the Babylonian exile. The author of Isaiah xiv. assures his race that " It shall come to pass in the day that the Lord shall give rest from your labor, and from your trouble, and from the hard service which men laid upon you, that you shall take up this taunt-song against the king of Babylon, and say: ' How is the oppressor stilled — the raging stilled!'" (verses 3 and 4). The great prophet of the exile condemns the Babylonians because they " showed no compassion; upon the aged they made their yoke very heavy " (Isa. xlvii. 6). Although the language is highly poetical, there must have been a painful basis of fact in his pictures of the woes experienced by his race under the degenerate rule of Nebuchadrezzar's successors: " It is a people robbed and plundered; snared are all of them in holes and hid in prison houses; they are become a prey, and there is none to rescue; a spoil, and none who says, Restore" (Isa. xlii. 22). 34. While some of their number became the object of Babylonian oppression, the lot of most of the Jews in the East was far better than that of the ordinary exile forced to live alone among strangers, for they were citizens of the little Jewish state which Nebuchadrezzar established within the shadow of his great capital. What was

the extent of this kingdom within a kingdom, and whether all the Jews in Babylon at first were permitted or chose to dwell together, can only be conjectured. Ezekiel speaks of preaching to the colony who lived at Tel-Abib (" Storm-hill"), one of the many artificial mounds upon which the towns of the Euphrates basin were located in ancient times, precisely as they are to-day. In the list of those who THE ORGANIZATION OF THE JEWISH EXILES 41 returned to Judah, certain groups came from Tel-Melah (" Salt-hill") and Tel-Harsha ("Forest-hill "). Whether the territory belonging to these little towns was contiguous or not, the different Jewish colonies constituted an independent social unit, the different members of which were in closest touch with each other. As in Judah, the elders were their civil representatives (Jer. xxix. 1; Ezek. xiv. 1). The earlier family organization was maintained. The more wealthy possessed servants. The authority of the princes was still acknowledged, and at their head was a descendant of the house of David, Jehoiakin, who, after 561 B. c., was officially recognized by the court at Babylon (II. Kings xxv. 27-30). As long as they paid the imperial tax and remained loyal to Babylon, they were probably allowed to rule themselves in accordance with their own laws. Capital punishment — at least if the offence was of the nature of rebellion — was executed in the name of the Babylonian king, and in a manner calculated to inspire terror in the minds of all evil-doers (Jer. xxix. 22). 35. Within this little Judah, unfortunately, the same evils nourished as in the parent state. False prophets, whose personal characters were not above reproach, misled the people with deceptive messages, purporting to be from Jehovah (Jer. xxix. 21-23; Ezek. xiii. 1-7; xiv. 8-10). The exiles in the East, as well as those in Egypt, carried with them many idolatrous practices, which they were slow to abandon (Ezek. xx. 30-32). The faithful prophets were still compelled to combat this old error, strongly fortified as it Avas by the practices of their conquerors (Ezek. xiv. 3-7; Isa. xlii. 17).

Everywhere an even more insidious danger, which threatened to undermine the very foundations of their faith, assailed the scattered remnants of the Jewish race. It was the doubt as to whether Jehovah was able or willing to deliver them. " My strength is perished and my expectation from the Lord" (Lam. iii. 18), was the cry of many earnest, perplexed souls. The mass of the Judeans, before the great catastrophe, had regarded the temple at Jerusalem as inviolable (Jer. xxvi. 9). While it stood, they could endure all personal afflictions, because they were assured that Jehovah was dwelling in their midst; but when they witnessed its complete destruction, they felt that Jehovah had indeed abandoned them as a nation. " Wherefore dost thou forget us forever, and forsake us so long time?" (Lam. v. 20), was the wail of one who perhaps at the moment gazed upon the ruins of the sacred city. Even the prophets accepted the popular belief that "the Lord had forsaken the land " (Ezek. viii. 12), and had for a time retired to his " mount in the uttermost parts of the north " (Isa. xiv. 13,14; Ezek. i. 4). It was this sense of separation from Jehovah, combined with the feeling that they were ceremonially unclean, that constituted the horror of the exile. With the temple in ruins, it was no longer possible to worship Jehovah as a nation. No more could they sacrifice to him their firstlings; consequently they felt that everything which they ate was unclean. Daily they were polluted by contact with the heathen about them. The very soil itself was unclean. Shame saddened every moment, for they regarded their lot as the sign of Jehovah's displeasure. It is not strange that at first a despair which developed into a spirit of rebellion, and became at last a source of apostasy, seized many. THE RELIGIOUS LIFE OF THE JEWISH EXILES 43 36. Gradually, however, under the wise guidance of their inspired prophets, a hope was implanted in their hearts, and they learned to adapt themselves to their changed surroundings. It is to be noted that no one ever suggested the building of a temple to Jehovah in the land of their adoption. Much later, in Egypt, the experiment was tried; but at this earlier stage in the development of the Jehovah religion, such a thing vras inconceivable. Until they were free again to rebuild on the sacred site, all that religious life which had centred about the temple, was impossible. For the present " the Lord had cast off his altar, he had abhorred his sanctuary" (Lam. ii. 7). As a result, sacrifice took the form of fasting. By denying themselves their ordinary food, they gave expression to the intensity of their feelings, and at the same time laid before Jehovah a gift which could be presented at any time and at any place. From the beginning of the Babylonian exile, fasting became a common religious institution among the Jews (Ezra viii. 21; Neh. i. 4; Joel i. 14; Zech. vii. 3-5). Naturally, as the observance of the great feast days fell temporarily into abeyance, more and more stress was laid upon the institution of the Sabbath, which could be observed equally well beyond the limits of Canaan (Ezek. xx. 12-21; xxii. 26; xxiii. 38). Ezekiel was the first of the prophets to assign to it a position of transcendent importance. The example of the Babylonians, who also observed the seventh as " a day of rest for the soul," may have strengthened this tendency, which ultimately became so strong as to prove one of the most powerful motives in Judaism. 37. Unfortunately there is no direct evidence as to how the Sabbath was observed. Probably, at first, if they followed the example of the Babylonians, much attention was given to the propitiatory services. In the light of later developments among the Jews of the dispersion, it is extremely probable that families and communities gathered together, not only to offer atoning sacrifices, but also to read and study the Book of Deuteronomy and the writings of their prophets, which they then learned to value as never before. Certainly there must have been some such popular study of their scriptures to inspire the great literary activity of their leaders. If so, the origin of the synagogue service is to be found in this period. It is certain that the practice of pub-

licly reading the scriptures in connection with great propitiatory feasts was already familiar to the Jews (Jer. xxxvi. 6-8), and that the synagogue came into existence as a result of just such peculiar conditions and needs as existed among the exiles. The other element in the synagogue service, prayer, public and private, now became a far more important feature of the religious life of the Jews than hitherto (Dan. vi. 10). Each individual became in a sense a priest, presenting in person his offering of praise and his petitions to Jehovah. The need of such communion was certainly never in the history of the Hebrew race felt more keenly. Thus, while the Babylonian exile was a period of sorrow and doubt, it was also one of rapid change and progress; as the dangers which confronted the Jews multiplied, so did their opportunities; the nation of peasants had been projected into the great stream of the world, and thereby an entirely new epoch in their development was inaugurated. THE PERSONALITY AND WORK OF THE PRIEST-PBOPHET EZEKIEL 38. The man who appreciated most profoundly the dangers and the possibilities of the Babylonian exile, was the prophet Ezekiel. Born in Jerusalem of a well-known priestly family, he saw the first temple with his own eyes, and, judging from the vividness with which he remembered details, probably assisted in its services. Perhaps, also, as a youth he listened to the earnest sermons of Jeremiah, and at the feet of the great prophet drank in those prophetic truths which are the foundations of his later teachings. In his character and work these two currents of influence — the priestly and prophetical — constantly appear, and their harmonious blending is one of the great sources of his power. It was an age when the faithful priest joined with the true prophet in a common struggle against the waves of heathenism which threatened to engulf the higher religion of Jehovah. One effective product of that union was the Book of Deuteronomy and the reformation of Josiah, which followed its promulgation (II. sects. 168, 182-186); the other was Ezekiel,

who represents a later development of the same so-called Deuteronomic school of thought. By virtue of the combination, the lofty ideals of the prophet were presented in the concrete, popular imagery of the ritual, so that the uneducated masses could appreciate and act in conformity with them. Ezekiel is the type of teacher who appeals directly to the greatest number of hearers. 39. In his character also he combined those qualities which fitted him to be a leader of his own and immediately succeeding generations, but which do not commend him so strongly to the present. That intensity, bordering almost upon insanity, which led him to sit seven days in blank amazement among the Jewish colonists at Tel-Abib, before delivering his message of denunciation (iii. 15), seems incongruous, except in the tense atmosphere of the exile. His language frequently seems mere hyperbole until the situation, which called it forth, is appreciated (compare, for example, xvi.). His repetitions and minute details are only tiresome to one who does not realize how obtuse were his readers. Ezekiel was not an orator nor a rhetorician, but an organizer and a practical man of affairs. His words appealed to his contemporaries because they recognized their truth and helpfulness. He stood so close to them that he clearly appreciated and was able to supply their spiritual needs. His reverence for the written law, and his full acceptance of the current theory of its origin (xx. 10, 11; xxxiii. 15; contrast Jer. vii. 22; viii. 8), put him into touch with his readers. The fanciful apocalyptic imagery, which he first introduced into Jewish literature, and which we now find only thought-obscuring, was also very popular in his day. The deeper sources of Ezekiel's influence, however, are qualities which are effective in all ages. His intensity was the out- THE CALL AND MISSION OF EZEKIEL 47 ward expression of a moral earnestness, inspired by a stern sense of justice. Opposition never daunted him, but only revealed his unflinching devotion to right (iii. 9). A certain fiery impetuosity characterized all that he did. At the same time, his high sense of Jehovah's exaltation and holiness begat in his heart a deep humility, which finds expression in the term, "son of man," with which he always speaks of himself. 40. Carried to Babylon in 597 B. c., among the first group of exiles, Ezekiel appears to have remained silent until 592 B. c., when, like Isaiah, he received his distinct call to the work of a prophet. His account of this important event reveals the powerful motives which then influenced him. On the one hand, he was oppressed by the defiant folly and mistakes of his countrymen in the exile, and especially of those left behind in Judah; on the other, the character and will of Jehovah was impressed upon his receptive mind so vividly that he realized, as never before, the startling contrast between the divine ideal and the human reality. Henceforth his life-work was to " go to the house of Israel and to speak Jehovah's words unto them " (iii. 4), that they might realize that divine ideal. Until 586 B. c., when Jerusalem was destroyed, he devoted himself to combating the false hopes of deliverance from Babylonian rule which were entertained by the remnant of his nation in Canaan, and by many of the Jews in the East. His message, like that of Jeremiah, was, in the circumstances, one of denunciation and proclamation of impending ruin. At first his fidelity was rewarded only with rejection and personal violence (iii. 25) at the hands of his fellow exiles, whose minds were filled with vain hopes of immediate deliverance from Babylonian rule; but when his predictions came true, there was a great revulsion of popular feeling, so that henceforth he enjoyed the veneration and respectful attention of all the Jews in Babylon, and his influence extended to his race throughout the world. Thus an opportunity was given him which was vouchsafed to no other prophet except, perhaps, to Isaiah. He improved it nobly. The Hebrew state, which his predecessors had addressed, was no more. Out of the wreck only detached communities remained. To these Ezekiel turned. Not the nation, but individuals, commanded his attention. 41. One of the many revolutionary changes

introduced by the destruction of the Jewish commonwealth was the elevation of the individual into a position of importance, which he had never enjoyed before. Jeremiah, in his closing messages of consolation, proclaimed this truth when he declared that in the coming day Jehovah would implant in each heart a knowledge of his law. Ezekiel adapted himself to the changed conditions, and became a pastor, devoting himself primarily to the culture of the souls of those under his immediate charge. There is clear evidence that he fully appreciated the new nature of his mission. It was he who first developed the figure of the " Good Shepherd" who gathers and tenderly cares for his scattered flock (xxxiv. 10-17). Ezekiel frequently designated himself as a watchman, appointed by God, whose duty it is to "hear the word from the mouth of Jehovah and to give the divine warning to the people " (iii. 17). Elsewhere he speaks of the exiles EZEKIEL'S METHODS OF TEACHING 49 as children (ii. 4). They also recognized the pastoral relation, for they came freely in person, or through their elders (xiv. 1), to consult him in regard to matters of individual faith, and to "hear what is the word that cometh forth from the Lord " through the mouth of their trusty pastor (xxxiii. 30). He also clearly defined his pastoral responsibilities: if he faithfully warned those under his charge, he felt that he was innocent in the sight of God even though disaster overtook them; but if it came because of any remiss-ness on his part, then "their blood would Jehovah require at the hand of his watchman " (xxxiii. 1-9). In his complete surrender to his work, he set an example for all times. So entirely did he identify himself with his message, that he speaks of eating and digesting the roll on which it was written (iii. 1-3). 42. In the variety of the methods which he employed to impress his words upon those under his charge, he surpassed all other prophets. Like Jeremiah, he frequently sought out groups of his countrymen, and by public address endeavored to reach them. We can see him in his earnestness "stamping with his foot" and gesticulating with

his arms, to add force to his words (vi. 11). More frequently, perhaps, deputations of Jews visited him in his home with questions which they freely discussed together (xiv.). In the literary atmosphere of Babylon, he trusted chiefly, however, to pastoral letters or tracts, copies of which were probably also distributed among the Jews of Canaan and Egypt; for Ezekiel felt that they, too, belonged to his flock. In all his writing that strongly dramatic element, which characterize everything that he did, found expression in the variety of rugged figures which he employed. The false prophets are "foxes which undermine rather than build up their nation" (xiii. 1-7); the sense of security inspired by their lying messages of peace is " like a wall of defence laid in untempered mortar, which will crumble at the first attack " (xiii. 10-12). Not content with words, he often acted his prophecies. To convince his people that the downfall of Jerusalem was inevitable, he represented on a tile the city in a state of siege, and pictured all the details of its capture (iv. 1-3). At another time he was commanded to shave off all his hair and to burn one-third in the fire, one-third he was to smite with a sword, and the remaining third he was to scatter to the winds. Of these he was to preserve only a handful, thus symbolizing the fate in store for his race. Again he tells us that, in the sight of a gaping multitude, he carried all of his household furniture to a place beside the city wall, and then in hot haste dug a hole in the soft clay, through which, under the cover of night, he bore away his possessions. Having in this manner aroused the curiosity of his fellow-citizens to the highest pitch, he explained that even thus their rebellious brethren in Jerusalem would soon be only too glad to escape from their doomed city (xii. 1-16). 43. Although born a priest, and an ardent advocate of ritualism and the written law, Ezekiel, as a faithful pastor, was a preacher of practical personal righteousness. He ever placed deeds first and form second, regarding the ritual and law as aids in the development of upright character (xxxiii. 15).

He MORAL ASD RELIGIOUS TEACHINGS OF EZEKIEL 51 predicted the fall of Jerusalem, not because the temple service was neglected, but because of the crimes and apostasy of its inhabitants (v. 5-11; vii. 1-27). To the exiles who came to inquire of him the divine will, he preached fundamental and complete conversion, declaring: "Return, turn yourselves from your idols; and turn away your faces from all your abominations " (xiv. 6). Repeatedly he impressed upon them the truth that an external change was not sufli-cient, but that the heart, the mainspring of action, must be transformed (xxxvi. 26). One recognizes in his denunciations of the corrupt rulers of his nation, and in his unsparing attacks upon those who had been unfaithful to the marriage bonds, or forgotten their obligations to their neighbors (xxii. 6-12), the same bold, uncompromising spirit that inspired John the Baptist and Savonarola. In the presence of sin his " forehead was as an adamant, harder than flint" (iii. 9), but the seeming harshness of the prophet was prompted by the desire that " the wicked might turn from his way and live " (xxxiii. 11). 44. Like every true pastor, he wails that "the people hear his words, but do them not; for with their mouth they show much love, but their heart goes after their gain" (xxxiii. 31). False prophets and prophetesses were found among the exiles, who undermined the influence of Ezekiel and destroyed the peoples' faith in the prophetic message (xiii.; Jer. xxix. 21-28). Certain popular errors gained wide acceptance. The proverb: " The fathers have eaten sour grapes, and the children's teeth are set on edge," which Jeremiah branded as a lie, was still current in the exile. Ezekiel resolutely met these dangers with assertions of the divine truth as it had been revealed to him. " No man shall suffer for his father's sins, but shall be rewarded according to his own deeds " (xviii. 20). If he overlooked certain individual exceptions to this general principle, which are emphasized by the author of the Book of Job, his teaching was far truer and more practical than the error which it combated. No one in his flock was allowed to shirk personal responsibility. Each one was led directly before the bar of divine justice. The false theory that righteous deeds would save from the consequences of wrong-doing was also mercilessly attacked (xviii. 24). At the same time he taught the efficacy of repentance and reformation, no matter how deeply the penitent had sinned (xviii. 21). " Divine justice and judgment are but an expression of God's love, for their aim is to turn the sinner from his evil way that he may live " (xviii. 23). 45. Although he was influenced by the experience of the exile, which led men to conceive of the Lord as far removed from them and to meditate more upon his judgments than upon his favor, Ezekiel never failed to appreciate that Jehovah was a God of love and mercy. Together with all the true prophets, he regarded the exile as merely a temporary stage in the moral and religious evolution of his race. As he demonstrates at length, it was the natural and inevitable consequence of the political, social, moral, and religious crimes of the Hebrew people during their national life (xiv. to xvi.; xxiii.). It was also intended in divine providence to efface the effects of those crimes, and to prepare the Jews for the realization of their mission. Until they were thus prepared, THE GLORIOUS FUTURE FOR THE JEWISH RACE 53 that mission could not be accomplished. In the light of this truth, the intense earnestness with which Ezekiel devoted himself to the moral education of his scattered flock, receives its full explanation. In them he saw the germ upon whose proper development depended mankind's future. 46. One of the many elements, inexplicable from a human point of view, is the unanimity and absolute certainty with which the prophets of the period declared that their race would be again restored to Canaan. In the details, their portrayals of the nature of the restoration varied, but respecting the essential facts, they were in perfect agreement. Before the final fall of Jerusalem, Ezekiel announced that Jehovah would surely gather his scattered people.

Later, when the sacred city was in ruins, and the Jews were in exile or in the grave, he reiterated the same prediction in the striking parable of the valley filled with dry bones. By this he declared that the nation, then morally and physically dead, would yet be raised and revivified by Jehovah, and endued with a new and more glorious life (xxxvii. 1-14); while all heathen foes which opposed it, would be completely destroyed. For the sake of his honor, which was sadly tarnished by the infidelity of those who represented him before the world, Jehovah would give them a new heart of flesh, instead of their hard heart of stone (xxxvi. 21-26). The old and broken covenant he would renew, and he himself would return again to dwell in Jerusalem among his people (xvi. 62). It is also interesting to note that in Ezekiel's picture of the restored Hebrew kingdom the descendants of the northern Israelites, as well as the Judeans, are to have a share (xxxvii. 16-22). Each of the ancient tribes is to be assigned a definite portion of the land of Canaan (xlvii. 13). Over the united people is to rule Jehovah's faithful servant, a scion of the royal Judean line, who shall be dominated by the same noble purposes as guided Israel's great conqueror-king of blessed memory (xxxiv. 23, 24; xxxvii. 24-28). Ezekiel portrays the unbroken peace and unbounded prosperity which will ultimately come to the restored people, in colors even more glowing than do the earlier prophets (xxxiv. 25-29; xxxvi. 8-15); but being a discerning pastor, who did not shut his eyes to the imperfections of his flock, he recognized that a long process of purification was necessary before they would be prepared to become worthy citizens of the kingdom which Jehovah purposed to establish, with Jerusalem as its centre. 47. Profiting by the experience of the past, and following the tendency toward greater ceremonialism, which found expression in Deuteronomy and the reformation of Josiah, Ezekiel outlined for the restored state a plan calculated to correct the imperfections of the earlier system, and to impress by form and ceremony the great truths which he deemed essential. Naturally it was in general modelled after the pre-exilic Hebrew kingdom and temple, with which he was so familiar; but his fertile mind suggested much that was entirely new, and not a little that proved impractical in the presence of actual facts. His purpose, however, is evident. By detailed regulations lie aimed to close all the gaps in the law of Deuteronomy, whereby the old heathenism had found admission, and to surround the members of the restored EZEKIEL'S PROGRAM FOR THE HIERARCHY 55 community with influences which would insure their perfect development. According to his vision, the life of the community centred, not about the palace, but about the temple, where dwelt Jehovah, the acknowledged King of his people. To guard his holy abode from too close contact with the life of the city, and to impress the idea of his holiness, it was to be enclosed by two series of broad courts, shut in by encircling walls, and guarded by imposing gates. Within this space, contrary to earlier usage, no foreigner was to be allowed to set foot; even the non-Hebrew servants who performed the menial duties at the pre-exilic sanctuary were to be excluded. Their place was to be filled by the Levites, who, in accordance with the regulations of Deuteronomy, were continued in charge of the temple (Deut. x. 8, 9; xviii. 1-8). Now, however, since they had formerly been connected with the high places, they were to be degraded (Ezek. xliv. 10-14). The higher functions henceforth were to be performed only by the descendants of Zadok; that is, by the original priests of the sanctuary at Jerusalem. The number of sacrifices in the name of the nation was to be greatly increased, and the ritual made more elaborate; while the private offerings of earlier times almost disappeared. A prominence which they never possessed before was also given to the atoning sacrifices. At the beginning of the first and seventh months special atoning services were appointed. In fact, almost all the sacrifices offered in the name of the nation were now to be of this nature. From

this time forth, the prophetic teachings respecting the hideousness of sin were to be forcibly driven home to the hearts of the people through the services of the ritual. 48. In Ezckiel's system the priesthood completely overshadows the monarchy. The chief r6le of the prince, who represents the king of earlier days, was to provide for the stated sacrifices in behalf of the nation. For this purpose alone, he was to receive fixed dues from the people. His old right of appointing and regulating the priests of the sanctuary vanished, the situation was completely reversed, and he became merely a servant of the sanctuary. In the new division of the territory of Judah, Ezekiel assigns to the priests and Levites the most desirable land immediately surrounding the temple. Thus it was that this energetic priest-prophet of the exile formulated the first constitution of a purely ecclesiastical state. The subsequent temper and political fortunes of his people favored its institution. It was, of course, laid aside until the second temple was built, but, from that time on, many of its suggestions were adopted entirely or in modified form. 49. Ezekiel, it may truly be said, presented the rough draft, which, when elaborated, became the program of later generations. With him began the codification and gradual — possibly almost unconscious — expansion of the older ritualistic laws, which culminated in the minute regulations of the scribes. Most of the ideas which they emphasized — the exaltation of the priesthood, the sanctity of the temple, the careful distinction between clean and unclean, and the atoning sacrifices — are also prominent in Ezekiel's system. He, therefore, occupies an important mediating position between, the earlier and simpler code HISTORICAL VALUE OF EZEKIEL'S PROGRAM 57 contained in Deuteronomy and the Book of the Covenant (Ex. xx. to xxiv.), and the more detailed regulations which are known as the Priestly or Levitical Law (see sect. 201). Later circumstances and re-visors modified Ezekiel's program in many particulars. The day had not yet arrived when any system was considered final. His regu-

lations were revised as freely as he had modified those of Deuteronomy. " The Law " was still in the process of formation. For example, the power and duties which he assigned to the Davidic prince were absorbed by the high priest, who, in the program of the priest-prophet of the exile, had not yet appeared. Later generations also assigned quite another historical reason why the Levites, the priests of the old high places, were made subservient to the Zadokites, the original Jerusalem priests (sect. 231). Many other regulations calculated to increase the revenues of the temple and of its ministers were added, as new needs arose and as the ritual became more complex. On the other hand, many of the more impracticable elements in Ezekiel's plan, as, for example, the arbitrary assignment of the territory of Canaan and the design of the temple, were simply ignored in the face of later conditions. It was but natural in the first century of the Christian era, when the traditional origin of the law was generally accepted by the Jews, that they should recognize the many differences between Ezekiel's and the still more elaborate Priestly Code, and should question the authority of the prophet. In the light of history, however, he figures as the most prominent of the many who, during the critical period of the exile, were thinking of the future as well as of the present, and devising those systems of law, which, when finally revised and combined, became the guiding norm of Judaism. Ezekiel was indeed the potter who took up the tools of preceding priests and prophets, and on the wheel of his age moulded the external religious life of his race. THE LITEKAKY ACTIVITY OP THE EXILE 50. While their state existed, the attention of the Jewish people was almost wholly engrossed by the stirring political events which followed each other in rapid succession. They had scarcely time to listen to the voice of their prophets, much less to that of their past. During the exile, however, for half a century their life was barren of events. They lived, not in the present, but in the memory of bygone experiences, and in the hopes which they projected into the future. The more intensely they thought of that future, which they firmly believed held for them the possibilities of a renewed national life, the more earnestly they studied the past, to learn how they might avoid its mistakes. The work of Ezekiel, who is the most perfect representative of the better class of Jews in the exile, forcibly illustrates this dominant tendency. The sixteenth and twentieth chapters of his prophecy, as well as many other passages, are devoted to a review of Hebrew history, with the aim of drawing from it lessons, helpful for the present and future. The same motives that led them to study their previous history, impelled them to collect and preserve the literary productions of preceding generations. Chief among these motives was the horror which the faithful felt, lest Babylon's policy of disintegration should prove successful, and the Jews be absorbed and lose their identity among the peoples within whose territory they found themselves. The danger was at that time far greater than it is usually considered to have been. The high wall of separation which has kept the Jew during the succeeding ages from the Gentile was not yet built. The inhabitants of Samaria, deported by Assyria in 722 B. c., were quickly absorbed by the kindred Semitic races among whom they settled. The moment the Jews began to engage in trade, their temptations multiplied, for the Babylonians introduced their gods and religion into every department of business. Babylonian priests were the scribes who wrote their legal contracts, and Babylonian gods were invoked to witness the oaths which sealed their agreements. As long as the Jews refused to acknowledge the deities of Babylon, they were naturally subject to many restrictions. Thus self-interest, as well as the potent, persistent example of the rich and powerful, with whom they came into daily contact, prompted them to forget the austere God whom they or their fathers had worshipped on the hills of Palestine. The Babylonian worship itself offered many strong allurements. In the magnificence of its

services it completely overshadowed anything hitherto known to the Jews. The inspired prophets of Jehovah could declare, especially when Babylon's end was near: " Bel has bowed down, Nebo has crouched, their idols are given up to the beasts and the cattle " (Isa. xlvi. 1); but to the ignorant during the years of Babylon's glory the testimony of facts seemed only to confirm the claims of their boastful conquerors. The religious faith of such kings as Nebuchadrezzar also contained many ideas which are admirable. The INCENTIVES TO LITERARY ACTIVITY 61 same was true to a certain extent of the religion of Egypt, which must have proved even a greater temptation to the ordinary Jew, because it was that of a friendly people. The earnest sermons unveiling the nothingness of the gods of the Babylonians, which appear in the literature of the exile, are conclusive evidence that the temptation to apostasy was a real one, and the terror which the faithful felt in the face of it, well grounded. Nothing was so calculated to arouse the loyalty of the race as the memory of common national experiences. If the knowledge of those experiences were to be preserved, it must be through the medium of written records. The scattered condition of the Jewish people made writing the only means whereby it was possible to communicate with all of them. This fact undoubtedly gave a great impetus to the literary art. The atmosphere of both Egypt and Babylon fostered the same tendency. Nowhere in the ancient world was writing more commonly employed in the everyday affairs of life. In Babylon, at least, every important commercial transaction was sealed by a written contract. Rulers communicated with their subjects by means of public inscriptions. A large class of scribes devoted their entire time to literary composition and to copying public and private documents. Already the royal libraries possessed a literature representing a period of over three thousand years, and consisting of royal decrees, national annals, hymns, mythological tales, epics, magic formulas, and laws. Thus it was that their condition, their

needs, their patriotism, and their environment all conspired to make the Jews in the exile a literary people. 51. The best energies of the Jewish people now-found expression in writing, as the Books of Ezekiel, Lamentations, and the exilic chapters preserved in the Book of Isaiah, conclusively demonstrate. For the first time also they learned fully to prize the literary treasures inherited from the past. An important part of their work, therefore, was the collecting and editing of that which had already been written. On a larger scale than had Ezekiel, some unknown editor or editors essayed the task of preserving, in the form of a connected and detailed history of their nation from earliest time to the present, those records which probably already existed in written documents. The aim was to kindle a national spirit, and above all to enforce the great prophetic truths which that history so clearly illustrated. The result was the narrative contained in the Books of Samuel and Kings. Introductory to this, and edited from the same point of view, is the Book of Judges. While this great history traces the life of the Hebrew people down to the year 560 B. c., and, therefore, in its final form comes from the latter part of the exile, it is composed of extracts from much earlier writings. Fortunately the exile was not unexpected, at least by those who heeded the words of the prophets. The blow did not fall all at once, so that ample opportunity was given to the refugees in Egypt, and to the first group of exiles in Babylon, to preserve copies of their sacred writings. In Samuel-Kings the work of the final editor is chiefly that of a compiler. His own contributions, aside from the arrangement of the material in a chronological framework, appear in the didactic sections, which are intended to enforce the prophetic truths current in this later age, and EDITING OF EARLIER HISTORICAL RECORDS 63 which are easily recognized because of their peculiarities of style and thought (see I. sect. 34; II. sects. 2, 3.) 52. The Book of Joshua, although in part parallel with the Book of Judges, presents an entirely different picture of the history and contains fewer citations from primitive records. The style and point of view also are much more uniform than those of Judges. It represents in general the conception of the period which was current during the exile (compare Ezck. xx.). It is extremely probable that the older prophetic sections, preserved in the book, were edited at this time, although its final composition dates from a still later period. 53. The return to Babylon, the traditional home of the ancestors of the Hebrews, undoubtedly kindled a new interest in the narratives of the patriarchs; just as the Jews in Egypt recalled the stories of the sojourn of their forefathers in the land of the Nile, and of their return to Canaan. How far we are indebted to this new interest and literary activity for the preservation of the inspiring prophetic narratives contained in the opening books of the Old Testament, can never be definitely determined. That some debt exists can hardly be questioned. The same is true of the accounts of creation, the garden of Eden, and the flood, which reveal so many striking points of likeness and unlikeness with the corresponding traditions current among the Babylonians. To the same influences we undoubtedly owe the development of the parallel priestly narratives, which were later united with the older prophetic to form our present Pentateuch. 54. Ezekiel was only one of many priests deported to Babylon. There is evidence that others, like himself, during the period when the temple lay in ruins, were preparing for the promised restoration. The process of codifying, expanding, and adapting the law was greatly accelerated by the exile. While the temple remained and its services were continuous, its regulations and customs were preserved chiefly in oral form, but after its destruction they were in imminent danger of being forgotten through disuse. The danger impelled those who were familiar with the ancient usages to take the pen. In so doing they also recognized their opportunity for improving upon the old. While they felt the influence of the growing reverence for the past, in the exile they were free from the

tyrannical rule of existing custom. This freedom may have given rise to systems differing from Ezekiel's, as his in turn differs both from the earlier Deuteronomic and the later Priestly Code. At first there may have been much confusion. It was necessary that many regulations be modified before they could be practically applied to later conditions. The outlines, however, of that which ultimately became the accepted code, were probably developed at this time, and the task of uniting existing codes with the new systems begun. 55. In estimating the literary, and especially the editorial work of the exile, it is necessary to remember that the extreme reverence for the letter, as well as for the spirit of earlier writings, was a growth of later times. The Jews still had prophets in their midst whose words they recognized as authoritative as those of olden days. The consecrated priests and prophets who edited and expanded the writings of RE-EDITING OF EARLIER PROPHECIES 65 their predecessors, considered themselves equally inspired by the spirit of the same God. The message of Jehovah to mankind through the Jewish race was not yet complete. New conditions constantly called for a new interpretation of the old. At first the close student of the Bible is dismayed to find the older writings interspersed with changes and additions from later hands. Dismay is soon exchanged for thankfulness, when it is recognized as an index of the great truth that divine revelation never ceased, but that each age received a new message from the Eternal. Fortunately the canon of the Old Testament was not forever closed until centuries after the exile. More than half of its books, however, bear the imprint of the work of the faithful editors who, during the period of their nation's deepest humiliation, labored to preserve the inestimable treasure intrusted to their race, and, in so doing, preserved the race itself. VII THE CLOSING YEARS OF THE BABYLONIAN KTTLE 56. After a strong reign of forty-three years, in 561 B. c. the great Nebuchadrezzar died, leaving a powerful and well-organized empire to his son

Evil-Merodach (Babylonian, Amil-Marduk, " man or servant of Marduk"). The new ruler seems to have been one of the many weak products of the Oriental harem. Berosus states that he was dissolute in character and unjust in his rule. This statement is confirmed by the brevity of his reign. None of his inscriptions have been found; but, according to the biblical narrative (II. Kings xxv. 27-30), it was he who liberated the Jewish king, Jehoiakin, after he had been confined for thirty-seven years in Babylonian prisons, and gave him a place at the royal table. This act of clemency may have signalized the accession of the new ruler to the throne, although the author of Kings dates the event in the latter part of the year 560 B. c., when he had already been reigning more than a year. The liberation of Jehoiakin does not appear to have possessed much, if any, permanent political significance, for during the years immediately preceding the dissolution of the great empire, the hatred of the Jewish exiles toward their masters was intensified rather than mollified. NEBUCHADREZZAR'S SUCCESSORS 67 57. The first blow against Babylon was struck when Nergal-sharuzur, the Neriglissar of the Greeks, slew Evil-Merodach, after he had reigned but two years; for, although the assassin, who mounted the throne, was a stronger ruler than the murdered king, it introduced a regime of anarchy which destroyed the vital strength of the empire. The new ruler was probably the Nergalsharezer of Jeremiah xxxix. 3, who, as one of the chief officers of Nebuchadrezzar, directed the final capture and destruction of Jerusalem in 586 B. c. Two Greek historians state independently that he was the brother-in-law of Evil-Merodach, and therefore the son-in-law of Nebuchadrezzar. Their testimony is probably authentic, for, from the inscriptions of Nergalsharuzur, it is evident that he followed closely the policy of the great king. For a brief interval he maintained the integrity of the empire. His entire attention, however, was devoted to building enterprises. Nabonidus attributes to him the rebuilding of certain temples (Nab., Cor. Cyl.

iv. 3-6). The old palace of his predecessors, which had fallen into decay, he thoroughly restored (Cambridge Cyl. ii. 15-39), and further developed the canal system of Babylon. He alludes to the rebellions and conspiracies which disturbed his short reign, and, in a prayer at the close of one of his inscriptions, suggests the well-grounded fears which oppressed him: "0, Mar-duk, mighty lord, strong prince, omnipotent and invincible, light of the gods, to thee I pray. Be kindly disposed to the gracious work of my hands, and grant as a gift forever a long life, many offspring, a stable throne, and a lasting rule, in accordance with thy eternal and unchanging will, to me, Nergalsharuzur, the king, the builder, the one who cares for thy sanctuaries " (Ripley Cyl. ii. 28-38). 58. Four years only he reigned, leaving his throne to his young son, Labashi-Marduk, who, according to the Nabonidus inscription, "as a little child was taken from the harem, and not in accord with the desire of the gods was seated on the throne of sovereignty " (Cor. Inscript. iv. 8). Within nine months the conspiracies which his father had feared, ripened, and the young king was murdered by his nobles. They then conferred the royal power upon one of their number, Nabuna'id, better known as Nabonidus, a prince of Babylon. It is difficult to ascertain what determined the choice of the conspirators. Perhaps it was because, as he claims, he was a descendant of the family of Nebuchadrezzar and Nergalsharuzur (Cor. Inscript. v. 6), or, possibly, because, recognizing that he had few of the qualities of a statesman or ruler, they hoped to retain more power and independence for themselves. In his coronation inscription, Nabonidus states that " into the midst of the temple of the sceptre they brought me, and their offerings they poured out at my feet, my feet they kissed, and they worshipped my majesty. By the decree of the lord Marduk, I am raised up to the dominion of the land. Now they cry, 0, father of this land, thou hast no equal " (v. 1-5). 59. From his inscriptions, as well as from the statements of the Greek his-

torians, it is evident that his interests were all religious and antiquarian. In the face of the imminent danger from invasion, he strengthened the huge wall along the Euphrates; but otherwise all of the recorded activity of his reigii of THE ANTIQUARIAN ZEAL OF NABONIDUS 69 seventeen years consisted in the restoration of temples. In him this tendency was so extreme that it became grotesque. Like Nebuchadrezzar, he repaired and adorned the sanctuaries of Babylon. He recognized Marduk, Bel, and Nebo, the favorite gods of his people, but his chief interest centred in the revival of the worship of the ancient deities. Not contented, as his predecessors had been, with rebuilding ancient temples on their traditional sites, he made careful excavations to find their original foundations. In the great cylinder from Abu-Habba, he tells us: "I summoned my distant subjects from Gaza, on the borders of Egypt, by the upper sea on the other side of the Euphrates, even to the lower sea (Persian), kings, princes, governors and many men, which Sin, Shamash, and Ishtar, my lords, had intrusted to me, to build the temple of Sin, my lord and savior, which is situated in Harran." Cedars were brought from Mount Amanus, and bronze, silver, and gold were freely used in beautifying this ancient shrine. Similarly the temple of Shamash at Sippar, originally founded thirty-two hundred years before by the son of Sargon L, was lavishly rebuilt. Here an entire year was devoted to excavating for the original site, while each day the king uttered fervent prayers for the success of the undertaking. When not only the original foundation of the temple was unearthed, but also the cylinder of its first builder, the joy of the royal antiquarian knew no bounds. 60. The same interest in the past seems to have led him to collect many of the images of the gods, and to transfer them to places where they would receive better care. His aim may also have been to concentrate their protective power in Babylon. In one of his inscriptions he prays to Shamash, his favorite god: "Be gracious to me, receive my sighs, grant

my petition; the legitimate crown and sceptre, which you have allowed me to grasp, may I hold in my hand forever and ever" (Nab. Abu-Habba, Col. iii. 19-21). Although there is no evidence that he was deliberately attempting to set aside the popular worship, the old Babylonian gods, which were also those of the Assyrians, receive far more attention in his inscriptions than do Marduk and Nebo. His subjects, naturally, could not understand his zeal for the old, and, therefore, viewed his acts askance; while the priests and worshippers at the shrines which he despoiled swelled the army of those who were bitterly opposed to him. Perhaps it was because he recognized his growing unpopularity, that he retired from Babylon altogether, making his home at a town whose location is no longer known. Thus absenting himself from his capital, the great religious feasts, which were regarded as a most important element in the worship of the national gods, and for which the presence of the king was essential, were not observed. Nothing was more calculated to alienate a religious people like the Babylonians, than these wide departures from the current tradition. Cyrus states in one of his inscriptions (I. Raw. 68, 4; 33, 4): "The gods of Shumir and Akkad, whom Nabu-na'id, arousing the anger of the chief of the gods (Marduk), had carried away to Shuannaki, I, at the command of Marduk, the great god, caused to be restored to their places in accordance with their desire." THE FALSE CONFIDENCE OF NABONIDUS 71 61. There is something exceedingly tragic in the picture of this last king of proud Babylon giving his whole attention to the gods of the dead past, thereby neglecting his duties as a king and arousing the suspicions and hatred of his subjects; while from the north, apparently little heeded by him, the dark war clouds were approaching ever nearer. The prominent mention of his oldest son, Belsharuzur, in his inscriptions, as well as the policy of the king, indicate that he assigned to him an important place in the empire, and possibly in his latter days shared with him the royal authority. His apparent indifference in the face of an overwhelming danger may be explained by his absolute confidence in the impregnability of the walls of Babylon on the one hand, and, on the other, by his blind confidence that the gods would never desert one who had served them so faithfully and untiringly. A sudden and sad awakening awaited the royal dreamer. 62. The Assyrian kings, in conducting campaign after campaign against the freedom-loving tribes living among the mountains to the east of their broad empire, felt that they were conferring a great service upon their race in exterminating or carrying away into slavery those peoples who most seriously menaced their peace and independence. Their policy resulted far differently from what they had imagined. Its very thoroughness defeated its end, for the inviting territory bereft of inhabitants by their arms, like a loadstone attracted the Aryan peoples, who during the eighth century came streaming down from southern Europe and the highlands of central Asia. At first they were intent only upon gaining homes, and were united by no common bond. In most cases they affiliated readily with the surviving peoples whom they found already in possession, and who represented earlier waves of invasion. In time the different tribes began to coalesce. Before the fall of the Assyrian empire, large bodies of these northern invaders had established themselves among the mountains to the north. According to the recently discovered inscription of Nabdnidus, which chronicles the destruction of Nineveh (see Appendix I.), rude Aryan hordes, the Umman-Manda, at the summons of Nabopolassar, who had raised in Babylon the standard of revolt against Assyria, completed in 605 B. c. the destruction of that great world power. The conquerors divided the territory thus acquired with the Babylonians. Whenever this new northern power er is referred to in the contemporary cuneiform inscriptions it is called the empire of the Umman-Manda. The term Umman-Manda means "nomadic hordes," and is the regular Babylonian designation of those fierce northern in-

vaders known to the Greeks as the Scythians and the Cimmerians. The state which they founded on the ruins of Assyria must, however, be identical with the Median kingdom of the late Greek writers. The Madai, during the flourishing days of the Assyrian empire, occupied the territory to the south of the Caspian Sea. Before or soon after their conquest of Assyria, the northern hordes must have overrun Media, conquering and partially uniting with the older population. The amalgamation was the easier because they were of kindred blood. The designation " Median " may therefore have an historical basis or may simply be due to the confusion in later times of the somewhat similar but fundamentally different terms, Manda and MadS. About 585 B. c., THE RISE OF CYRUS 73 according to the Greek historians, a treaty was concluded between Nebuchadrezzar, the son of Nabopo-Jassar, Alyattes of Lydia, and the Median king Cyaxares, the conqueror of Nineveh, which brought nearly thirty years of comparative peace and prosperity to western Asia. It was, however, an armed peace. Nebuchadrezzar improved the years of quiet to fortify his capital and land strongly against his northern ally. The overthrow of the house of Nebuchadrezzar and the accession of Nabonidus marked the severance of friendly relations between Babylon and the kingdom of the Umman-Manda. A kingdom like the latter, which had come into existence so suddenly, and which included many heterogeneous elements, was destined as quickly to collapse, whenever the power which held it together devolved upon a weak or mediocre ruler. Astyages, the successor of Cyaxares, obviously possessed little of the ability of his predecessor. There can also be little doubt that the old Median population was only awaiting a strong champion about whom it might rally in an effort to throw off the hated yoke of the conqueror. 63. The deliverer came, not from the Median, but from the kindred Persian stock. Cyrus is designated in the inscriptions as " the king of Anshan " or " Anzan." Anshan is mentioned in a very ancient

inscription of Gudea (Sarzec, Ddcouvertes en Chalde"e, pi. 19, Col. 3), and frequently in later Assyrian inscriptions, and appears from these references to have been a little state located in northwestern Elam and to the south of Media, among the mountains northeast of Babylonia. Cyrus gives a long list of his ancestors, who, like himself, had ruled in Anshan, and tells us that he became king in 559 B. c. It is exceedingly probable that before he suddenly emerged into world-wide prominence, his sway was acknowledged by the Elamite tribes who had survived the calamities which had overtaken their nation (Ezek. xxxii. 24). In the great cylinder of Nabonidus it is stated that " Cyrus, the king of Anzan, his (Astyages) insignificant vassal, scattered with his few troops the numerous Scythians (Umman-Manda). Astyages, their king, he captured and carried away in bonds to his land " (i. 28-33). The inscription evidently dates from soon after this event, for the victory of Cyrus over the Scythians is viewed by the Babylonians, not with alarm, but as in perfect accord with the will of their god Marduk, and, therefore, as an occasion for rejoicing. The Nabonidus-Cyrus Chronicle gives a fuller account of the great victory whereby " the insignificant vassal" of Astyages became master of the old Median empire. " Astyages assembled his army and advanced against Cyrus, king of Anshan. ... The people of Astyages rebelled against him; he was taken captive and handed over to Cyrus. Cyrus advanced toward Ecbatana, the capital; the silver, gold, and possessions of the territory of Ecbatana he carried forth and brought to Anshan " (i. 1-4). The date of this event was 549 B. c. The cause of the revolt of the Median subjects of Astyages was evidently their dislike for the barbarous rule of the Umman-Manda. The facts also explain why the Modes were regarded as co-partners with the Persians in the empire which resulted from this victory. The statement of the Persian historian, Ctesias, that most of the successes of Cyrus were purchased by intrigue and deceit, may not be entirely without foundation. THE EARLIER CON-

QUESTS OP CYRUS 75

The most probable basis for the tradition of Herodotus, that the Scythian princes were treacherously murdered, is found in the events of 549 u. c. Henceforth Cyrus figured as the regular successor to the Median throne, and devoted the years immediately following to establishing his claim. It is not strange that the biblical writers continued to speak of the new empire as the Median. In 546 B. c. Cyrus appears for the first time with the title " King of Persia."
64. The new conqueror combined with the ability of a great commander the skill of a diplomat and the prudence of a wise statesman. He knew how to wait as well as how to lead a sudden attack. In the year 547 B. c. he crossed the Tigris and conquered and subjugated the broad plains of Mesopotamia, lying to the north of Babylon, which had been held by Astyages, but temporarily seized by Nabonidus (Nab.-Cyrus Chr. i. 15-17). Thus he established early in his career a base for an attack upon his still powerful rival; but there is no positive evidence that he ventured it at that time. Apparently recognizing the impregnable nature of the huge walls which encircled Babylon, he wisely hesitated to press at once his conquests in that quarter. Instead he seems to have instituted intrigues calculated to alienate still further the lukewarm loyalty which the Babylonians felt for their strange king.
65. Cyrus meantime, in 546 B. c., turned his attention to the old fend between the Medes and the Lydians, who, under their wealthy king, Croesus, were masters of central Asia Minor. The Lydian king assumed the offensive, and in Cappadocia an indecisive battle was fought (Herod, i. 76). When Crresus retired, deeming the campaign of the year at an end, Cyrus followed him, met and defeated his army, and was soon in possession of his capital, Sardis. The Greek colonies in Asia Minor were next attacked. Some of them submitted readily, while others made a valiant resistance; but the lack of united organization among the Greeks gave Cyrus the advantage, so that in time he was able to extend his rule to the Egean Sea. Returning to his capital, he next successfully directed his armies against the half-civilized hordes to the east of his empire. Not until 538 B. c. were conditions ripe for the conquest of the proud mistress of the lower Euphrates. The ultimate result of the impending struggle had long been evident to all who recognized the marked superiority of Persian arms over those of any other people in southwestern Asia. To those who were cognizant of the internal weakness and corruption of the Babylonian empire, it was obvious that the fruit for which Cyrus had waited so long was ripe for the plucking. 66. The hopes and expectations of the Jewish exiles in Babylon, while Cyrus was engaged in his career of conquest, can be imagined; but, fortunately, we are not left to conjecture. Through all the dark period which had preceded this promise of a dawn, the more faithful ones, like Ezekiel, had cherished the firm belief that an opportunity would yet be given to them to return. Jeremiah's bold assurance that Jehovah would not forget his loving purpose toward his scattered people, and that he would again plant them in Canaan, never again to be torn up, had kept alive their much-tried faith. Babylon's rule was recognized by all as the first barrier which must be removed before the way would be opened for a return, for " they JOY AT THE PROSPECT OF BABYLON'S FALL 77 who took them captives held them fast; they refused to let them go " (Jer. I. 33). When the mighty city began to totter, it is not strange that joy filled every Jewish heart. Sighs of relief and cries of thanksgiving burst from many lips. If these found too open expression, and brought upon the exiles the persecutions of their masters, it only made them the more eager for the consummation. 67. A chorus of minor prophets, disciples of Isaiah, Jeremiah, and Ezekiel, made Babylon's approaching downfall the theme of their message. They present vividly the hopes and fears of the exiles in the East. At Jehovah's command, they saw his consecrated ones, the multitudes of the nations, headed by the Medes, whom no bribes would turn back, advancing to execute judgment upon guilty Babylon (Isa. xiv.; xxi. 1-10). Graphically they pictured the details of the siege: "The land trembles. The mighty men of Babylon cease to fight. They remain in their strongholds. Their might has failed. They are become as women. Her dwelling-places are on fire. Her defences are broken. One post shall run to meet another, and one messenger to meet another, to show the king of Babylon that his city is taken on every quarter" (Jer. li. 29-31). Complacently they described the complete ruin and desolation soon to overtake the city, which they regarded as the personification of greed, corruption, oppression, and idolatry. Prom their high towers they perceived that Babylon had ceased to be a useful instrument in the hand of Jehovah, and hence it must be destroyed. From their point of view, it was not strange that they regarded this act as a punishment for the wrongs done to their city and temple (Jer. li. 11, 24). In a sense they were right, for Babylon's downfall was the direct consequence of the cruel, rapacious policy which brought to the great city its wealth, and with that, the resulting luxury and corruption which, in turn, proved its undoing. Its conquest by Cyrus introduced a new and nobler chapter of human history. Above all, it made possible the re-building of Jerusalem and the temple, which were destined again to give to the Jewish race a centre about which their national and religious life might crystallize. THE MESSAGE OF THE GREAT PROPHET OP THE EXILE 68. Op all the exiles who eagerly watched the victorious progress of Cyrus, none understood so fully its true significance as the great unknown prophet from whom came the messages preserved in chapters xl. to lv. of the Book of Isaiah. Rising above the confusion and humiliation of the present, he caught glimpses of the eternal purpose which was being worked out in human history, and of the principles in accordance with which it must be realized. Forcibly and beautifully he interpreted to his own and succeeding ages the results of his inspired

vision. In him Hebrew prophecy reached its highest expression. Accepting the principles enunciated by his great predecessors, Isaiah, Jeremiah, and Ezekiel, he heralded the universal kingdom of God, in which, not might, but self-sacrifice was to be the ruling force. While he was an idealist, living in a future which proved far more distant than he anticipated, he recognized and dealt most practically with the needs of the moment. His first aim was to arouse the enthusiasm and patriotism of his apathetic fellow-exiles, that they might turn their backs upon the comforts of Babylon, and, in the face of seemingly superhuman obstacles, devote themselves and their all to the noble task of reviving their dismembered state. He fully realized that the future of their race and of the religion of Jehovah depended largely upon their action when the opportunity came. It was a crisis even greater than that which arose when Jerusalem was destroyed, for if the Jews neglected their supreme opportunity, their end would be far more shameful than that of the northern Israelites. The prophet's words were primarily addressed to his fellow-countrymen in Babylon, but the appeal was to all who would respond to the needs of the hour, wherever the upheaval of 586 B. c. had cast them. 69. The prophet's message opens with the joyful proclamation that Israel's period of hardship is over (xl. 1, 2). With the combined power of logic and rhetoric, the awful doubts which paralyzed the exiles were met, and glorious hopes substituted. We can hear him, like Ezekiel, reasoning with his flock: "Do you fear that Jehovah has forgotten and will not vindicate you (xl. 27)? Already he is preparing to accomplish for you a mighty work of deliverance (xl. 3-5). Like a tender shepherd he will gather his people (xl. 11). Do you fear that your masters will not let you go? At Jehovah's command the peoples who now hold you in slavery shall themselves bring you back. Kings and queens, bowing humbly before the Lord, shall supply your every want. Then you shall know that Jehovah is a God who never fails those who wait

for him (xlix. 22, 23). Do the perils of the long journey back to your native land appall you? Jehovah declares that he will make the desert a paradise before you, so that you will be able to return without danger or discomfort (xli. 18-20). Does the THE CERTAINTY OF DELIVERANCE FROM BABYLON 81 present desolation of Judah discourage you? Barren Jerusalem shall again be inhabited and the land, as of old, studded with prosperous cities (xliv. 26). As suppliants, shall proud and rich nations come bringing to you their wealth. Best of all, that peace and prosperity shall continue, not for a passing moment, but forever; and your present woe shall be but a horrible dream of the past (xlv. 14-17). Upon your descendants also shall rest Jehovah's blessing and the benign, reviving, transforming influence of his spirit (xliv. 3). 70. " But some of you question, ' What proof is there that these glorious predictions will be fulfilled?' The sole and sufficient assurance is found in the character of the God who thus promises. He, who proclaims himself to be your Redeemer, is also your Creator. Jehovah is he who rules the universe and guides with omnipotent hand all human events (xliv. 24, 25). Consider the utter folly of fearing the Babylonians, your present masters, whose gods arc the creations of their own hands and fancies, and who possess no power to deliver either themselves or their devotees. The proud nations of the earth are but infinitesimal particles in the great universe which Jehovah directs with such wisdom and precision (xl. 12-26). If you question his ability and readiness to save, remember how he has revealed himself in your past history (xliii. 2). Above all, he is a God of absolute righteousness (xlv. 19). Recall also how, from the earliest history of your race, he has tenderly cared for you. His love has far surpassed that of a mother toward her helpless child (xlvi. 3, 4; xlix. 15, 16). Surely you cannot, for a moment, doubt the promise of such a God, infinite in power, all wise, all just, and all loving. 71. " If you but open your eyes you will see the instrument wherewith he is to accomplish

your deliverance. For your sakes he is giving victory after victory to that obscure eastern prince, who already has be-come master of the powerful Median empire (xli. 1-4, 25). It may not be in accord with your expectations, but I tell you that this Cyrus is, indeed, Jehovah's Messiah, anointed to prepare the way for your restoration (xlv. 1-13; xlviii. 14-16). In view of Jehovah's purpose to deliver — a purpose which already is on the verge of being accomplished — the fall of proud Babylon is imminent. No longer, 0 arrogant Babylonians, will you compel the nations to pander to your love of luxury. For your cruelty toward his people, whom he for a time intrusted to your care, destruction shall fall upon you. Vainglorious, corrupt, superstitious city! All your boasted wisdom, your far-famed magical formulas, and the skill of your astrologers, shall not deliver you from the vengeance which Jehovah will speedily visit upon you (xlvii.). 72. " Do you wish to know, 0 exiles, why Jehovah has chosen you as a race from all the peoples of the earth, and why, therefore, he will surely redeem you? It is because it is his immutable and righteous purpose to lead all mankind to know and worship him (xlv. 23). You, he has called to serve him, in realizing that purpose. You, indeed, are his witnesses before the world. He has created and trained you, that you may set forth his praise (xliii. 10, 12, 21). For the uplifting of mankind he requires a servant who, JEHOVAH'S PEOPLE CHOSEN FOR SERVICE 83 amidst persecution and humiliation, ever responsive to the divine teaching and direction, will devote himself wholly and completely to the exalted task of proclaiming his divine will (xlii. 1-4, 6, 7; xlix. 3, 5-13). That you might be prepared for that sublime service, 0 Israelites, Jehovah has spared no effort. With that end in view, he chose you, the seed of Abraham, and brought you from the ends of the earth, cared for and designated you as his servant. Indeed, he is still upholding you, protecting you from your foes, and encouraging you in face of danger (xl. 8-13). Freely he has forgiven your sins, and now he is eager to have you return to him (xliv. 21, 22). Throughout your history he has bestowed upon you all the tender care and solicitude which a loving heart can give (xlvi. 3, 4). When blessings failed to lead you into the path of loving obedience, his tender care for you found expression in discipline, that it might awaken you to your duties and opportunities (xlii. 23, 25). 73. "Justly does Jehovah expect you, his chosen people, to be a faithful servant, prepared for any service; but alas! what does he find? Like your forefathers, to whom the great Isaiah spoke, you are blind, so that you do not see the truth, and deaf, so that you do not hear the call to service. Even the refining fire of discipline has failed to arouse you from the deep lethargy which has taken possession of you (xlii. 18-25). Instead you only say, despondently: ' Jehovah has abandoned me ' (xlix. 14). Your God has not demanded costly sacrifices; but you have not even presented what was easily in your power to give. The only offerings which you have brought to him have been your sins (xliii. 23, 24). Submission and purity of life are the first requisites for service; but alas! you are obdurate and far from righteousness (xlvi. 12). With your lips you profess allegiance to Jehovah, but your acts belie your words. Obstinately you have refused to give heed to his commands. Treacherously have you dealt with him" (xlviii. 1-4, 8). 74. Thus when the prophet, with his enlightened eye, reviewed the past history of his people and studied the character and attitude of those to whom he wrote, he was forced to admit that they were by no means prepared to perform the great service necessary for the salvation of their race and of mankind. Hence, while still speaking to his contemporaries, he was led repeatedly to turn from the imperfect and discouraging reality to describe the perfect type of servant who must appear before Jehovah's loving purpose could be accomplished. Many analogies might be cited from the history of Hebrew prophecy. Hosea frequently paused in the midst of his bitterest denunciations to portray the glories of the day when the Israelites would again be reconciled to Jehovah. Jeremiah, as he sat among the ruins of Jerusalem, painted in most glowing colors the picture of the restored city and people (Jer. xxx.: xxxi.). Indeed, the form of most Messianic prophecies, which are but the foreshadowing of the one great divine purpose being realized in human history, is determined by the conditions and, especially, the needs of the age in which the prophet lived. Naturally he placed the ideal and the sad reality side by side, and thus, by contrast, brought out each in stronger colors. MEANING OF THE TITLE "SERVANT OF JEHOVAH" 85 75. It is significant that in Isaiah xl. to lv. there is no reference to a Jewish Messiah. The term had come to be associated with the royal house of David, which had already begun to sink into merited oblivion. The one Messiah mentioned is Cyrus, and his mission is clearly denned. The prophetic conception of the divine purpose had so far expanded that it could no longer be represented by the imagery of a temporal kingdom. A new and more comprehensive terminology was demanded to describe the fuller revelation. Thus it was that the familiar title, "servant of Jehovah," became the keynote of the prophecy. Already it had been applied to the patriarchs, to Moses, Joshua, David, Solomon, and most of the pre-exilic prophets. In Deuteronomy xxxii. 36, 43, the people of Israel are addressed as the " servants of Jehovah;" while to the prophets as a class the designation was often given. In its origin the Hebrew word translated "servant" also means "slave." Its essential idea is that of the complete dependence and submission of the one thus designated to his master. Vassal princes spoke of themselves as the slaves or servants of their conqueror. A high official or commander-in-chief of an army was addressed as the "servant of the king." In something of the same sense Moses is spoken of as the "servant of Jehovah. " So, also, the prophets were Jehovah's ambassadors, intrusted with an important mission, which they were under obligations to perform at any cost to themselves. The term "servant of Jehovah," therefore, suggests the relationship, on the one hand, of the divine master commanding and supporting, and, on the other, the attitude of careful attendance and ready, faithful obedience. 76. The original of the familiar term "Messiah, anointed," as used by the prophets, was practically the same, for whoever in the Old Testament was called a Messiah — whether he was a king, like Saul, or whether he was one of the patriarchs, or the whole people Israel — was so designated, to indicate by the use of the familiar figure of anointing, that he was especially chosen and consecrated to do a certain work. The best illustration of the practical identity of the two terms is the fact that of the two most prominent men of the age, the one, Nebuchadrezzar, is called "the servant of Jehovah," and the other, Cyrus, "Jehovah's Messiah." In Psalm lxxxix. 50, 51, also, the terms " servants " and " Messiah " are used as interchangeable synonyms, both being applied to the faithful in the Jewish community. 77. The four passages in which the prophet portrays his ideal of the perfect servant of Jehovah, who alone can accomplish the divine will, constitute in themselves a unit, each adding to the completeness of the picture. Placing ourselves among the exiles, we can hear in imagination the inspiring message of the prophet: " Behold, mankind, the type of servant who will receive Jehovah's complete approval and support, and upon whom he will bestow the light and power of his own spirit, that the one thus equipped may make known his divine law to all nations. Quietly and unostentatiously, with none of the destructive methods of the old prophets, but carefully considering the needs of the weak, in perfect accord with the standards of truth, shall the faithful servant of Jehovah go about his spiritual mission of proclaiming God's law to men. He shall not waver nor be discouraged until he has THE MISSION OF THE SERVANT OF JEHOVAH 87 established on the earth this divine law, of which the nations are in such need. Jehovah, the creator of the universe and the source of all human life, declares that, in accordance with his righteous purpose, he will uphold his servant and make him the medium for the establishment of a covenant between himself and his people, and a source of spiritual light to all nations. His servant, surpassing his yoke-fellows, the former prophets, shall also be instrumental in opening to truth, eyes now blind, in bringing freedom to those now imprisoned, and in delivering from bondage the victims of suffering and sin (xlii. 1-7). 78. " Give 'heed, 0 peoples far and near, to the declaration of the servant respecting his relation to Jehovah and concerning the character of his mission: ' From my birth Jehovah called me, prepared me for effective service, and protected me from all harm. To me he has said: " You are my servant, the true Israel, by whom I shall be honored." I replied: "Alas! it seems as though my strenuous efforts (to regenerate Israel) had been in vain; but I can rest calmly in the assurance that they will be vindicated and rewarded by Jehovah." Then he, who created, strengthened, and intrusted me with the mission of bringing back his people, Israel, into loving accord with him, responded: " You are capable of a greater service than the mere restoration of the remnant of your kinsmen, the Israelites. I accordingly appoint you to bring spiritual enlightenment to all peoples, and a knowledge of my salvation to the ends of the earth." ' Jehovah further declared to his servant, now so heartily despised by mankind and the slave of rulers: ' The time is yet coming when you shall accomplish the work in which you now seem to have failed. Then kings shall be eager to do you homage, because I, who appointed you to your mission, am faithful. Verily, I will not fail you, but will cause you to establish a new covenant between me and my people, and to bring about a glorious restoration of the exiles now so widely scattered' (xlix. 1-13). 79. " Listen again to the testimony of the servant: 'Jehovah has given me the facility, which alone comes from attentively heeding his teaching, so that I am able to impart a message of help to those who need. Daily, constantly he instructs me, and

I have ever eagerly listened and been ready to respond to the call to service. Patiently have I submitted to persecution, humiliation, and derision. Serenely confident that Jehovah would help me, I faltered not; for I knew that I should never be put to shame. He, who will vindicate me, is at hand, so that no one can condemn me. Indeed, complete destruction shall come upon those who attempt it.' Such is the experience and testimony of the true servant of Jehovah. Avell do you who fear the Lord, and are seeking amidst darkness for light, heed and profit thereby (1. 4-10). 80. " Know also Jehovah's final testimony respecting the character and work of his servant: ' Behold, supreme success shall crown the wise efforts of my servant, so that he shall be greatly exalted. Just as in the past many were astounded because of the overwhelming afflictions which were visited upon him, so shall nations and the rulers of the earth stand reverentially before him, realizing in the light of his exaltation what no one had suspected before' (lii. 13-15). Succeeding generations also shall look back upon his work and exclaim: ' Who believed the prophetic SERVICE PERFECTED THROUGH SUFFERING 89 revelation respecting the servant, and understood the divine purpose which was being accomplished through him? Unattractive, despised, afflicted by disease, avoided by his fellows as an outcast, we turned away from him in horror. Deluded by the old theory of suffering, we despised him. And yet, there is no doubt that he was sick that we might be well; this one, whom we deemed cursed by God, was bearing our pains; he was wounded because we had transgressed. The peace which we enjoyed was secured through his punishment. We had wandered far from Jehovah, doing our own will, while upon him the Lord caused to fall the consequences of our sins' (liii. 1-6). When persecuted, this martyr servant of Jehovah voluntarily, submissively, in silence endured, while tyranny, under the guise of law, unjustly condemned him. Thus for the sins of humanity he was prematurely and violently cut off. Although ab-

solutely innocent, even after death he was entombed with criminals. And yet, this was no mere accident, but in perfect accordance with the divine will, for by being thus afflicted and by giving his life as an offering for others' guilt, the servant was destined to live immortally in the lives of his spiritual offspring and to realize the eternal purpose of Jehovah. After his pain and trial is over, he shall enjoy the consciousness of having made many righteous. His shall be the glory of a mighty victor, because by humiliation and a supreme self-sacrifice, he bore the sin and successfully interceded for the guilty " (liii. 7-12). 81. No one will deny that the character of the servant of Jehovah, as portrayed in these sections, presents many perplexing questions. The first one usually asked is: "Avho was this unique servant of Jehovah? " Surely the prophet could not have meant to identify himself with that servant; nor did any prophet who had preceded him, even the great Jeremiah, do more than suggest, by character and experience, certain outlines of the portrait. Much less can it be the Jewish people as a whole of which he is speaking; indeed, it is repeatedly stated that one of the chief aims in the mission of the servant is to restore the remnant of Israel to their true relations with Jehovah (xlii. 6; xlix. 5, 6). Even the faithful few within the nation, who heard and heeded the words of their prophets, cannot be the original of the picture before us. But we may further ask, Was the prophet necessarily describing a definite person or groups of individuals? In practical human experience, the presentation of an ideal usually long precedes its realization. The Hebrew prophets were constantly drawing new sketches of a perfect ruler and political state, although the best the world had yet seen were imperfect in comparison. They continued to present new ideals, because, being wise teachers, they recognized that the only way to lead humanity to rise above its low standards, was by holding up before it the higher which had been revealed to them. The great prophet of the exile was in this respect no exception. By the most effective means at his command, he was endeavoring to influence his fellow-exiles, and especially the more faithful, to strive themselves to be true servants of Jehovah. In one suggestive passage, after presenting most graphically the experience of the servant, he turns to those of his readers " who fear the Lord " and urges them to learn from the experience of the servant the lesson of submission and fidelity (I. 10). THE REALIZATION OF THE IDEAL OF SERVICE 91 82. Like all the prophets who caught glimpses of the perfection, ultimately destined in accordance with the divine plan to succeed existing imperfection, he was obliged to look to the future for the fulfilment of his supernatural ideal. It is obvious that he did not foresee that fulfilment as do we who stand in the full light of history. Like the architect of a great mediaeval cathedral, he saw only in imagination the marvellous creation which he outlined. It was his privilege to indicate the processes by which it was to be reared, but not to know personally the men and forces who, in succeeding ages, were to make the divine plan a material reality. As we follow the history of Judaism, we find a partial realization, in the experiences and work of the faithful few, who resisted the temptations offered to the Jews to forget their nationality and to enjoy the opportunities offered by the land of their adoption, and who went back to join their poverty-stricken kinsmen in rebuilding, amidst persecutions and distress, the city of sacred memories. It is interesting to note that the builders of the second temple publicly styled themselves "the servants of the God of heaven and earth " (Ezra v. 11), for the term suggests a familiarity with the message of the great prophet. By their voluntary self-sacrifice they did the work which their less devoted countrymen spurned, and revived that community which became the repository of God's supreme revelation to the human race. In time, too, Judaism began, as a body, to recognize its prophetic mission to humanity, and to seek to lead the heathen to a knowledge of the one true God. Their attainment of the ideal, it must be con-

fessed, was incomplete and partial compared with its fulfilmeiit in the character and work of the great teacher of Nazareth, who, both as prophet and martyr, completely realized and eclipsed the sublime portrait of the suffering servant of Jehovah. Alone sinless, he stood before humanity as its sin-bearer, transforming the hard heart of mankind by the irresistible influence of a love expressed in voluntary and complete self-sacrifice. In the light of history, Christianity has rightly recognized in him the supreme agent for the realization of the divine plan so marvellously presented by the unknown prophet of the exile; but until that divine plan takes final form in the kingdom of God on earth, the ideal of the servant of Jehovah will continue (as Paul clearly realized; see Acts xiii. 47) to call men to offer themselves willingly, completely, for the uplifting of the human race. THE POLITICAL AND RELIGIOUS SIGNIFICANCE OF THE BABYLONIAN EXILE 83. While the Babylonian exile was the briefest, it was also in many ways the most important period in the life of the Jewish people. It was more than a crisis; it represented a fundamental transformation in the political, social, and religious character of the race. The struggling community which ultimately centred about Jerusalem, had in reality little in common with the nation to which Jeremiah prophesied a few decades before. The ancient Hebrew state had proved in many ways a failure. Its leaders had been as blind to the higher religious truths presented by the prophets, as they were to their sagacious political counsels. From the vantage ground of the exile, the more enlightened recognized with shame that the fate which had overtaken their nation was well merited. It had sinned; for, according to the meaning of the expressive Hebrew word for sin, it "had missed the mark " which had been set before it by its inspired teachers. The wreck of the ancient state cleared the way for the construction of the new. Naturally in the reconstruction, the architects sought to eliminate all that had proved worthless. The exile demonstrated that the Jewish

people could maintain their racial integrity without political organization, and that the religion of Jehovah was not dependent upon the monarchy. In the eyes of those who labored for and participated in the revival, the ancient kings and their advisers had with few exceptions traduced their nation, and were, therefore, set aside as useless. Ezekiel and his fellow-workers anticipated the change, which subsequent circumstances enforced, and devoted themselves to formulating the constitution of a purely ecclesiastical state. In the place of the monarchy rose the hierarchy. The old military and royal aristocracy also vanished, and instead appeared a priestly nobility, with the high priest at its head. Israel became literally "a kingdom of priests and a holy nation " (Ex. xix. 6). The radical change in the external organization of the Jewish race was but an index of the deeper fact that its energies had been turned into entirely different channels. Ritual and religion, not politics, commanded the attention of its leaders. 84. In the calm and leisure of the exile, even the masses found time to meditate and to listen to the messages of their prophetic teachers. Torn from their old associations, they no longer felt the spell of the high places and heathen customs, consecrated by the usage of centuries. The advantages of the new situation were on the side of the progressive prophetic party. The reformation of Josiah had practically failed in Judah; but during the exile the principles proclaimed by the pre-exilic prophets won the day. A few remnants of the old idolatry survived in Canaan, but otherwise the ancient heathen gods ceased to attract them. The victory of the THE RELIGIOUS INFLUENCES OF THE EXILE 95 prophets was the more complete because they had consistently foretold the approach of the exile, so that when it came, it furnished a testimonial to the truth of their words which even the masses, who must see and touch before believing, appreciated. Later, the liberation by Cyrus, which they had long predicted, still further established the prophets' authority. The exiles, crushed by the calamity which had overtaken them, were also in a condition to receive the stern, uncompromising messages of their spiritual guides. Since they regarded the misfortunes which overwhelmed them as the punishment of their nation's guilt, they loathed more and more the sins of the past, and welcomed with eagerness anything which promised to bring absolution and reconciliation with Jehovah. Unconsciously they must have been influenced also by the example of their Babylonian masters, who were constantly offering propitiatory sacrifices to their deities. The result was that, from the period of the exile on, atoning offerings and prayers for forgiveness assume a far more important place among the Jews. Henceforth the ruling passion with the faithful was the desire to regain their lost national and individual purity. 85. Finally, in Babylon the Jews freed themselves not only from idolatry, but also from the half-heathen conception of Jehovah, which placed him nearly on an equality with the gods of the other nations, and restricted his influence to Canaan: Such a belief had sufficed for the Hebrews while they lived undisturbed among the secluded hills of Palestine, but when Jehovah's people bowed low in the dust before the Babylonians, who attributed their victories to the intercession of other gods, the popular conception of Jehovah was likewise cast to earth. The inspired prophets, however, had anticipated this crisis and were prepared to turn the eyes of the people from the fallen Jehovah of their imagining to the God who rules supreme in the universe. At this time the religion of the Jewish people became pure monotheism. Absorbed among races more powerful and more highly civilized than they, the Jews were forced to admit that they were only one of the weak families of the earth. The experience was painful, but valuable. It not only broadened their conception of Jehovah's character, but also led them to recognize their complete dependence upon him. They saw for the first time that they were unique among the nations simply because of their unique relation to the God of the universe. That rela-

tion, in turn, was the result of no worthy action on their part, but simply of Jehovah's choice. Thus was begotten in the minds of the thoughtful that attitude of genuine humility which comes from appreciating facts as they are, and which is the necessary pre-requisite of true development and service. 86. As these simple but important truths gradually impressed themselves upon their consciousness, the attitude of the exiles to the great heathen world about them changed. No longer could they ignore their neighbors, or merely consider them when they disturbed the peace of Israel. Beginning with the period of the exile, the nations figure prominently in the utterances of the prophets. From the same epoch dates the rise of a broad religious philosophy of history. The nations, drawn together by force, began THE NEW CONCEPTION OF THE RACE'S MISSION 97 dimly to recognize that they belonged to one family; while certain inspired Jews grasped the greater truth that one Father stood at the head of that family, and that Cyrus was Jehovah's anointed as truly as was Jehoiakin. Hence it became impossible for them to regard the heathen merely as objects of divine vengeance. Instead of constantly brooding upon their own wrongs, they began to think of Jehovah's relation to the peoples about them, and then of the role which they, as his chosen people, were called to enact in the realizing of the divine purpose in human history. Thus in the mind of the great unknown prophet of the exile, the heathen world figured as a vast missionary field and the Jews as Jehovah's chosen messengers, to proclaim abroad his name. It was difficult for him to abandon the old hope of a temporal world kingdom with the Jewish people at its head, but in his best moments he realized and taught that, not by the sword nor by force, was the rule of Jehovah to be made universal, but by the self-denying service of his despised yet faithful countrymen. Himself afflicted and the apostle to the oppressed, he learned to appreciate the value of suffering, voluntarily endured, as a transforming influence in the life of the sufferer, and as the most powerful

conceivable force in the redemption of sinful mankind. In his ideal of the suffering servant of Jehovah, he taught his kinsmen that, in the hour of their greatest humiliation, it was possible for them to conquer the world by loving sacrifice. 87. His ideal was too exalted for his contemporaries fully to understand, much less to appreciate. In the slow-moving Orient, a nation is not re-born in a day. To most of his readers a teaching which made service through suffering the weapon whereby the world was to be conquered, seemed only folly. His message, however, was true, and it was a significant moment in human history when it found lodgment in a human heart and expression from the lips of a man. Henceforth, it was destined to attract mankind more and more until the truth became an objective reality in the character and work of the great teacher of Nazareth. Thus during that half century when the Jewish race was pinioned hand and foot, mighty changes were going on within its throbbing heart. Then those ideas found full expression which were destined to shape and control its future. The tortures of the prison house also tested and brought each individual into a prominence, unknown before. The exile proved, as Amos predicted (Am. ix. 9), a sifting process, for it effectually separated the faint-hearted and sceptical from the brave and true. Many — perhaps the majority — were found wanting; but those who endured the ordeal and remained faithful were devoted to the worship of the Jehovah of the prophets with a passionate zeal, which was in striking contrast to the popular indifference that daunted pre-exilic prophets like Isaiah and Jeremiah. Bound together, not by political bonds, but by common suffering and common faith, the loyal few proved the nucleus out of which, during the succeeding centuries, grew the Jewish church. PART II THE PERSIAN PERIOD OF JEWISH HISTORY THE HISTORICAL SOURCES AND LITERATURE OF THE PERIOD 88. The record of the life of the Jewish people during the two centuries following the conquest of Babylon by Cyrus in 539 B. c. is found in a great variety of writings, chief among which are the Books of Ezra and Nehemiah. Originally, in the Jewish canon, they together constituted one book, and their striking points of similarity leave no doubt that they are from the hand of the same author. Furthermore, a comparison of their marked peculiarities with those of the Books of Chronicles demonstrates that these four books constitute one connected narrative, written in the same style and from the same unique point of view. The close connection between 'the two main divisions of this history is also indicated by the fact that the opening verses of Ezra-Nehemiah (i. 1-3") are the same as the closing section of Chronicles (xxxvi. 22-23). The characteristics of the author, who is commonly designated as the chronicler, are well known (sect. 255; see also II. sects. 7-11). He was an ecclesiastic rather than an historian. His primary aim in writing was to emphasize the institutional side of Israel's history. He lived in an age which idealized the past. Like his contemporaries, he unconsciously read the institutions and conditions of his own day into the earlier and more primitive periods, since he did not fully realize that Israel had enjoyed a progressive religious development, extending through many centuries. The result is that the original contributions of the chronicler are of value to the discriminating historian, chiefly as they reveal the conditions of the later time. 89. In determining the date at which he lived, we note that he refers to the "days of Nehemiah and Ezra" (Neh. xii. 26, 47) as if they belonged to the distant past. Unlike the older writers, whom he quotes, he describes Cyrus and his successors as " kings of Persia," which he would not have done if the Persian empire was still the one dominant power in southwestern Asia (Ezra i. 1, 2, 8; iii. 7; compare the usage in an older passage which he quotes, v. 13-vi. 3). In Nehemiah xii. 11, 22, he mentions Jaddua, who was high priest until 331 B. c., and in the twenty-second verse of the same chapter he speaks of Darius the Persian, who must be Darius Codoman-nus, the last king of the great empire founded by

Cyrus. His ignorance of the exact order of the earlier Persian kings (compare Ezra iv.) likewise points to a late date. Certainly he did not live before the Greek period. The first half of the third century, B. c., furnishes the most probable background for his work. 90. Living as he did, centuries after most of the events which he records transpired, the question as to what was the nature of the sources from which he gained his data becomes exceedingly important. Hitherto this subject has been somewhat overlooked by scholars; but within the last few years it has EARLIER SOURCES USED BY THE CHRONICLER 103 received the attention which it deserves (see Appendix III.). Fortunately, like most ancient historians, he frequently cites, with little or no change, from the earlier records at his command. In Ezra iv. 8 to vi. 18 are found two such quotations. Instead of translating them into Hebrew, in which the rest of his book is written, he retains the original Aramaic in which he found them. Prom the time of the exile, Aramaic became the language of official communication between the Semitic subjects in the Persian empire; during the last century of the Persian period it gradually became the common language of Palestine, so that the Aramaic document, from which the chronicler quotes, may well have been written only a few generations after the events which it records occurred. That it was written some time during the Persian period is established by the fact that, unlike the sections originating with the chronicler, it refers to Persian monarchs, such as Darius, as the king, without the addition "of Persia." The chronicler evidently introduced the first section, iv. 8-23, into its present context to explain why the building oj: the temple was not begun immediately after permission was granted by Cyrus, for the twenty-fourth verse of chapter iv., as well as v. 1, 2, which connect the two citations, and which are from his hand, refer only to the temple; while the first passage thus introduced is dated from the reign of Artaxerxes, and relates to the building, not of the temple, but of the walls. In verse 12 it is definitely

stated that the walls had been finished and the foundations repaired. The statements of the officials in Samaria may have been somewhat exaggerated, but the incident finds its most complete historical setting in the reign of Artaxerxes I., when the great work of Nchemiah in rebuilding the walls was nearly accomplished. Restored to this setting, so clearly indicated by the passage itself, it furnishes valuable facts supplementing the Nehemiah history. 91. The other quotation, v. 3 to vi. 14, may have been taken from the first part of the same collection of Aramaic documents, recording the official relations between the Jewish colony and the Persian government. It tells of an incident in connection with the building of the temple during the reign of Darius. While the Jewish rather than the Persian point of view is apparent in the form in which the imperial decrees are reported (compare vi. 9, 12), there is no reason to doubt that the Judean paraphrase has faithfully preserved the chief historical facts. The statistical and ecclesiastical notices contained in vi. 15-22 are expressed in the language of the chronicler. Whether his source was an earlier document or a tradition current in his day cannot be determined. The fact that the king of Assyria is regarded as still the overlord of Palestine points to a very late date, when the memory of conditions obtaining in the Persian period had become indistinct. The account of the observation of the passover suggests the chronicler's well-known tendency to describe such ceremonials as they were conducted in his own time. 92. Chapters i. and iii. are recognized, by all as the work of the chronicler. The fundamental facts presented in them — the permission from Cyrus to rebuild the temple at Jerusalem, the appointment of Sheshbazzar as governor of Judah, and the return of CHRONICLER'S CONCEPTION OF THE HISTORY 105 some of the vessels of the sanctuary — are closely parallel with those suggested by the quotation from the Aramaic document (v. 3 to vi. 14). The variations— as, for example, the r6le of a devout worshipper of Jehovah, which is assigned to Cyrus, the size and details of the list of sacred vessels returned to the Jews, the account of the immediate institution of elaborate services at Jerusalem (compare especially iii. 3-5), and the prominence given to the priests and Levites — are all distinctly characteristic of the chronicler and of his time. Furthermore, the picture which they present of conditions in Jerusalem differs widely from that contained in the oldest sources, the prophecies of Haggai and Zechariah (see sect. 119); the differences again are those which distinguish the age of the chronicler from that of Zerub-babel. The same is true of iv. 1-6. The prophets, who inspired the temple building, make no reference to the opposition of the people of the land, but plainly declare that the long delay in the work was due to the selfish neglect of the Jews themselves (Hag. i. 2-11). The language of the section is certainly that of the chronicler. In his day, when Samaritan opposition was so bitter, it was but natural that he should regard this as the cause of a delay which seemed to him otherwise inexplicable. Hence Ezra i., iii., and iv. 1-6 represent only the chronicler's conception of the first two decades of the Persian period. This conception was based upon the testimony of the Aramaic document and the Books of Haggai and Zechariah, and was naturally modified by his peculiar point of view and by traditions then current. 93. An examination of the genealogical list pre- served in Ezra ii., and its parallel in Nehemiah vii., reveals conclusive evidence that in its present form it is also from the chronicler. His love for minute genealogical tables, which became a characteristic of later Judaism, is shared by almost no other Old Testament writer. In the list, the priests, the singers, the porters, and the Nethinim, in which he was especially interested, are introduced in his usual order, and receive a major part of the attention (Ezra ii. 36-58). The clan designated as "the children of Solomon's servants " is mentioned only by him. Although their order and historical setting arc entirely different, there are too many repetitions in this list of the names in I. Chronicles

ix. 10-34 and Nehemiah xi. 3-36 to be explained as a mere coincidence. The Hebrew student also recognizes in the unusual order in which the compound numbers are written another peculiarity of the chronicler. In the first part of his list (Ezra ii. 3-35) it ia probable that he cites from an earlier census. The question of the date of this census can best be treated in connection with the history, and is, therefore, reserved for later consideration (sects. 117-119, 214, 215). The aim of the chronicler in presenting this genealogical list twice in his narrative was evidently to emphasize his thesis that the Judean state was revived, not by the ignorant, idolatrous Jews who were left behind, but wholly by those who returned from the East. To this end he introduces it just before the building of the temple, and then again in connection with the restoration of the walls of Jerusalem (Neh. vii.). 94. The latter part of the Book of Ezra is devoted to an account of the mission of Ezra. Chapter vii. THE SOURCES OF THE EZRA NARRATIVES 107 1-10 is an introduction from the hand of the chronicler. As usual, he begins with a genealogical list. He makes Ezra the son of Seraiah, the chief priest put to death at Riblah by the Babylonians at least one hundred and thirty years before (II. Kings xxv. 18, 21). If the term " son " is used in the sense common in late Jewish genealogies, of "descendant of," it at least suggests that tradition had not preserved the names of Ezra's immediate ancestors. The chronicler describes him in the language of the later age as " a ready scribe in the law of Moses." The decree in vii. 11-26 can hardly, in its present form, be from the hand of Ezra. Like the Cyrus decree in chapter i., it has at least been freely retouched by some one deeply imbued with the Jewish, legalistic spirit. The fact that it is in Aramaic, however, suggests that it was based upon an Aramaic original. 95. In the sections vii. 27 to viii. 34 and ix. 1-15 the first person is suddenly introduced. This has usually been regarded as conclusive evidence that these passages represent direct citations from a memoir of Ezra. An American scholar

(Torrey — The Composition and Historical Value of Ezra-Nehemiah) has recently shown, by a detailed study of the section, that it abounds from beginning to end in the peculiar words, idioms, and ideas of the chronicler. This fact alone, however, hardly justifies his inference that the story of Ezra is simply the creation of the same hand. Certainly, if anywhere a close similarity of style and thought are to be expected, it is in the writings of Ezra and of his followers who lived in the legal atmosphere generated by the movement which he represented. It is much nearer the truth to say that the chronicler is a later disciple of Ezra. Hence the similarity between the literary products of the two men confirm rather than disprove the authenticity of the sections. It is also a well-known fact that the chronicler, in transcribing, constantly introduces his own peculiarities of style. In the light of these considerations there is still good ground for believing that the passages before us are free citations from a memoir coming from Ezra himself. 96. The remaining sections of the book are in the third person, and bear on their face indisputable evidence that in their present form they come from the same school of thought as the Ezra memoir and the writings of the chronicler. Since the time of the editor of I. Esdras, who placed Nehemiah viii. immediately after Ezra x., it has been generally recognized that the sections contained in Nehemiah viii. to x. are another part of the narrative preserved in Ezra vii. to x. Many rearrangements have been suggested, but the one which alone removes the insuperable difficulties involved in the present order, and gives a connected and consistent history, is that presented by Professor Torrey. He makes the reconstructed order Ezra vii., viii., Nehemiah vii. 70 to viii. 18, Ezra ix., x., Nehemiah ix., x. (Composition and Historical Value of Ezra-Nehemiah, pp. 29-34). A satisfactory explanation of the present disordered arrangement is found in the characteristic desire of the chronicler to assign to the work of Ezra, the great priestly reformer, a position of priority with reference to that of the layman Nehemiah. To this end he transferred the account of Ezra's expedition and of the preliminary reform to a position before the citation from the memoirs of ORIGINAL ORDER OF THE EZRA NARRATIVES 109 Nehemiah, just as he placed the census of the returned (Ezra ii.) before the account of the building of the temple, and introduced the narrative regarding the interruption of the building of the walls during the reign of Artaxerxes (Ezra iv. 8-23), to explain why the temple was not built during the reign of Cyrus. He may possibly have been guided in the present rearrangement by the tradition that Ezra's expedition was in the seventh year of a certain Artaxerxes (Ezra vii. 8), whom he naturally concluded was the same as the one under whom Nehemiah rebuilt the walls of Jerusalem, or in the absence of distinct testimony he may have introduced the present date to establish Ezra's priority to Nehemiah (compare sects. 187, 188). The record of the great reformation, however, stands in its true chronological order after the account of the work of Nehemiah. The present extremely disconnected arrangement of these sections, which are in style and theme a unit, suggests that he was dealing with documents which he found already written. If he himself be regarded as their author, it is necessary to resort to the less probable hypothesis that the present remarkable disarrangement is due to some later copyist. The exact nature of the source which the chronicler reconstructed so freely can only be conjectured. It may well have been the Levitical Book of Chronicles (literally, " The Words of the Days") to which he elsewhere refers (Neh. xii. 23). In the archives of the temple some records were certainly kept of the great reform movement which revolutionized the character of its services. The style and point of view of such records would be closely analogous, if they did not, indeed, impart their peculiarities to the writings of the chronicler. There is good reason, therefore, for concluding that the source from which he gleaned the important data respecting Ezra and the

action of the Great Assembly, is substantially reliable. This conclusion is confirmed by the fact that the data are in harmony with the testimony of the independent sources. 97. Nehemiah i. to vi. contains literal quotations from the personal memoirs of Nehemiah. The vocabulary, style, and point of view are entirely different from those which characterize other parts of the book. The list in chapter iii. alone suggests the work of the chronicler, and even here the Nehemiah memoir probably furnished the chief data; or else they are from authentic and detailed traditions. The same source may be traced in vii. 1-4, and its logical continuation xi. 1, 2. The remainder of chapter xi. and the first part of chapter xii. (verses 1-26) consist of long genealogical lists edited by the chronicler (compare in detail I. Chr. ix.; Josh, xv.), but probably, in part, founded upon earlier records, preserved in the temple archives, to one of which he refers (" The Book of the Days;" xii. 23). The Nehemiah memoir reappears in xii. 31, 32, prefaced by an introduction (xii. 27-30) and followed by an insertion (verses 33-36) in which the chronicler attributes to the priests, the Levites, and the singers the prominent place which he considered to be their due in the dedication of the walls. The citation from the Nehemiah memoir in verses 31 and 32 find their original continuation in verses 37-40, and possibly in verse 43, which, unlike the insertions of the chronicler, are in the first person, and in thought and style closely resemble Nehemiah's other THE CITATIONS FROM NEHEMIAH'S MEMOIRS 111 writings. The remainder of the chapter is clearly from the hand of the editor. 98. The short passage xiii. 1-3 evidently does not belong in its present context. Its affinities are all with the Ezra narrative. The remainder of chapter xiii. concludes the citations from the Nehemiah memoirs. Its vocabulary and style indicate that it is not a direct quotation, for its language is, in part, that of the chronicler. At the same time, it contains many of Nehemiah's marked literary peculiarities. The deeds which it records, and the manner

and spirit in which they are performed, are characteristic of no other man of the period than the builder of the walls of Jerusalem. The section, therefore, is apparently a summary of the latter part of the Nehemiah memoir which the chronicler doubtless deemed too long to be reproduced in full. Its historical value is practically equal to that of section i.-vi., which is one of the most important and reliable historical sources in the Old Testament. 99. The fragmentary and often uncertain record of Bzra-Nehemiah is supplemented and rectified by the testimony of certain contemporary witnesses. Chief among these are the prophets, Haggai and Zech-ariah, who prophesied in connection with the building of the temple. The brief epitomes of their sermons, preserved in the books bearing their names, are carefully dated so that they present most exact information. 100. A vivid picture of conditions within the Jewish community is also furnished by the little book which bears the title "Malachi" (my messenger). This title was probably taken from the first verse of the third chapter (where the word occurs), and can hardly be the name of the prophet. Since he bitterly attacks the religious authorities and prevailing conditions, it is highly probable that the prophecy was originally issued anonymously. Its brief superscription contains no suggestion as to its date. Certainly it is much later than Zechariah's prophecy, for the temple has long been built, and both people and priests have begun to grow careless and corrupt in performing its services (i.). A bold scepticism has begun to find expression, The same evils are present that aroused the indignation of Nehemiah (with ii. 10 compare Neh. v. 1-5). The distinction between the priests and Levites, as established by the Priestly Code, is unknown. The law of Deuteronomy is still in force (ii. 1-9). Evidently the great priestly reformation recorded in Nehemiah x. had not yet taken place. The impulse toward reform, however, is strongly marked. Earnestly the prophet exhorts the people to ally themselves with the party of the righteous (iii. 16-18). The wall of separation is already being built about the true Israel. The unknown prophet was, therefore, one of the many messengers who arose not long before the rebuilding of the walls of Jerusalem under Nehemiah.in 445 B. c., and who by their faithful labors prepared the way for the later reformation. 101. In the closing chapters of the Book of Isaiah is also found a collection of prophecies coming from the anonymous co-workers of the author of Malachi. They were appropriately appended to the writings of the great prophet of the exile, because, although none of them attain to the same purity and exaltation of style, they abound in the same ideas, showing that DATE AND AUTHORSHIP OF ISAIAH LVI. TO LXII. 113 their authors were close students of his prophecies. Marked differences in teaching and in point of view, as well as in style, suggest that several different writers are here represented. For their use as an historical source, their date is the chief question. From the internal evidence this can be answered with comparative certainty. In chapters lvi. to Ixii. the temple has already been rebuilt, and the altar service is in full progress (lvi. 5-7). The designation "holy mountain," which is applied in late psalms to Jerusalem, as the site of the sanctuary, appears frequently (lvi. 7; lvii. 13). The problems considered are those of the restored Jewish community. Many Jews have returned; but lvi. 8 answers the common expectation: " The Lord God who has gathered the outcasts of Israel saith, yet will I gather others to him Israel beside his own that are gathered." The same evils within the community which were attacked by the author of Malachi (iii. 1-5) call forth the denunciation of the prophets (Ivi. 9-12; lvii. 1-2; lviii. 6, 7; lix. 2-8). Chapter lvii. 3-13 is a vivid portrayal of the abominable practices of the hostile foes of the Jewish colony. Many of the waste places are not yet rebuilt (Iviii. 12; Ixi. 4). A deep-seated discouragement in the presence of obstacles and persecution has weakened popular faith in the inherited hopes of the nation (lix. 1, 9; compare Mai. ii. 17). At the same time a faithful few

were looking for the God-sent messenger who would re-establish a new covenant between Jehovah and his people (lix. 20, 21; compare Mai. iii. 1). The noble ideal of service presented by the great prophet of the exile is again held up before the people (Ixi. 1-3). The need of a fundamental reform is forcibly presented, and the delay of the promised redemption explained by it (lix. 3-15; Ixi. 8). The age is kindred to that of Nehemiah; but in some of the passages the fervent hope is expressed that the walls of Jerusalem will speedily be built, indicating that Nehemiah has not yet appeared in Jerusalem (lviii. 12; Ix. 10). These chapters, therefore, reveal conditions within the Jewish community during the half century preceding the advent of the great pioneer reformer. 102. The background of the remaining four chapters (Ixiii. to Ixvi.) is quite different. The short section Ixiii. 1-6 is a prophecy of divine vengeance to be executed upon the Edomites. Here, as before, those inveterate foes of the Jews figure as a type of the hostile heathen world. It is therefore a message of deliverance to the Jewish race. Since the thought is so general, and one which was often expressed in late Jewish literature, it is impossible to date the passage with any degree of certainty. It may well voice the hopes of the community after the great reform of Ezra. The psalm of trust and supplication contained in Ixiii. 7 to Ixiv. was written after a terrible calamity had overtaken Jerusalem. " Our city is a desolation and our holy and beautiful house, where our fathers praised thee, is burned with fire; and our pleasant things are laid waste" (Ixiv. 10, 11). Only two occasions in early Jewish history seem to furnish a satisfactory background. The first is the destruction of Jerusalem in 586 B. c.; the other is the partial destruction and pillaging of Jerusalem by the army of Artaxerxes III. (Ochus) during the closing years of the Persian period. The language, the ideas, and the DATE OF ISAIAH LXV. AND LXVI. 115 expectations of the passage, as well as its position in the Book of Isaiah, all point conclusively to the later date. 103. Chapters Ixv.

and Ixvi. consist of a series of loosely connected passages which introduce us to the hopes and hostilities of the Jews during the last century of Persian rule. The first part of the sixty-fifth chapter, as well as the related passages, Ixvi. 3, 4, 17, suggest the nature of those half heathen practices which led the stricter Jews to exclude the Samaritans from the temple at Jerusalem. The latter part of chapter Ixv. and Ixvi. voice the expectations of a general return and exaltation of the Jewish race which filled the hearts of the faithful after the reformation of Nchemiah and Ezra had been instituted. The same general hopes of a speedy downfall of hostile world-powers, to be followed by the long delayed vindication of Jehovah's people (xxvi. 20-21; xxvii. 1), characterize chapters xxiv. to xxvii. of the Book of Isaiah. The ideas as well as the style of this remarkable section are entirely foreign to those of Isaiah, the son of Amoz. Representatives of the Jewish race are scattered to the uttermost parts of the earth (xxiv. 14-16; xxvii. 12, 13). The reign of the written law has begun (xxiv. 5). The hope of a general resurrection of the dead for the first time finds clear expression in Jewish literature (xxvi. 19). The present moment was for the Jews one of sadness; but already they seem to see the agents of their deliverance approaching (xxvi. 20, 21; xxvii.). The last two decades of Persian rule furnish the most satisfactory historical background for these chapters; since then the Jewish community was visited with bitter persecutions at the hands of the Persians, while the corrupt empire began to show evidence of its approaching dissolution, before the victorious advance of the Greek. 104. Were we better informed respecting the details of the life of the Jews during the century following the great priestly reformation, we should probably be able to assign an exact date to the brief prophecy of Joel, the son of Pethuel. Like all the prophets of the later age, his outlook is broad and general. He still expects a complete restoration of the scattered members of his race (iii. 1). This is to be followed by an overwhelming judgment upon all the foes of Jehovah's people and by the glorification of Jerusalem (iii.). Unlike the prophets of the days of Nehemiah, Joel finds nothing to criticise in the life of the community. The temple is the centre of its activity. The priestly reformation has evidently been firmly established. The allusion to strangers passing through the land may refer to the hostile march of the armies of Ochus, but the general picture which the prophecy presents is peaceful. The occasion of the prophecy is simply the appearance of a great swarm of locusts. Judah has no more grievous complaint against the nations than that they have traded unjustly in Jewish captives (iii. 2-8). The Greeks figure, not as advancing conquerors, but as slave-traders (iii. 6). Hence the prophecy may with considerable confidence be assigned to the opening decades of the fourth century B. c., when peace and prosperity followed the institution of the Priestly Law. 105. Two other Old Testament books, Ruth and Jonah, afford new points of view for studying the DATE OF THE BOOKS OF JONAH AND RUTH 117 thought of the period. Although so different, they both deal with the question, whether or not Judaism should be exclusive and expel from its midst all foreign elements and assume toward the encompassing heathen world an attitude of uncompromising hostility. The hot discussion of the question was first opened at Jerusalem in the days of Nehemiah, and practically answered in the affirmative by the reformation instituted under the direction of Ezra. The presence of Aramaisms in the Book of Jonah, which otherwise is characterized by its good Hebrew, points to the latter part of the Persian or the earlier part of the Greek period as the time of its composition. While the Book of Ruth is famous for the classical beauty and simplicity of its style, it contains certain Aramaic idioms which also proclaim its post-exilic origin. Although the story may rest upon authentic tradition, it idealizes, after the fashion of post-exilic writers, the semi-barbarous period of the Judges which forms its historical background. The genealogical list at the close of the book also strongly

suggests the ago of Ezra, which was characterized by its antiquarian tastes. 106. Unquestionably the most baffling of all the vexed problems which confront the student of Old Testament literature is the date of the Psalms. The problem is doubly complicated, first because the historical allusions are so rare and indefinite, and secondly because we are so ignorant respecting the details of many of the periods from which they come. The superscriptions also afford little assistance, for most of them were obviously added by later scribes, who were in the habit of giving an early date to all anonymous writings and of associating them with the names of men famous in antiquity. A great majority of the psalms, like the proverbs, were originally anonymous, for they simply voiced common human experience and were written for the immediate use of the temple or of the community. Poetry certainly was one of the earliest forms of literary composition among the Hebrews, and frequent references are found to music in connection with worship in early times; but the language, ideas, and historical allusions contained in the psalms which have been preserved support the conclusion that a large proportion of them come from the centuries following the exile. The psalms, like the Priestly Law, represent the fruitage of prophecy. Conditions during and after the exile were particularly favorable for the production of lyric poetry. The Book of Lamentations and the half lyrical writings of the authors of Isaiah xl. to lxvi. are significant illustrations of this fact. In Babylon also the Jews probably became familiar with the penitential psalms of their conquerors, many of which resemble very closely those of the Hebrew Psalter. If the exile gave the first strong impetus to psalm-writing, the Persian period fostered it, and must be regarded as the background of a large number of the psalms in our present collection. In this form the repressed feelings of the faithful found expression. Their disappointments, their longings, their hatreds, as well as their joys, were all voiced in psalms. Song service also formed an in-

creasingly important element in the worship of the second temple, and therefore created a great demand for liturgical literature. The dedication of the temple, the rebuilding of the walls, the institution WRITINGS OF THE GREEK HISTORIANS 119 of the Priestly Law, and the persecutions of Ochus, each called forth psalins which reveal the inner life of the race and which will be studied in connection with the events themselves. 107. In addition to the histories of Josephus and the ancient fragments preserved by the Church Fathers, which throw some direct light upon the life of the Jewish people, the period is brilliantly illuminated by the writings of the Greeks. The relations between Greece and Persia were so intimate that their mingled life constitutes the real background of Jewish history during this epoch. Since it was the golden age of Greek thought, we are far better informed respecting the background than we are regarding the details of Judah's history. The absence in the writings of the Greeks of any definite facts regarding the personal life of the Jews is not in the least surprising when we fully realize how little they came into contact with each other during the Persian period. The Greeks were known to the Jews at this time only as a distant people or as pirates (Isa. lxvi. 19; Joel iii. 6). It is not strange, therefore, that Herodotus was not acquainted with the name of that peculiar people "who practise circumcision" (ii. 104). The inscriptions of Cyrus, and especially the great Behistun Inscription, in which Darius tells of the mighty revolutions which convulsed the empire at the beginning of his reign, also supplement our knowledge of Persian history at a most important crisis in the life of the Jewish race. n THE CONQUEST OF-BABYLON AND THE POLICY OP CYRUS 108. In October of the year 538 B. c. Cyrus at last turned his victorious armies towards the tottering capital of southwestern Asia. His base of operation was Mesopotamia, the fertile territory between the upper waters of the Tigris and Euphrates, which he had apparently conquered in 547 B. c. (Nab.-Cyrus Chr. i. 16-18). Persian intrigue, favored by the resentment and suspicion aroused among the Babylonians by the strange conduct of their king Naboni-dus (see sect. 60), had prepared the way for an easy conquest. On the northern borders of Babylonia, beside a certain river, a battle was fought between the Persians and Babylonians. The army of the latter was defeated, and Nabonidus fled. A few days later, the north Babylonian town of Sippar surrendered without resistance to Gobryas, the commander of the forces of Cyrus. Within two days more (about October 10th) the Persian general was in possession of Babylon. As the chronicle distinctly states, the gates of the city were opened to the Persians without a battle (ii. 8-16). The only resistance, if any, was offered by the garrison occupying the great temple within the walls. In the clear light of the inscriptions, it is evident that the elaborate tale of HerodoTHE CAPTURE OF BABYLON 121 tus to the effect that Cyrus turned the waters of the Euphrates into the great basin made by Nebuchad-.rezzar and entered the city while its inhabitants were so engaged in a feast that they neglected to close the water gates, has been given a wrong setting. It must refer rather to the second capture of Babylon by Darius about twenty years later. 109. The inscription of Cyrus states that Nabonidus was among the captives. According to the Greek traditions he was banished to Carmania. About two weeks after its capture by his army, Cyrus made his triumphant entrance (about October 24th) into Babylon. Then the hopes, which had led the inhabitants to throw themselves upon his mercy, were not disappointed. " Peace he gave to the town. Peace he proclaimed to all the Babylonians" (Nab.-Cyrus Chr. ii. 19, 20). Zealously espousing the cause of the religion of the conquered, he carefully restored to their sacred sites the images of the gods which had been transported to Babylon by Nabonidus. In the remarkable cylinder, which comes from Cyrus himself, he expatiates at length upon his clemency toward his new subjects and upon his devotion to their gods. Great precautions were taken that wrong should be done to none, and that individual rights should be respected. The fortifications of Babylon, which under Nabonidus had been allowed to fall into partial decay, were repaired. The temples of the gods of Babylon were restored and embellished. Repeatedly and unreservedly Cyrus proclaimed himself and his son Cam-byses, whom he associated with himself as king of Babylon, to be devoted worshippers of Marduk, Bel, and Nebo, the gods of his new subjects (Cyrus Cyl. 33-36). Indeed he introduces into his inscription a message, which he claims to have received from the great Marduk, directed to " Cyrus, who reveres him " (lines 27, 28). Any monotheistic tendencies which the conqueror of Babylon may have had, evidently did not exert a very potent influence in determining the nature of his public acts. The inscriptions reveal, not only the supreme skill of Cyrus as a diplomat, but also the nature of the policy which governed his relations with subject peoples. It was the antithesis of that of the Assyrians and Babylonians who had endeavored to establish their supremacy by crushing the nations under them so completely that all opposition was impossible; for Cyrus, by acts of clemency and toleration, appealed to the gratitude and loyalty of the conquered. It was in the practical development of this policy that he and his immediate successors ever figured as the nominal worshippers, as well as the generous patrons, of the gods of the nations under their rule. 110. It was, therefore, with real joy that the princes of the western cities and provinces, formerly tributary to Babylon, hastened to send their ambassadors to kiss the feet of this new master in token of submission. Equally significant, in the light which it sheds upon Jewish history, is the statement of Cyrus, which follows the account of the reception given these ambassadors: " The gods, whose sanctuaries from of old had lain in ruins, I brought back again to their dwelling places and caused them to reside there forever. All of the citizens of these lands I assembled, and I restored them to their homes" (Cyrus Cyl. 31-32). The most natural inference to PERMISSION TO REBUILD THE TEMPLE 123 he drawn from this passage is that general permission v.'as given to all exiles found in his newly conquered province to return to their native lands, taking with them the booty stripped from their temples by the avaricious Babylonians. 111. To the Jews, as well as to their neighbors, Cyrus proved a mighty deliverer, for to them all the same general concessions were undoubtedly granted. In carrying out the details of the policy, which the great conqueror so plainly outlines, special enactments were also required. It is therefore more than probable that a decree, relating especially to the Jewish people, was the original of the one which the chronicler cites in Ezra vi. 3-5 from the older Aramaic document, and which purports to be a citation from the state records found in Ecbatana during the reign of Darius: " In the first year of Cyrus the king of Babylon, Cyrus the king made a decree: 'Concerning the house of God at Jerusalem, let the house be builded, the place where they offer sacrifices, and let the foundations thereof be strongly laid; the height thereof sixty cubits and the breadth sixty cubits, with three rows of stones and a row of new timber: and let the expenses be given out of the king's house: and also let the gold and silver vessels of the house of God, which Nebuchadrezzar took forth out of the temple which is at Jerusalem, and brought unto Babylon,-be restored and brought again into the temple which is at Jerusalem, every one to its place, and you shall put them in the house of God. ' " The influence of the Jewish thought and form of expression is plainly evident, but in general it is in harmony with the known decrees of Cyrus. 112. The same Aramaic document which the chronicler has quoted, with little if any change, in v. 13-16, states that Cyrus instituted measures for the restoration of the Jewish temple. To a certain Sheshbazzar, whom the great king appointed governor of Judah, were intrusted the vessels of gold and silver found by Cyrus in Babylon, where they had been carried by Nebuchadrezzar from the former temple at Jerusalem. Although the narrative is late, its testimony is substantiated by the fact that Cyrus in his inscriptions distinctly states that he devoted his attention to restoring the idols found in Babylon to their original temples. In the absence of idols, the sacred vessels from Jehovah's temple would most naturally be returned. Undoubtedly the acts of Cyrus were prompted by politic motives. His general policy of conciliation has already been noted. In the case of the Jews, aside from the possibility that he recognized in their religion a cult kindred to that of the Persians, there was an added reason for their being special objects of his royal favor. Egypt was the third and last of those great empires which had sought by joining forces to check him at the beginning of his career of conquest. Already he was contemplating the conquest of Egypt, which his son Cambyses carried into execution. To accomplish this project successfully, the loyal adherence of the states of Palestine was essential. Thus the old rivalry between the East and the West again became a determining factor in the history of the Jews. As has already been noted (sect. 23), the religious faith of both the Samaritans and the Jews in Canaan centred about the ruined site of the temple at Jerusalem, as about no other shrine. If the long- THE CONSTRUCTIVE POLICY OF CYRUS 125 ing to see the temple rebuilt was as intense among the exiles in Babylon, as is suggested by their writings, it must have been still stronger among the " remnant in the land." No action on the part of Cyrus, therefore, was better calculated to command the grateful loyalty of a strategically important body of his subjects than to figure as a patron of their revered sanctuary. 113. Incidentally such a policy would also powerfully attract the large body of Jewish refugees in Egypt. It is a noticeable fact that the oldest version of the decree of Cyrus respecting the rebuilding of the temple makes no reference to the return of the Jews in Babylon, but considers only the Jews living in the province of Judah (Ezra vi. 3). The Persian monarch was seeking to solve a po-

litical not a racial problem. The policy whereby he attempted to undo the desolation wrought by Babylonian armies, and to cement into a united whole even the extreme provinces of his empire, was most commendable. The restoration of the Jewish race, as the great unknown prophet of the exile clearly proclaimed, depended only upon whether or not its individual members were ready to make personal interests secondary to those of their race and religion. The political barriers had been completely swept away; the exiles were at perfect liberty to return, indeed there is good reason to believe that Cyrus would have welcomed a general influx of people into the territory of central Canaan. The real question of the age is, Did the Jews, and especially those in Babylon, improve their opportunity?

Ill THE REVIVAL OF THE JEWISH COMMUNITY IK

PALESTINE

114. The widely-accepted tradition of the immediate return of a large body of Jews from Babylon rests solely on the doubtful testimony of the chronicler. Living two or three centuries later, when the popular memory of those distant events was very shadowy, it was but natural that he should think that the foundations of that temple which he revered so highly, were laid by loyal exiles who returned for the purpose, instead of by those who remained behind, whom he, with his generation, intensely despised. The hopes so frequently expressed in the prophecies contained in Isaiah xl. to lv., of another exodus into Canaan, undoubtedly encouraged him to entertain a theory so acceptable to him (compare the language of Ezra i.).

115. A closer study, however, of Isaiah xl. to lv. indicates that the attitude of his fellow-exiles toward a return chilled the prophetic enthusiasm of the author and aroused grave doubts in his mind whether they would respond when the opportunity came. Repeatedly he chided them for their obstinacy (xlvi. 12; xlviii. 4). Above all, he lamented the lack of a leader to rally them. "There is none to guide her REASONS WHY THE EXILES DID NOT RETUKN 127 among all the

sons whom she hath brought forth; neither is there any that taketh her by the hand " (li. 18). If portions of chapters xl. to lv. were written a little after the capture of Babylon, then I. 2 voices the disappointment which filled the soul of Jehovah's messenger: " Wherefore when I came was there no man? When I called, was there none to answer? Is my hand shortened at all that I could not redeem? or had I no power to deliver? " It requires little imagination to appreciate the reasons which deterred the exiles from returning. The long, dangerous journey across the desert, which they or their fathers had made as captives under the guidance of their Babylonian captors, was in itself enough to appall the bravest. Palestine, with its desolate ruins and treacherous foes, offered far more terrors than attractions. Their brethren who remained behind were repeatedly declared by Jeremiah and Ezekiel to be far inferior to those who were carried away, and their r6Ie in post-exilic history furnishes no reasons for changing this estimate. 116. On the other hand, their homes and friends, all that was dear to them except their native land itself — and that was still desolate — bound them to the country of their adoption. Under the rule of Cyrus, any restrictions which before may have limited them were removed, and they were free to enjoy, on an equality with the Babylonians, the opportunities and pleasures offered by the rich valley of the Euphrates. As a result of their own choice, the exile for most of them never ended. True to their national instincts, they continued to live in colonies by themselves, retaining their social organization, their customs, and their religion, constituting so many individual units in the great Persian empire. The recent excavations at Nippur have unearthed a wealth of cuneiform tablets, from the reigns of Artaxerxes and Darius, bearing many familiar Jewish names, such as Samson (Samshanu), Nathanael (Natan-ili), Shimeon (Shamakkunu), Gedaliah (Gadaliama), and Menahem (Minakh-Khimmu). Traces of the presence of a large Jewish colony living in Nippur long after the

Christian era have also been found. Babylonia, as is well known, immediately after the beginning of the present era, continued to be recognized as one of the three most important centres of Judaism. From this point the Jews rapidly spread to Ecbatana, Susa, and other great cities of the Persian empire. For the next century, in wealth and intelligence, and probably also in numbers, they certainly far surpassed their kinsmen in Judah. Although for a variety of reasons they refused to return in person, they were by no means all apostates to the faith of their fathers. Their interest still centred about Jerusalem, and they were ever ready to assist by their gifts the work of national revival. When in time conditions became more unfavorable in the East, or more favorable in Judah, many of their descendants improved the opportunity to return. 117. Aside from the setting given to them by the chronicler, there is nothing to support the conclusion that the list in Ezra ii. and its parallel, Nehemiah vii., contain the census of those who returned together, immediately after 538 b. c. According to its superscription, the census purports to include those found in the province of Judah who had returned from Babylon. It is not distinctly stated when they returned, DATE OF THE CENSUS OF EZRA II. 129 but this must be inferred from the list of the leaders which immediately follows. The names of Zerub-babel and Joshua, whom we know were in Jerusalem at least by 520 B. a, stand first. Then follows that of Nehemiah, who is, in all probability, the Nehemiah who in 445 B. c. returned, bringing back a retinue of servants and some loyal patriots like himself. Next in the list, found in the Book of Nehemiah, follows the na«ie of Azariah, which in the Hebrew is practically identical with Ezra. This name originally was, in all probability, that of the priest who was associated so closely with Nehemiah. He, according to Ezra viii. 1-20, led back exiles enlisted from different clans, whose names correspond throughout very closely with those in the lists before us. The name " Seraiah," found in the corresponding passage,

Ezra ii. 2, may be due to the mistake of a copyist or of the chronicler, who had in mind Ezra vii. 1, where Seraiah is mentioned as the father of Ezra. Among the names of other leaders, who, from their order in the context, it is to be inferred, led back companies of exiles, subsequently, to the age of Nehemiah and Ezra, appears that of Mordecai, derived from the name of the Babylonian god Marduk. It also reappears in the Book of Esther as the name of a prominent Jew of the Persian period. At least one of the names in the list, Bigvai, is generally recognized as of Persian origin, being derived from *Baga,* god. Obviously a Persian name would not be given to a Hebrew chieftain until Persian influence had been paramount in the land of the exile for a generation at least. The fact that this non-Hebrew name is also borne by a tribe numbering over two thousand (Ezra ii. 14), as well as that the name of Joshua the priest has become the designation of a priestly tribe, numbering nine hundred and seventy-three (Ezra ii. 36), all strongly suggest that the census reported in these lists was taken late in the Persian period. 118. This conclusion is confirmed by the character of the lists themselves. A large proportion of the citizens of the province of Judah are classified according to the towns which they inhabit (see Ezra ii. 20-29, 33-34; compare Nehemiah iii.), being designated as the " sons" of Gibeon or of Bethlehem or of Jericho, or else as the " men" of Michmash or of Bethel. Since it is a well-established fact (sect. 215) that these nineteen towns were certainly not all in possession of the Jews before the latter part of the Persian period, the inference is obvious that the census was taken nearer the time of Alexander the Great than that of Cyrus. As has been shown, the long list of the priests, singers, porters, Nethinim, and the children of Solomon's servants is, in its present form, from the chronicler and, if based upon an earlier list, points to a period when the temple service and equipment was much more highly developed than even in the days of Nehemiah (compare Neh. i. to vi.; also chronicler's list, Neh.

xii.). 119. Obviously, therefore, the present lists throw little light upon the number and character of those who returned immediately after 538 B. c. That they were few and unimportant is also evident from the testimony of our only contemporary records, the prophecies of Haggai and Zechariah. Surely about forty thousand could not have returned at this time without receiving the slightest reference in either of these EVIDENCE AGAINST A RETURN FROM BABYLON 131 prophecies, which portray so vividly conditions within the Jewish community about 520 B. c. Not only is there no reference to anything suggesting a general return, but the prophets constantly address their audiences as "the people of the land" (Hag. ii. 4; Zech. vii. 5), or as "the people who have been left" (Hag. i. 12, 14; ii. 2; Zech. vii. 6, 11, 12). Thus they refer to them in the same terms as Jeremiah did to those who remained with him in Judah after the first captivity (Jer. xlii. 2, 15, 19; xliii. 5; xliv. 7, 12, 14). A few generations later, when a deputation visited Nehemiah at Susa, his inquiry was not: "How are the returned? " but, " What is the condition of the Jews in Judah who escaped, who were left behind from the captivity? " The reply of the men, who had come direct from Palestine, is also conclusive evidence that there had been as yet no general return of the Jews from Babylon (Neh. i. 3). The community to which we are introduced through the Aramaic document in Ezra, as well as through the prophecies of Haggai and Zecha-riah, and the memoirs of Nehemiah, is small, poor, and struggling. Zechariah, in 520 B. c., regarded the years that had followed the great victory of Cyrus as discouraging for Jerusalem and the cities of Judah as the half century that had preceded. For seventy years the shadow of Jehovah's displeasure had rested upon them, and there had been no riffc to lighten their gloom (i. 12). If half of forty thousand loyal Jews returned from Babylon in 537 B. c., such words as these would have been impossible. Like the great prophet of the exile, Zechariah still urges: "Ho, Zion, escape thou that dwellest with the daughter of Babylon" (ii. 7). The general return of the exiles is yet in the future. Incredulous as are the prophet's hearers, "the people who have remained in the land," he declares: " Thus saith the Lord: Behold, I will save my people from the east country, and from the west country; and I will bring them and they shall dwell in the midst of Jerusalem " (viii. 7, 8). Then he trusts that the barren city and the encircling towns will again be inhabited and prosperous (vii. 7). 120. At the same time the evidence does not preclude but rather supports the conclusion that some of the Jewish exiles in the East before long availed themselves of the permission of Cyrus to return from Babylon and so had a part in the building of the temple. The first governor of Judah, Sheshbazzar, whom the chronicler designates as the " prince of Judah" and seems to identify as a son of the captive Jewish king Jehoiakin, and therefore as an uncle of Zerubbabel (I. Chrs. iii. 16-19), probably took some Jews with him in his retinue. His successor, Zerubbabel the son of Shealtiel, and the grandson of Jehoiakin, was undoubtedly born in Babylon. " Begotten in Babylon " is the most probable meaning of his name. Joshua, who belonged to the leading priestly family, must have been a descendant of one of the large number of temple priests who, together with the royal captives, were carried to Babylon by Nebuchadrezzar. Each of these leaders, as the list in Ezra ii. (Neh. vii.) suggests, must have brought some of their brethren to assist them as I hey returned to enter upon their duties at Jerusalem. Zechariah also refers to " those of the captivity; " and gives the names of three men, Heldai, Tobijah, and Jedaiah, who had recently come from Babylon, bringing silver and gold, presumably as a contribution from PERSONNEL OF THE JEWISH COMMUNITY 133 the Jews remaining there, toward the building of the temple. Together these little bands of Jews, who returned at different times during the fifteen or twenty years following the revolutionizing victory of Cyrus, constituted such a small part of the colony in Judah that the prophets in preaching to the people

could properly ignore them. At the same time the intellectual and religious influence which they exerted, was undoubtedly far greater than their numbers. 121. In the light of the conditions which existed in Palestine during the earlier days of the exile, it is clear that, as Haggai and Zechariah imply, the community which they addressed consisted almost entirely of those Jews, Calcbites and Jerahmeclites (sect. 22), who had been left behind in 586 B. c., and of those who had fled to the lands immediately adjacent to Palestine. When Sheshbazzar was made governor of Judah, and the benign policy of Cyrus became known, undoubtedly many more Jews who had taken refuge among the surrounding nations, and who were eagerly awaiting a favorable opportunity to return, rallied to his standard. Egypt certainly contained thousands of such exiles, who were in closest communication with their brethren in Palestine, and who were only a few-days' journey from the land of their nativity (sects. 24, 25). Since they had not been carried into exile, they would naturally be reckoned as " the people of the land" or as " the people who had been left behind." 122. The testimony of these cumulative facts furnishes the true starting point for the appreciation of the history of the revived Jewish community during the next two centuries. The possibilities presented by the great unknown prophet of the exile were only partially realized. Jehovah, through his " Messiah," Cyrus, prepared the way; a certain number improved the opportunity; but the majority of those in Babylon were, as their enlightened prophet feared, unequal to the sacrifice. The growth of the community in Judah, after it received its first accessions, was gradual, and its life proved to be a long, painful struggle. The term " Revival" describes the real facts better than either " Restoration " or " Return;" for no sudden transformation signalized the fortunes of the little Jewish colony in Judah immediately after 538 B. c. Darius I., not Cyrus, reorganized the Persian empire. Only in time did the Jews of Palestine realize fully what a marvellous change had

come over their political horizon. Judging from later usage, as well as from the testimony of the chronicler, from the first they were allowed to have over them a governor of their own race. The more just and kindly rule of Persia gave them new opportunities for development. With a recognized leader, they were in a position better to defend themselves against their neighboring foes. Their hearts were doubtless also gladdened by the appearance of bands of refugees returning from Egypt. At times also they were inspired with hopes of a complete national restoration by the return of exiles from distant Babylon, laden with gifts for their poor kinsmen in Judah (Zech. vi. 9-15). Above all, these returning exiles brought the rich fruitage of the higher religious life which they had experienced in the East. Thus there are good grounds for believing that at this early period the Jews of Babylon began to exercise upon their kinsmen in Palestine that powerful religious CONDITIONS IN JUDAH BETWEEN 538 AND 520 B.C. 135 influence which was destined in time radically to transform the character of the Judean community. 123. Already we have seen that, during the period of the Babylonian exile, a rude altar had been built, and solemn services were performed on the site of the ruined temple. The Cyrus decree, which must have been issued about 538 B. c., reads: " Concerning the house of God at Jerusalem, let the house be built, the place where they offer sacrifices, and let its foundations be strongly laid." The prophet Haggai also refers to the system of sacrifices which was in force long before active work was begun on the rebuilding of the house of the Lord (ii. 14). Since its foundation was formally laid in 520 B. c., as a result of the preaching of Haggai, it is difficult to trace much definite religious progress during the first decade and a half of the Persian period. Possibly the form of laying a foundation of the temple was gone through with under the direction of Sheshbazzar, soon after 538 B. c., so as to satisfy the conditions of the decree of Cyrus. It is also reasonable to conclude with the chronicler that the zealous Jews who returned from Babylon established henceforth a simple but more regular service on the sacred site (Ezra iii.; compare Hag. ii. 10-16; Zcch. vii.); and that they probably made some preparations for the rebuilding of the temple. In one section of the Aramaic document, it is claimed by the contemporaries of Haggai that it had been building since the conquest of Cyrus (Ezra v. 16). In the light of the context, however, and of Haggai's plain assertion that before 520 B. c. not one stone had been laid upon another (ii. 15), the statement appears to have been made to avert the dangers of the moment. The reasons why really nothing had been accomplished were probably, not so much because of the opposition of "the people of the land" (as the chronicler suggests in Ezra iv. 1-6), for, until the time of Nehemiah, the Samaritans at least were allowed to worship with the Jews at Jerusalem (see sects. 146, 205), but, as is clearly stated by Haggai, they were because the little community was still desperately weak, both in resources and influence. It was but natural that, as soon as Cyrus granted them permission, they should devote themselves first to building better houses which would protect themselves and their families from the inclement climate of Palestine. In barren Judah this task required considerable time, for the returned refugees at least were obliged to begin as pioneers, and those who had remained were pitiably destitute. They were dependent upon the soil for subsistence, and in those opening years their labors bore little fruit. About 527 B. c. the armies of Persia began to march through Palestine to Egypt, and upon the Jews undoubtedly fell in part the burden of their support. Sadly discouraging seemed the contrast between the glowing promises of the great prophet of the exile and the dark reality. Memories of the glories of the past temple still lingered in their minds, and they could not decide to rear such an insignificant structure as the materials at their command alone made possible. "The time has not come for the Lord's house to be built" was the commonly

accepted conclusion. Not until 520 B. c. did the man arise to proclaim to them that " now is the acceptable day of the Lord." THE REBUILDING OF THE TEMPLE AND THE

SERMONS *OF* HAGGAI

124. In 529 B. c. Cyrus, the founder of the Persian empire, died. The chief event in the reign of his son, and successor, Cambyses, was the conquest of Egypt, which was completed in 525 B. c. By his almost insane acts of cruelty the new king alienated his subjects and drove them to rebellion. When in 522 (or in 521) B. c. he set out to return from Egypt to his capital, news came that a certain Gaumata, known to the Greeks as Goma,tes, the Magian, had announced himself to be the brother Bardes, whom Cambyses had caused to be secretly slain, and that he had attracted to his standard a majority of the people in the empire. Although in command of a well-trained army, Cambyses, when he had returned as far as Hamath in Syria, preferred to take his own life rather than contest the throne with the impostor. 125. Left without an open rival, Gaumata, by granting popular concessions and by establishing a system of terrorization, succeeded in maintaining his authority for a few months (Behistun Inscript. i. 12). In the autumn of 521 B. c. the Persian nobles formed a conspiracy and slew the impostor. The leader of the conspirators was Darius, who claimed to be a descendant, through a parallel branch of the royal family of the Achaemenidee from which Cyrus had come. He was at once elected by his colleagues to the vacant throne. His first act was to strengthen his position by marrying Atossa, the daughter of Cyrus. If he was to rule supreme over the entire Persian empire, ability even greater than that of its founder was demanded, for the slain Gaumata begot a brood of false pretenders, and his death was the signal for revolt in many parts of the empire. In Susiana a certain Athrina led a rebellion which was quickly put down, only to be followed a little later by another in the same province. A more formidable revolt was that of the Babylonians head-

ed by Nidintubel, who assumed the popular title of Nebuchadrezzar III. While Darius was personally engaged in subduing the Babylonians, a Phraortes appeared among the Medes, who took the historic name of Cyaxares, and among the Persians arose another pseudo-Bardes, both of whom commanded large followings. In the summer of 520 B. c. Babylon was captured by Darius, and he was then able to give his personal attention to subduing the Medes. The Babylonians soon revolted again under the leadership of another pretender, who also assumed the name of Nebuchadrezzar III. During this period of chaos, many of the more distant provinces improved the occasion to throw off the Persian yoke. Against such odds the ultimate success of the youthful Darius must have seemed very questionable. That the integrity of the Persian empire, composed as it was of heterogeneous elements only imperfectly organized, could be maintained, was exceedingly doubtful. Not until the spring of 519 B. c. did it become evident that Darius was master of the situation. THE INFLUENCE OF THE CRISES IN THE EAST 139 126. It was no mere coincidence that the prophets Haggai and Zechariah came forward with their exhortations and predictions in the autumn of 520 B. c., when each message which came from the East told of a new rebellion and greater political confusion, so that the Persian empire seemed about to be torn to shreds. Almost every earlier prophecy which has been preserved was called forth by some political or social crisis. Those of Haggai and Zechariah are no exceptions. For more than two centuries the political life of Judah had been determined by the influence which proceeded from beyond the Euphrates. A large proportion of the Jewish race was still found in the valley of the great rivers. It would have been strange indeed, if the feelings of the struggling community in Palestine had not been powerfully affected by the mighty convulsions which were then shaking the world. 127. Not a few reflections of these great world-movements are found in the prophecies of Haggai and

Zechariah. Haggai, for example, declares that Jehovah will soon shake the heavens and the earth and the sea and the dry land and the nations (li. 6-9). In a second message he repeats the thought and adds that, "Jehovah will overthrow the throne of kingdoms and will destroy the strength of the kingdoms of the nations; and will overthrow the chariots and those that ride them; and the horses and their riders shall come down, every one by the sword of his brother." A more vivid reflection of the impressions which the waves of revolution sweeping over the Persian empire made upon the receptive mind of the prophet, can not be imagined. Haggai's colleague, Zechariah, also looks beyond the boundaries of Judah to read her fate. The angel who delivers to them his message, comes " from walking to and fro through the earth " (i. 11). Already he beholds the four smiths who are to destroy the horns of the nations which have scattered Judah (i. 18-21). His exhortation to the Jews in Babylon to escape, suggests that he regarded the moment as peculiarly opportune (ii. 7). In vi. 1-8 the prophet directs the eyes of his readers toward the great political movements which were agitating the world. 128. Undoubtedly the startling events which were transpiring near the centre of the Persian empire had also aroused the prophets' hearers. The apathy which had paralyzed the poor Jewish community was at last shaken. Action begets action. A new era seemed about to open. Poor crops and drought, which were ever regarded by the Jews as clear evidence of Jehovah's displeasure (see Amos iv. 4-11; I. Kings xviii.), had already appealed to the consciences of the more thoughtful (Hag. i. 6, 9-11; ii. 16, 17). Conditions were at last ripe for the building of the temple. All that was needed was for some one to take the initiative. The degenerate house of David, with the exception of Josiah, had shown little energy during the latter days of the Judean kingdom, and less religious zeal. Sheshbazzar and Zerubbabel give no evidence of being exceptions to the rule. It was simply because he was the legal heir to the throne of Judah that at

this critical epoch the eyes of the more ambitious Jews were fixed upon Zerubbabel. The great actions of the past were performed at the instigation of the prophets, and it was most fitting that an earnest prophet of Jehovah should be the one to arouse both leaders and people. THE FIRST APPEAL OF HAGGAI 141 129. Haggai wisely selected for his appeal the first day of the sixth month (September, 520 B. c.), when the people were assembled to celebrate the feast of the new moon. One fails to find in the prophecies of Haggai the literary beauty and originality of his predecessors; but they are characterized by a certain directness and practicability befitting a situation which called not for rhetoric, but for action. When he first stood before the assembled people his message was: "Zerubbabel the governor and Joshua the high priest, leaders of the Jewish community, do not listen to the words of this discouraged and apathetic people, when they say, ' The time has not yet come to build the temple.' Consider, men of Judah, whether it is right for you to enjoy your own comfortable homes while you allow the house of Jehovah to lie in ruins. Meditate and you will clearly perceive that Jehovah has sent you these poor crops and hard times to show his displeasure at your conduct and to arouse you to action. His command to you is: Go up to the hill country and secure wood and build the temple according to your means, and you can be assured that I will be pleased therewith and will be glorified in the evidence of my people's fidelity " (i. 2-8). 130. The response on the part of the people was immediate and hearty. By the twenty-fourth of the sixth month the work was instituted. Since after the exile the Jews adopted the Babylonian system of reckoning time, and in 520 B. c. the Babylonian year seems to have begun on the first of May, the building of the second temple was commenced in October. Haggai, who was the moving spirit in all the work, promptly assured the people: " Since you have listened to Jehovah's command, he is with you in your undertakings " (i. 13). A month later, when the people showed signs of

discouragement, he delivered to them at the Feast of Tabernacles another cheering message: " Do some of you, who saw the first temple in its glory, disparage this humble structure which we are rearing? Be courageous, 0 leaders and people! Jehovah, who led your forefathers, a nation of serfs, from Egypt and covenanted to care for and guide you, is still working in your midst. Indeed, he will soon revolutionize existing political conditions. The heathen nations, which now oppress you, shall come bringing their treasures to beautify this humble sanctuary, so that its glory shall far exceed that of the former temple. Then, instead of the present discord, Jehovah will give to this city perfect peace " (ii. 3-9). 131. It was in the following month (December) that Zechariah is first reported to have appeared before the people, possibly at another moment of discouragement, calling them to duty, assuring them of Jehovah's co-operation, and fortifying his words with familiar teachings and illustrations drawn from the writings of earlier prophets and from the past experience of their race (i. 1-6). Under the inspiration of these two prophets the preparation for the building of the temple slowly progressed, until late in December, 520 B. c., the foundation was laid (Ezra v. 2; Hag. ii. 18). With the Assyrians and Babylonians such a ceremony was solemnly celebrated. Whether the Jews imitated their former masters so far as to place within the cornerstone inscriptions describing the work and immortalizing the names of Zerubbabel and Joshua, is an interesting question. Haggai certainly improved the LAYING OF THE FOUNDATION OF THE TEMPLE 143 occasion to deliver two more sermons. The first was addressed to the people. Turning to some priests, he inquires: "If the skirt of one of you, who is bearing consecrated flesh, touch ordinary food, will it become holy? " Of course they answer, " No." " Or if one profaned by contact with a dead body touch any of these things, will they not become unclean? " As the priests answer, " Yes," he applies the illustration: " So are this people, both in their deeds and in their offering, unclean, vitiated as they have been by their selfishness, and consecrated by no true sacrifice. By failure of crops, blasting, mildew, and destructive hailstorms, Jehovah has endeavored to impress this truth upon you. But now that the foundation of the temple is laid, all is changed. Henceforth he will bless you with prosperity. And concerning you, 0 Zerubbabel, Jehovah declares that in the coming overthrow of the heathen powers, he has chosen you to perform a peculiar service for him, and therefore, as a king treasures his signet ring, so will he protect and cherish you " (ii. 6-23). THE HOPES AND DISCOURAGEMENTS OP THE TEMPLE-BUILDERS 132. No more addresses of Haggai are recorded, but in February, 519 B. c., two months after the laying of the foundation of the temple, Zechariah presented a series of visions, or, more properly, allegories, intended to inspire hope in the hearts of the people. Although the two prophets were one in purpose, their methods of teaching present striking contrasts. The difference is partially explained by the fact that, while Haggai was a simple layman (Hag. ii. 11), Zechariah was by birth a priest. The chronicler suggests that he was, during the high priesthood of Joshua, at the head of the priestly tribe of Iddo (Neh. xii. 4, 16). In his opening address he manifests the characteristic priestly reverence for the past history and literature of his race. Like Ezeldel, whom he resembles in so many ways, he was a prophet in spirit and aim; but in the form in which he announced his message, he reveals his priestly training. Following the example of the priest-prophet of the exile, he preferred the obscure apocalyptic style to the plain statement. Possibly the fear that his teaching might be regarded with suspicion, if reported to the Persian satrap, also influenced him so to express his ideas that they would be Intel- ZECHARI-AH'S MESSAGES OF ENCOURAGEMENT 145 ligible only to his countrymen. It is significant that the date of his first vision corresponds with that at which Darius first succeeded in repressing the more formidable rebellions which had been convulsing the empire. The angel

who spoke to the prophet reports that " all the earth sitteth still, and is at rest" (i. 10). The hopes of the downfall of the world-powers and the speedy inauguration of the Messianic kingdom, which had found expression in Haggai's predictions, uttered four months before, and which had stirred the Jewish community into activity, seemed blighted. The people felt that, although in beginning to build the temple they had done their part, Jehovah had failed them, for Jerusalem's exaltation seemed more distant than ever before. Their faith and energies relaxed accordingly. There waa sore need of a new prophetic message. 133. In his first vision Zechariah is informed by the angelic messengers that, although the nations are at rest, and there are no signs on the horizon of a speedy deliverance for Jerusalem, Jehovah's interest in his beloved city is not abated. Already he has returned to take up his abode in his restored temple, and he will yet comfort and bring prosperity to his land (i. 8-17). In the second vision the prophet pictures, in his allegory of the four smiths, those who will destroy all the nations which have scattered Judah (i. 18-21). In the succeeding vision he sees one going forth to measure Jerusalem with a view to rebuilding it on its old foundations. Soon an angel interrupts him with the glad assurance that so great will be the population of Jerusalem that no walls will encircle it, but, instead, Jehovah himself will be a wall of fire about it and its glory within. It requires little imagination to hear the bitter complaint of the people because their city is still without walls and apparently neglected. True prophet that he was, he chided them because their expectations of what Jehovah would do for them were material and circumscribed; and proceeded to urge the Jews in Babylon to escape from the rebellious city, now doomed by Jehovah to destruction, and to find refuge within Zion, blessed and guarded by his protecting presence, and destined to become the centre of his universal kingdom. 134. As Zechariah fixed his eyes upon conditions within Jerusalem, there arose before him a vision of Joshua the

high priest, charged by the adversary with the sins of the priesthood and of the community which he represented. Then the prophet heard Jehovah absolve Joshua of the sins with which he was polluted, and appoint him to the care of his temple, on condition that he prove faithful to his trust. The solemn consecration and instalment of the priestly family are accompanied by a reiteration of the promise of free forgiveness to the people, of Jehovah's continued care for the service of his sanctuary, and of the advent of his Messianic servant, whom Jeremiah had designated as the " sprout" (Jer. xxiii. 5). The next vision also stands in close connection with the institution of the temple service; for its chief symbol is that of the candlestick, representing the restored temple and its service, which are to be supported by the two anointed ones ("sons of oil"), Zerubbabel and Joshua, the heads of the civil and religious organization. Already Ezekiel had advanced the same thought in his program of the restored temple (sect. 48). THE CROWNING OF ZKRUBBABEL AS KING 147 135. In his last vision the prophet returns to the consideration of the political outlook. In imagination he beholds Jehovah's messengers of vengeance going forth to the north against Babylon and Persia, and to the south against Edom and Egypt, to destroy the world-powers which oppose the realization of his purpose. The details of this world-judgment are indefinite. The old martial spirit of the race has disappeared. The prophet is a man of peace. The central truth which he proclaims is that Jehovah rules in human affairs, and in his own good way he will put down the wrong and vindicate the right. Haggai and Zechariah evidently hoped to behold with their own eyes the exaltation of their race. The atmosphere was tense with expectation. Nations were rising and falling almost in a day. The fact that they had been permitted to begin the rebuilding of their temple seemed in itself a miracle. It was but natural that they should regard it as an earnest of still greater glory. This hope found expression in a command which came to Zechariah, probably immediately after the last vision. Unfortunately the text has been changed by later editors. The main ideas, however, are clear. He was ordered to make, from the gold and silver which had been sent by the Jews in Babylon, a crown, and place it on the head of Zerubbabel. The meaning of the act, in the light of ancient Hebrew usage, was unmistakable, and the prophet's words removed all doubt: "The builder of Jehovah's temple shall bear the glory and sit and rule upon his throne; and there shall be a priest (Joshua) on his right hand, and there will be a counsel of peace between the two of them." His message also throws much light upon the hopes cherished by those to whom he spoke. It was but natural that the should crave political liberty. Other peoples had for a time succeeded in throwing off the yoke of Persia, and in placing the crown upon princes of their own blood. Jehovah was omnipotent. His people had atoned for the sin which had dethroned the house of David. Now, indeed, they were doing his will. Surely from their point of view independence under Zerubbabel, the hereditary heir of the throne of Judah, was not beyond expectation. 136. Fortunate were the people, if they were influenced by the peaceful spirit of Zechariah to leave the fulfilment of their aspirations to Jehovah, for the future brought them no independence under their hereditary prince. For the details of their disillusionment we are left to conjecture; the fact alone is preserved that at the moment when the crown was held out over the head of Zerubbabel, he, and with him the Davidic family, disappear forever from public life. When the fragmentary records next throw their flickering light upon the Jewish community, the descendants of Joshua the high priest have absorbed nearly all of the civil, as well as the ecclesiastical, authority resident in the community in Judah. 137. The Aramaic document quoted by the chronicler supplements the facts presented by Zechariah. When the work on the temple had progressed so far that the timbers were being placed on the foundation (Ezra v. 8), and there-

fore several weeks, if not months, after the formal laying of the foundation-stone, Tattenai (in the Greek version, Sisiunes), the Persian satrap of the trans-Euphrates province, with his officials visited Jerusalem on their tour of inspection. Undoubtedly a FINAL DEPOSAL OF THF, DAVIDIC FAMILY 149 report of the unwonted activity of the Jewish community was the cause of their formal visit. The empire had been torn by so many revolts that any unusual act was viewed with great suspicion. In the course of the investigation, the elders of the Jews claimed that they were merely rebuilding the ancient sanctuary, and in so doing were acting in accord with an earlier decree of Cyrus, authorizing its construction. They further suggested that the royal archives be searched, that the truth of their words might be substantiated. Fortunately, Darius I., as his inscriptions, discovered in Egypt and Asia Minor, demonstrate, was, like Cyrus, disposed to patronize the temples of the peoples under his rule. A knowledge of this fact may have have influenced the Persian satrap not to interfere with the work at Jerusalem until he had received instructions from the great king. The presence of the satrap, and the cloud of suspicion which rested upon the Jewish community until their claim was substantiated by the discovery at Ecbatana of the Cyrus decree, was sufficient to dispel all secret hopes of elevating Zerubbabel to the position of independent kingship. If the purport of the preaching of Haggai and Zechariah became known to the Persian officials, doubtless steps were at once taken to remove Zerubbabel from his position as governor. Zechariah's early prediction, that Zerubbabel would be allowed to participate in the completion of the temple (iv. 9), suggests that his tenure of office was none too secure. That his authority was but slight is apparent from the prophet's words (iv. 6, 7). If not at once, probably in the general reorganization of the empire, which was soon instituted by Darius, the family of David was quietly set aside. 138. Although in divine providence, the temporal hopes of the Jews were unful-

filled, they were permitted, unhindered, to complete their temple. It is noticeable that in the latest sermons of Zechariah, dating from the latter part of the year 518 B. c., both the apocalyptic language and all references to Zerubbabel and to a temporal kingship disappear. Plain, earnest exhortation and promises of a universal kingdom of God take their place (vii.; viii). Evidently the temple was so far completed that certain of its services had been instituted. This fact gave rise to the natural question as to whether the fast appointed in the fifth month, in commemoration of the destruction of Jerusalem and of the temple, should continue to be observed. The subject was formally laid before the priests and prophets of the city by a visiting deputation. Zechariah answered the question in the true spirit of a prophet rather than that of a priest, by asking what the motives were which prompted the fasts observed in the exile. Was it to serve Jehovah or to gratify their own desires? If for the latter cause, the sooner the selfish forms were discontinued the better. Now that the revived community was entering upon a new life, the real question was, Were they going to avoid the mistakes of the old Hebrew state and offer God not empty forms but deeds of justice, mercy, and kindness, which represent the demands of the original prophetic torah. Their future was intrusted to their own keeping, and depended upon their own conduct. The foundations had already been laid for a glorious state. Jehovah was ready to co-operate in every way. If they but proved true to their opportunity, their noblest aspirations would be more than realized. Peace at last would come to the afflicted THE COMPLETION OF THE TEMPLE 151 Jerusalem, so that men and women would live to a ripe old age. The mournful fasts of the past would become joyful feasts. Above all, the day was coming when many people and powerful nations would make pilgrimages to Jerusalem to worship Jehovah. Then would the despised Jew be courted by foreigners eager to learn of the true God.

139. According to the chronicler, the temple was completed in March of the year 516 B. c. Undoubtedly the act was celebrated by the offering of sacrifice and by appropriate ceremonies. It must have called forth songs of thanksgiving, some of which have probably been preserved in our Psalter. Psalm xlvii. expresses the exultation which the little community naturally felt when their work was done. Their feeling, like that of Zechariah at this time, is voiced in the couplet (verse 8):

God reigneth over the nations:
God sitteth upon his holy throne.

140. The historical importance of the rebuilding of the temple can not be over-estimated. Judaism again had a home. The thought, so often expressed in the prophecy of Zechariah, that Jehovah had returned to dwell in their midst, was a source of joy and hope, not only to the Jews in Judah, but also to all members of the race, wherever they were. Now that daily sacrifices were offered for their nation, they felt with relief that at last the burden of national guilt which oppressed them, was removed. Again, they could raise their heads in the presence of the nations. The temple also proved a strong bond keeping alive in the heart of every Jew the sense of racial unity, thus binding together all the scattered members of the nation. It also gave a definite form to their religious development. Exalted far above all other institutions, the sanctuary and its service commanded the attention of the most able spirits in the dispersion, where the tendency toward ritualism, so strong during the Babylonian period, now carried all before it. The result was, that from the first, in their eyes, the humble structure, reared by the struggling community, far eclipsed in importance the more imposing temple of Solomon. In time they also imparted their deep reverence to the Jews of Palestine, so that its prestige completely overshadowed all other religious institutions in Judah.

THE SEVENTY YEARS OP SILENCE FOLLOWING THE BUILDING OF THE TEMPLE
141. Concerning the life of the Jewish community after the completion of the temple in 51G, until the appearance of Nehemiah in 445 B. c., the chronicler says not a word. The silence is as significant as that with which the Hebrew historians pass over the long reactionary reign of Manasseh. The two epochs have not a little in common. Each was preceded by a brief period of intense popular and prophetic activity, during which expectations of an immediate and glorious exaltation of their nation stirred all hearts. Mankind had not yet learned the lesson of patience, so that when the coming years brought no fulfilment, hopes were succeeded by the bitterness of disillusionment. The Messianic predictions of the prophets seemed but empty dreams to men bowed down under a foreign yoke. They lost faith, not only in the predictions, but also in the God of their prophets. That their feelings found bitter expression is evident from the extracts of contemporary sermons preserved in Isaiah Ivi. to Ixii., as well as in the Book of Malachi. 142. The political status of the Judean community was not perilous, but only hopelessly discouraging to men who were longing for independence. After Darius succeeded in quelling the many rebellions which disturbed the opening years of his reign, he devoted himself to organizing his vast empire. It was divided into provinces, over each of which were appointed a satrap or governor, a commander-in-chief of its forces, and a secretary, who were directly responsible to the king for the discharge of their respective duties. Eoyal judges and inspectors were also sent out to right grievances and to anticipate possible uprisings. Members of the royal family were usually appointed to the more important satrapies. By these regulations the king was able to exercise an absolute control over the entire empire. The system was so perfectly organized that the Persian state continued to exist long after the reigning family had become weak and degenerate. To the smaller nations the rule established by Darius was a great blessing, compared with that of the Babylonians which it supplanted. 143. In theory, at least, equal rights were accorded by the Persians to all subject peoples. As long as they paid their allotted taxes, they were assured peace and the privilege of worshipping their gods without molestation. Only under the powerful arm of Persia would it have been possible for the weak Jewish colony to have survived in the midst of strong and malignant foes eager to destroy it. As a matter of fact, its very insignificance protected it. Wars agitated different parts of the great empire, but made little impression on the Jewish community. During the reign of Darius I. the Hellespont was bridged and Persian armies invaded Europe. If the news of the battle of Marathon reached the Jews in Palestine, it only intensified their helpless discontent. The rebellion of POLITICAL EVENTS IN THE PERSIAN EMPIRE 155

Egypt in 48G B. c. undoubtedly aroused their interest, for, not only was it at their doors, but Egypt was also one of the lands of the Jewish dispersion. Soon they saw from their western headlands the armies of Xerxes, who at this time succeeded his father Darius on the Persian throne, marching to suppress the great uprising. A few years later came the fatal insurrection in Babylon which led to the practical destruction of the mighty metropolis. Whether or not any of the Jewa who had found a home there were influenced by this calamity to return to Judah is an interesting but unanswered question. In the vast array which Xerxes summoned from all parts of his empire, for the purpose of crushing the Greeks, the levy from the province of Syria was included; but, if Jews were in its ranks, they were too few and unimportant to be referred to in the lists. Persian prestige in Europe fell at Thermopylae and Salamis before Greek skill and courage, but in southwestern Asia the Great King continued to be the one recognized authority.

144. In 464 B. c. the weak, degenerate Xerxes was assassinated and his third son, Artaxerxes I., who is distinguished by the title Longimanus, succeeded him. The new ruler came to the throne as the result of palace intrigues. In later tradition he has the reputation of having been good-natured but weak, and ruled

by the favorites of his court and harem. Caprice, not justice, henceforth determined the policy of the great empire. The weakness of the central authority occasioned numerous revolts. Chief of these was the one in Egypt about 460 B. c., led by a certain Inarus. It was put down by Megabyzus, the satrap of Syria, who then found himself strong enough for several years by these lukewarm friends of the Jewish colony to the Great King, whereby with the free use of gifts and lies they sought to gain some advantage for themselves, at the expense of their kinsmen in the south. The reason why the open rupture between the Jews and Samaritans did not come before the time of Nehemiah was simply because the Jewish community was too weak, and because the conservatives within it had no energetic leader. 147. On the east were the Ammonites, represented in the days of Nehemiah by a prince whose name was Tobiah. There is evidence that they, like the Edomites, had been partially driven from their old homes by the Arabians, and had profited by the destruction of the northern kingdom to move westward and occupy the fertile Hebrew territory on the east of the Jordan (Jer. xl. 14; xli. 10), so that now they were near neighbors of the Jews. On the south, in possession of Hebron, and occupying many ancient Judean cities, which they had seized soon after the destruction of Jerusalem (sect. 22), were the most hated foes of all, the Edomites. The author of the Book of Malachi refers to their expulsion from their own territory by the Arabians (Nabata3ans), who invaded Edom from the south, and to their vain hopes of recovering their desolate land (Mai. i. 2-4). Associated with the Edomites, and ever pressing and harassing the "feeble Jews," were the same Arabian tribes which from dim antiquity until the present have never failed, when not resisted by a strong local government, to gain a foothold in Palestine. Some of them may also have been descendants of the Arabian colony which Sargon in the eighth century settled in Samaria (II. sect. 105). The Jews, CHE JEWISH COXMCMTT Df PALESTINE DURING Tilt:

PERSIAH Imi OBEKK PERIODS. EXTENT OF THE PROVINCE OF JUDAH 159 therefore, were obliged, during these depressing years, constantly and against great odds, to contend for their native soil against the encroachments, the covert attacks, and the intrigues of crafty, treacherous foes; for while the Persian rule insured the integrity of the different peoples under it, it did not prevent frequent wars among them, especially when the central government became weak. 148. The territory held by the Jews, and known as the Persian sub-province of Judah, represented only a fraction of the old southern Hebrew kingdom. Its extent is indicated by the references contained in the third chapter of Nehemiah, which describes the building of the walls of Jerusalem. At the most, it extended only five miles to the north of the capital city. If the most probable interpretation of verse 7 be adopted, the town of Mizpah (about three and one half miles northwest of Jerusalem), although inhabited by some loyal Jews, belonged not to Judah but to the province of Syria. Jericho was the most eastern and Bethzur, about thirteen miles southwest of Jerusalem, was the most southern town. On the west the province included the mountain villages of Zanoah and Keilah. In all it was less than twenty miles in length from north to south, and about the same in width. It comprised the least desirable territory of Palestine. With the exception of the land in the vicinity of Jericho, the eastern half was barren and uninhabitable. Few springs, and almost no streams, were to be found within the entire province, so that at the best it was capable of supporting only a sparse and poverty-stricken population. 149. The position of the Jews was still more painful and discouraging because Jerusalem, the site of their sanctuary and their natural place of refuge and defence, was almost depopulated (Neh. vii. 4), and open to the sudden attacks of their foes. Their first thought after laying the foundation of the temple was to rebuild the walls about Jerusalem (Zech. ii. 4, 5); but for a variety of reasons they were deterred from undertak-

ing the great task. Although the statement has frequently been made by recent writers, who would assign Ezra iv. 8-23 to the period, there is no conclusive evidence that the Jews ventured to place one stone upon another before 445 B. c. The prayer which Nehemiah uttered after he learned from his kinsmen that "the remnant that are left of the captivity there in the province are in great affliction and reproach," and that " the wall of Jerusalem was broken down and its gates burned with fire," suggests that it was no recent calamity to which they referred, but the disastrous blow dealt their nation by Nebuchadrezzar (Neh. i. 5-11). His surprise and sorrow were called forth by the revelation of how discouraging conditions within and without the community really were. It also indicates how little connection there was at this time between the Jews of the East and West. The spirit of Nehemiah's address to the people on his arrival at Jerusalem was: " Come, at last let us build the fallen walls that we may no longer be an object of reproach as we have been during these long years " (ii. 17). The details of the building of the temple reveal the fact that within the community there was neither the requisite resources nor energy for the much more difficult work of building the walls. This is strikingly confirmed by the sneering words of Sanballat THE FOES WITHIN AND WITHOUT JTJDAH 161 (Neh. iv. 2). Even Nehemiah, with the authority at his command, would not have succeeded if he had not been a man of transcendent ability. As has already been remarked, the rebuilding of the temple was a work which the Persian authorities would not only permit, but favor, for it tended to foster the spirit of contentment and loyalty. The fortifying of such a naturally strong city as Jerusalem, however, would at once have been regarded as an act of rebellion against the Great King. This was precisely the interpretation which was placed upon the work of Nehemiah by the princes of Palestine (Neh. ii. 19). The experiences of Nehemiah also demonstrate how bitter and almost irresistible would have been the opposition of the hostile neighbors of the Jews, even though the attempt had been made with the full consent of the Persian king. 150. These facts enable us to understand and to sympathize with the community in Judah during these seventy years of disillusionment and discouragement. When we also recall that the colony was largely made up of the weaker remnants of the Jewish race, we can at least regard their faults with charity. The contentious, selfish, belittling atmosphere of Palestine was not calculated to develop broad, noble characters. No great national achievement and no great crisis aroused their patriotism or inspired their faith. The result was that the Jewish community was afflicted by those social evils which have always been the curse of the Orient. Its rulers, who should have guarded it from the foes which like "beasts of the forest came to devour," are described as "blind and without knowledge, dumb dogs that cannot bark, dreaming, n lying down, loving to slumber; yea, greedy dogs that can never have enough; who say, ' Conic, I will bring wine, and we will carouse with strong drink; and tomorrow shall be as this day, beyond all measure great' " (Isa. lvi. 9-12). Nehemiah condemned them to their face for "exacting usury from their brothers and for selling them into slavery " (Neh. v. 1-12). The author of Malachi charges certain of them with " oppressing the hireling in his wages, the widow and the fatherless, and for defrauding foreigners, resident among them " (iii. 5). Even the high priests were prominent offenders. The civic life of the Jews was little better than that of their enemies. Injustice, lawlessness, deceit, treachery, and false swearing characterized their relations with each other as well as with their neighbors (Mai. ii. 10; iii. 5; Isa. lix. 3-15). 151. As might be expected, their religious life was equally degenerate. The services of the temple were kept up, but the people did not hesitate to cheat Jehovah by bringing to him as offerings those animals " which had died a violent death, and the lame and the sick " (Mai. i. 13). Worst of all, the priests encouraged the people in their impiety, and

offered to their divine King what they would never have thought of tendering to their Persian governor (Mai. i. 8). As the result of their laziness and indifference, they neglected to instruct the people respecting their duty, so that the entire ceremonial service was corrupt and contemptible in the sight of God (Mai. ii. 8, 9). They also failed to pay their tithes, so that the worship of the temple was in danger of being abandoned for lack of financial support (Mai. iii. 8). 152. Still more insidious and deadly dangers threat- SCEPTICAL TENDENCIES WITHIN THE COMMUNITY 163 ened to extinguish the life of the Jewish state, since for the first time in the history of their race a defiant scepticism found open expression. The priests of the temple complained: " What a weariness is all this round of sacrifices?" (Mai. i. 13). The bitter cry: " What evidence is there that Jehovah has loved us? " could not be ignored by the prophets (Mai. i. 2-5). Some, having lost all faith in Jehovah, were raising the question which was treated so sublimely by the author of the Book of Job: " What is the use of serving God? what profit has come to us for all our fasting, our prayers, our lamentations and humiliation? The man who defies God, and is self-sufficient, and seeks only his own selfish ends by fair means or foul, is the one who is happy a.nd enjoys prosperity. One may defy God with impunity. What is the advantage of fearing him as the prophets and sages have taught? " (Mai. iii. 14, 15). The declaration was also made openly that it was all the same whether a man did right or wrong, at least God in no way showed his approval or disapproval of good or evil conduct (Mai. ii. 17). 153. In the psalms of this period, those who made these sceptical assertions are styled "the scorners." They seem to have been greatly in the majority, and to have numbered among their ranks not only the dissolute, oppressive, evil heads of the community, but also many of the leading priests. One of the results of this sceptical attitude was the disregard of the distinction between the worshippers of Jehovah and those of heathen gods. The interests of peace, as

well as of trade, prompted the leaders of the weak, unpopular Jewish community to make protective alliances with the nations surrounding them. The prevailing method of sealing such an alliance in the old Oriental world was by marriage. The temptation was a strong one, and the religious sentiment, which should have enabled them to resist it, was weak. When Nehemiah arrived, he found that many, including the priestly family, had yielded to it. Eliashib, the chief priest of the temple, was allied by marriage both with Tobiah the Ammonite and with Sanballat the Horonite (Neh. xiii. 5, 28). False prophets were also present, who supported the leaders in their apostasy (Neh. vi. 10-14). The condition of the Jewish colony was, indeed, pitiable and well-nigh hopeless. It was weak and persecuted; it had lost hope; it had lost character; it had lost courage; and finally it had lost almost all its faith in Jehovah, and was threatened with absorption among the heathen peoples which encircled it. 154. The one saving element, aside from the faith of the Jews who had remained in the dispersion, was the small but earnest party of faithful Puritans, who still cherished all that the community as a whole had lost. By the author of the Book of Malachi they are called " the righteous" and " they who feared the Lord " (iii. 16, 18). In the psalms they are variously styled "the pious," "the just," "the meek," or "the poor and needy." As these terms suggest, they did not belong to the rich and influential classes; nor were they popular with the community at large, for their piety was a constant protest against its pet sins. Persecution at the hands of their worldly brethren was for them a common experience. Many passages in the psalms of the period voice their woes: PERSECUTION OF THE RIGHTEOUS 165

They that hate me without cause are more than the hairs of my head.

They that would cut me off, being mine enemies wrongfully, are mighty.

I am become a stranger unto my brethren,

And an alien unto my mother's children.

They that sit in the gate talk of me;

And I am the song of the drunkards.

Evidently they were the victims of the oppression, the injustice, and treachery of the rich and ruling classes, whom the prophets of the period, as well as Nehemiah, so harshly condemn. The psalms reveal the intensity of the animosity between the two parties (see especially Ixix. 22-28; xxxv.). The meek were the reproach of their adversaries because their afflictions were regarded, in accordance with the old dogma of proportionate rewards, as indubitable evidence that they had committed grievous crimes. The sense of sin well-nigh crushed them (li.). Passionately and oft they prayed:

Let me not be ashamed,

For I put my trust in thee;

Let integrity and uprightness preserve me,

For I wait on thee.

The experiences of the hero of the Book of Job were those of the party of the " righteous." Although they seemed to be condemned by God as well as by their fellow-men, their trust in Jehovah's fidelity and love likewise rose triumphant and strong above their agony of doubt and despair. Thus, while the Jewish community as a whole had sadly degenerated, there was within it a group of " those who feared the Lord " who were drawn closely together by common hopes and afflictions (Mai. iii. 16). They were the ones who prayed most earnestly that the walls might, in God's good pleasure, be rebuilt, and they were the ones who deplored most deeply that the services of the temple were being neglected (Ps. li. 18, 19). By their fidelity and suffering they preserved the faith in Jehovah, inherited by their race, during the critical years preceding the advent of Nehemiah, and stood ready to unite in raising the standard of reform, when circumstances were favorable, and when the Lord " should send his messenger, who would prepare his way before him" (Mai. iii. 1). Ixix. 4, 8, 12; compare Ps. xxii.; xxv.; xxxii. xxv. 20,21. THE REBUILDING OF THE WALLS UNDER NEHEMIAH 155. At the most critical time in the history of the Jewish community in Palestine, a messenger of the Lord appeared, who, by his patriotic, unselfish action, turned the currents of its life into higher and nobler channels. It was probably the result of no mere chance, that a deputation of Jews from Palestine, with a relative of the king's cup-bearer at their head, were found in Susa, the distant capital of the Persian empire. Fortunately the man to whom they appealed, was lacking neither in energy nor in influence nor in devotion to his race. Nehemiah, the youthful son of Hacaliah, was one of the noblest representatives of Judaism in the East. Although reared far from his native land, and surrounded by the corrupting influences of the Persian capital and court, his fidelity to the God and laws of his fathers contrasted most favorably with that of his kinsmen who lived under the shadow of the temple. At the same time he was gifted with a tact and executive ability which enabled him to win a high place of honor and responsibility in the presence of the Great King. 156. The Jewish chronology of the Persian period must forever remain in some doubt because three rulers bearing the name of Artaxerxes and three bearing the name of Darius sat at different times on the throne of Persia; and the biblical writers never distinguish between them. The absence both in the memoirs of Nehemiah and in the Aramaic document (Ezra iv. 7-23), of any of those titles whereby Artax-erxes II. and III. were designated, perhaps suggests that the master of Nehemiah was Artaxerxes I. This inference is further confirmed by his reputation for being especially susceptible to the influence of the favorites in his court. The queen who "was sitting beside him" (significantly referred to in Neh. ii. 6) was in all probability the queen-mother Amestris, whose influence over her son was paramount. According to Nehemiah xii. 10, the Bliashib who continued to occupy the position of high priest in Jerusalem in the thirty-second year of the reign of Artaxerxes (Neh. xiii. 4, 28), was a grandson of Joshua, under whose administration the temple was rebuilt in 520 B. c. A grandson of Joshua would naturally be living during the reign of Artaxerxes I.; but the thirty-second year of the second king who bore this name was a century and a half after the completion of the temple, so that it is highly improbable, if not impossible, that Eliashib was then alive. On the other hand there is nothing except certain contradictory statements of Josephus to suggest that the king referred to was any other than Artaxerxes I. (464-424 B. c.). 157. The manner in which permission to rebuild the walls of Jerusalem was gained, is characteristic of the Persian court of the period. To Nehemiah, a Jew of the dispersion, who knew Jerusalem chiefly through the idealizing memories of his ancestors, a faithful portrayal of the actual conditions existing there natu- NEHEMIAH'S COMMISSION AS GOVERNOR 169 rally brought a severe shock. Oriental that he was, he gave expression to his feelings in fasting and lamentation. Fervently he prayed to Jehovah, acknowledging the burden of guilt which he, in common with all the pious of his race, felt still rested upon them because of the sins of their forefathers. Fortunately his prayer did not end with merely a general petition. Without hesitation he assumed the responsibility to his race, entailed by his comparatively exalted position as cup-bearer to the king, and besought divine aid in the difficult task which he set before himself. Three months he waited for a favorable occasion. It came in the first month (March-April) of the year 445 B. c. As he was serving in the royal presence, Artaxerxes detected a trace of sadness in the countenance of his trusty servant. His inquiry as to the reason gave Nehemiah his supreme opportunity to appeal to the well-known kind-heartedness of the king. In the language of a courtier, but in a simple, straightforward manner, he told the king of the pitiable condition of Jerusalem, " the city of his fathers' sepulchres." Artaxerxes, who could not tolerate sorrow in his presence, was moved to pity rather than anger, and asked the young Jew to make known his request. Strengthened by a prayer for help, Nehemiah petitioned for royal authority to rebuild the ruined city. The caprice of the moment inclined Artaxerxes to do a favor which cost him nothing but the temporary absence of one of his cup-bearers. A limited leave of absence was granted to Nehemiah, and he was appointed governor of Judah with full authority to rebuild Jerusalem. At his request, Artaxerxes provided him with royal passports addressed to the officials of the trans-Euphrates province, and with orders to the keeper of the royal forest, Asaph (whose name indicates that he also was a Jew), to furnish the timber necessary for the repair of the gates and walls of the city. 158. Apparently without delay, Nehemiah set out, attended by an escort of cavalry, detailed by the king, and also with a considerable following of patriotic Jews, who like himself were intent upon transforming conditions in Jerusalem (Ezra ii. 2; iv. 12; Neh. ii.). Over the great post-roads built by Darius, the journey was probably accomplished within a month. Arriving at Jerusalem, he devoted the first few days to studying conditions there. For the difficult task which lay before him, he fortunately possessed the qualifications of an experienced courtier as well as the ability of a man accustomed to command. The obstacles which confronted him within the community were even greater than ·those which were thrown in his way by the avowed foes of the colony. His personal sympathies were with the small and weak party of the " poor and needy;" while the resources with which the city must be repaired, were at the command of the leaders and the rich, who for most part belonged to the party of "the scorners." Even though he was proving himself their savior, he soon found that he was the victim of their treachery. Fortunately, with personal wealth at his command, he was able to relieve the community from the odious exactions to which it had hitherto been subjected for the support of the governor and his retinue (v. 14). From the first he also entertained at his table in royal fashion one hundred and fifty of the leading men of Jerusalem and of the outlying towns, NEHEMIAH'S PLAN OF OPERATION 171 in addition to the guests

who came from time to time from the heathen nations about (v. 17, 18). In the poor, struggling Jewish state, nothing was better calculated to disarm hostile criticism and insure the popularity of the new governor and his measures than the policy which Nehemiah pursued. 159. He did not, however, trust the details of his work to others. On the night of the third day after his arrival, with a few of his followers, and without the knowledge of the resident Jews, he personally inspected the state of the walls. Going out by the valley gate to the southwest of the city, he went along the southern wall to the fountain gate and the king's pool. Here he found the narrow valley of the Kidron so choked with rubbish that he was obliged to leave behind the animal upon which he was riding, and to proceed along the east side of the city on foot. Having satisfied himself concerning the magnitude of the task before him, he called an assembly of the priests, the nobles, the representatives of the different towns, and the able-bodied workmen. In a stirring address, he called their attention to the unprotected condition of the city, and urged them to arise and build, that their inactivity might no longer give their foes an occasion for bitter taunts. He aroused their wavering faith in Jehovah's help by calling attention to the remarkable concessions which the Great King had already granted to him. In the circumstances it is not surprising that they voted unanimously to begin at once the work of rebuilding. 160. His plan of operation illustrates the rare tact and executive ability of Nehemiah. Realizing that, if the work was to be effective, the entire wall must be built at once, and that to accomplish this all the energies of the community must be enlisted, he threw the responsibility upon the different groups in the community, and appealed to the spirit of mutual emulation and personal interest, as well as to the patriotism of the political body as a whole. To this end he divided the work into different sections. The rebuilding of the sheep gate at the north of the temple area, where the animals for sacrifice were led into the city, he intrusted to the

priests. The men from Jericho were held responsible for the building of the protecting towers on the north of the city. To prominent nobles and their families were assigned sections of the walls. Certain tribes also assumed the responsibility of completing other divisions of the work. Even the more important guilds, as, for example, that of the goldsmiths, were represented in the distribution. Many private individuals were allowed to repair the wall opposite their own houses. In this way the lazy, wrangling community was suddenly transformed into an intensely active working body. It is reported that of all the groups of workmen represented, the nobles from Tekoa alone did not faithfully discharge the task laid upon them by Nehemiah. 161-The constant danger of attack soon nerved all to put forth the most strenuous efforts. At first their foes, headed by Sanhallat the Horonite, who probably came from Beth-horon, located in the territory of Samaria, Tobiah, who seems to have been the Persian official hend of the Ammonites, and Gashmu (or Geshem), an Arabian, only jeered at the suggestion that the Jews would succeed in fortifying the ancient capital. Superlative contempt and probably a sneer THREATS OF THE NEIGHBORS OF THE JEWS 173 at the attitude of the party of the " meek " are expressed in the words of Sanballat: " Do these weak and lazy Jews think that all that is necessary is for them to gather together and propitiate their God by sacrifice, and that then, out of these charred ruins, walls will rise in a day?" " Yes, a fox leaping upon any wall which they will rear, would be able to tumble it over," was the equally scornful rejoinder of Tobiah. Their words aroused the hot anger of Nehemiah, and called forth from him a bitter prayer for vengeance. At the same time the implied menace impelled the workmen to redouble their exertions, so that in an incredibly short time the breaches in the walls were nearly closed. 162. Then the scorn of their neighbors, the Samaritans, the Arabians, the Ammonites, and the inhabitants of the Philistine town of Ashdod, was changed to alarm, for they recognized that a new spirit had been infused into the Jewish community, which hitherto they had found an easy prey. Accordingly they conspired together to make a sudden and overwhelming attack upon the workmen and to destroy the results of their labors. The formation of such a general league could not, however, be kept secret. Through those residing in the outlying towns, news came of the threatening attack. A panic seized the Jews, who for more than a century and a half had learned only the lesson of helpless submission. Messengers also came from the towns of Mizpah, Jericho, Tekoa, and other villages, demanding that the contingents which they had deputed to build the walls of Jerusalem be sent back at once to defend their own possessions. The work would forthwith have been abandoned, had not Nehemiah proved equal to the crisis. First, arming the people and placing the men in front of their wives and children, he appealed to their faith in Jehovah, and urged them to fight for their homes and their families. The report that the weak-kneed Jews were preparing to make a desperate defence daunted the zeal of the confederates. 163. Although the threatened attack never came, the possibility of it was ever present. Nehemiah was compelled to organize his forces on a military basis, and in so doing showed himself as able a general as he was a courtier. The work was resumed, but each man had his weapons ready at hand. At night none were allowed to leave the city. Nehemiah divided his immediate following into two companies, the one to relieve those who were exhausted in the work, and the other to stand constantly in arms. Day and night, neither they nor their devoted commander laid them aside; while the rest toiled from sunrise until darkness. Orders were also issued that the people rally to repulse the enemy at any point, wherever the alarm was sounded by the trumpeter, who never left the side of Nehemiah. Under the pressure of constant danger, the work progressed with marvellous rapidity, until before many weeks the line of the walls was complete, although the doors had not yet

been set in the gates. 164. When the facts were reported to Sanballat and Gashmu, they changed their tactics and sought to effect a compromise. They first proposed a conference at one of the villages of the plain of Ono, northwest of Jerusalem, on the southwestern borders of Samaria. The experienced Persian courtier at once CONSPIRACIES AGAINST NEHEMIAH 175 suspected a plot to gain possession of his person. There certainly had been nothing in the previous attitude of his foes to inspire confidence in the honesty of their purpose. It was indeed an unpleasant experience for them to be flatly told that they " had no longer any right in Jerusalem" (Neh. ii. 20); but Nehemiah was carrying through a religious policy which gave no opportunity for compromise, and therefore he sent back the curt reply that he was employed on a far more important work, and had no time for conference. When, after repeated attempts, their efforts to shake his purpose and remove him by treachery failed, they endeavored to implicate him in treason against the Persian government. With this end in view, they sent to him an open letter referring to the current report that in building the walls of Jerusalem he and the Jews contemplated making him king. They also charged Nehemiah with having induced certain prophets to proclaim him king of Judah. Since the report would ultimately reach the ears of the Great King, they intimated that they would be glad to take council with him that they might organize a successful conspiracy. Some of the over-zealous Jerusalem prophets may have hailed Nehemiah as a Messianic deliverer, and thus have furnished a certain foundation for the charge, although there is little doubt that the proposals of Sanballat and his associates were made in sarcasm. Nehemiah contented himself with simply denying their malevolent assertions. 165. The last plot against himself which Nehemiah reports, was the most insidious of all. One of the recognized prophets of Jerusalem, Shemaiah ben Delaiah, in the privacy of his own house declared to Nehemiah that a plot against his life had been divinely revealed to

him. Apparently in all honesty, he urged the governor to take refuge at night within the temple from his would-be assassins. To have done so would have destroyed forever his influence in Jerusalem. Fortunately Nehemiah's sense of honor, as well as his reverence for the sanctity of the temple, saved him. " Should a man of my character and position flee? Should I, a layman, enter the holy sanctuary to save my life? Most assuredly I will not," was his indignant reply. Subsequent developments demonstrated that Shemaiah, together with other prophets and a certain prophetess by the name of Noadiah, had been hired by Tobiah and Sanballat to betray the courageous governor. Although many of the most prominent men in Jerusalem were related by marriage, and so were in closest communication with these unprincipled foes of Nehemiah, he stoutly refused to listen to their suggestions of a compromise; and so escaped from all the meshes which they cast about him. In the face of secret opposition, he pushed the work of restoration so rapidly that about the first of September, 445 B. c., the walls were completed. The period of fifty-two days, in which he states that the great undertaking was accomplished, would seem incredibly short, were it not for the fact that the walls had been only partially destroyed, that the energies of the colony were thoroughly enlisted, that the cause for haste was most strenuous, and above all that the man who directed the work was as gifted as he was devout. 166. The walls were finished none too soon. We are not surprised to learn from the Aramaic document (Ezra iv. 8-23) that, even before the work was entirely PERSIAN DECREE STOPPING THE WORK 177 completed, the Persian officials resident in Samaria, probably at the instigation of Sanballat and Tobiah, who thus carried out the threat which they made to Nehemiah (Neh. vi. 7), sent to Artaxerxes a report of the work being done by the Jews. The servants of the Great King may have felt, as they claim (Ezra iv. 14), that they were only faithfully discharging their duties; but, if so, they were sadly misled by the malicious slanders of Sanballat and Tobiah. Their report asserted that the aim of the Jews in building the walls of Jerusalem was rebellion, and that if the work which had already progressed so far should be allowed to reach completion without royal interference, " they would not pay tribute, custom, or toll, and that in the end it would prove harmful to the interest of the king." They also called attention to the bad reputation for rebellion borne in the past by the Jews, and especially by the inhabitants of Jerusalem. In conclusion, they asserted as their united opinion, that if the king did not quickly put a stop to the work he would entirely lose his trans-Euphrates province. Nothing was better calculated to arouse the fears and anger of Artaxerxes than the points which they emphasized, for the memory of the successful revolt of Mcgabyzus, at the head of the same province, was still fresh in his mind. The mere suggestion of a danger that a similar humiliating experience might be repeated, called forth the most strenuous orders from the king to stop at once the building of the walls. 167. The Persian officials, for obvious reasons, did not mention the name of Nehemiah in their report. It is possible that Artaxerxes did not associate the work of the Jews with the concession which he had given to his cup-bearer, as the result of the generous impulse of *a* moment. If he did, the fears and suspicions aroused by the report of his officials only led him to regret his kindness. When the royal decree came, the Persian officers at Samaria lost no time in carrying it into effect by force; but at the end of the time required to communicate with the king, Jerusalem was encircled with walls, and the Jews were in a position to accept the terms of the royal decree, which gave authority to stop all building, but none to destroy the work already done. One cannot refrain from wondering whether Nehemiah's extreme haste was not prompted in part by the fear that there would be some such capricious change of policy, as soon as he left the Persian court. Apparently, a personal presentation of the facts re-established his good relations

with Artaxerxes, so that he did not deem the incident worthy of recording in his memoirs, or if he did mention it, the chronicler, in his work of epitomizing and harmonizing, failed to quote it, since, for reasons of his own, he gave the incident a different setting (sect. 90). 168. In vii. 1-4 of his memoirs, Nehemiah states, however, that when the gates as well as the walls were completed, he placed the city in the charge of two men, his kinsman Hanaui, and Hananiah, the commander of the castle, a faithful and God-fearing Jew. This act and the detailed commands which he issued for the regulation of the city, strongly suggest that he was making preparations for his departure. His statement in v. 14, that his appointment as governor continued twelve years, does not necessarily imply that the greater part of that time was spent in Jerusalem. On the other hand, the condition upon which he was THE REPEOPL1NG OF JERUSALEM 179 allowed to leave the Persian court was that he would return after a set time, presumably long enough to complete the rebuilding of the city of his fathers. In xiii. 6, he distinctly states that he had been away from Jerusalem during the period when the innovations which aroused his indignation were introduced. The character of these changes indicates that his absence extended through several years. 169. Nehemiah's regulations for the defence of Jerusalem indicate that he anticipated no abatement in the hostility of its foes. The city gates were not to be opened until the middle of the forenoon. Then they were to be strongly guarded. At night they were to be securely barred, while the different sections of the walls were to be watched by those residing near them. Even with these strenuous precautions, the city was still in danger, for the restored walls had been built in the days of its greatest prosperity, so that their length and the space which they enclosed, were great. No general return had yet brought back thousands of loyal Jews, so that the inhabitants of the sacred city were too few to defend it properly (vii. 4). Henceforth the rulers of the community were induced to dwell

in Jerusalem. To complete the full quota, it also was necessary to select by lot one tenth of all the Jewish population resident outside Jerusalem and to bring them into the city. Those who freely volunteered, enjoyed the gratitude of their fellow-countrymen. Far different from the hopes of the great exilic prophet was the prosaic manner in which Zion again became inhabited; but Nehemiah, for the first time since its destruction, laid the foundations for a stable development. 170. Before Nehemiah returned to Susa, and probably before the adverse decree came from Artaxerxes, the walls were solemnly rcdedicated. The chronicler, in connection with his extracts from Nehemiah's account of the joyful occasion (Neh. xii. 31, 32, 37-40), has given his conception of the event, wherein the classes most prominent in his day, — the priests, the Levites, the singers (and even Ezra the scribe),— are introduced as the chief actors; while Nehemiah and the civil rulers are relegated to the background. Fortunately, in the fragment quoted from his memoir, Nehemiah has given a vivid picture of the unique celebration. He first assembled the people and the princes at the valley gate at the southwest corner of the city, the most distant point from the temple. Then he divided them into two companies, each of which proceeded in opposite directions, following the wall, and, as they went, giving thanks to Jehovah for prospering the work. " One, under Hoshaiah and half of the princes of Judah, went eastward upon the wall towards the dung gate and by the fountain gate, and straight before them they went up along the stairs of the city of David even to the water gate on the east side of the city " (compare map facing page 172) and on to the open space by the gate of the guard before the temple. The second company, followed by Nehemiah, proceeded along the other half of the city walls, " past the tower of the furnaces to the broad wall, and past the gate of Ephraim, the gate of the old wall, the fish gate, the towers of Hananel and Hammeah, and the sheep gate to the gate of the guard. " There before the temple the two companies met and stood, uniting their voices in loud songs of thanksgiving; while probably from the THE REDEDICATION OF THE WALLS 181 porch and interior of the temple came the solemn chant of the priests and ministers of the sanctuary. " Then they offered great sacrifices that day and rejoiced; for God had made them rejoice with great joy; and the women also and the children rejoiced, so that the joy of Jerusalem was heard even afar off " (xii. 43). Well might they rejoice, for, after more than two centuries of shame and discouragement, the Jews again could securely dwell under the shadow of their temple and sing:

Our feet are standing within thy gates, 0 Jerusalem, Jerusalem, that art builded as a city that is compact together.

The subsequent development of Judaism rested upon the noble work of the great layman. Truly did Jesus the son of Sirach declare:

The memorial of Nehemiah is great;

Who raised up for us the walls that were fallen,

And set up the gates and bars,

And raised up our homes again. Ps. cxxii. 2, 3. Ecclus. xlix. 13.

vm PRELIMINARY REFORM MEASURES 171. The importance of the rebuilding of the walls and of the repopulation of Jerusalem cannot be overestimated, for without this preliminary work the political and religious future of the Jewish colony was almost hopeless. A fundamental reform in the character and practices of the community was still absolutely demanded before it could worthily represent either the Jewish race as a whole or the Jehovah which it formally acknowledged (compare sects. 150 to 154). With the exception of the faithful few, the sweeping charge of one of their prophets was true; the members of the little state were thoroughly depraved (Isa. lix. 1-8). Prophets were still found to denounce existing evils and to urge reform; but apparently they were obliged to shield themselves from malignant persecution behind anonymous writings. Many of the righteous were cherishing in secret the hope that Jehovah would speedily send his messenger of the covenant, who would suddenly come to the temple to purify, as with a refiner's fire and fuller's soap, the sons of Levi and the services of the sanctuary, and many were even hoping that Jehovah himself would appear to condemn the prevalent heathen practices, the false swearing and the oppression of the helpless by the strong (Mai. iii. 1-5). CHECKING UNJUST EXACTIONS 183 172. In Nchcmiah, the party of the righteous and the cause of social and religious purity found an effective champion. Fortunately, with his authority and in view of his services to the community, he was able to command, as well as to exhort. Apparently, while the walls of Jerusalem were still being built, the wrongs of the masses found expression (Neh. v.). Under the unjust rule of the leaders of the community, as a result of the prevalent system of exacting usury, the common people had been forced not only to mortgage their fields and crops, but also to sell their sons and daughters into shameful slavery to the nobles and to the rich, in order to meet the Persian tax and to get food with which to live. When Nehemiah learned the real state of affairs, he called a general assembly of the people, and turned upon the heartless oppressors in hot indignation. He first called their attention to the example set by himself and those who had returned with him, in ransoming, as far as their means permitted, their brethren who had for one reason or another been sold to the heathen. He also appealed to their sense of shame, by pointing out how, by their despicable conduct, they were making their state an object of reproach in the eyes of the heathen foes who surrounded them. To these charges the culprits could make no reply. Then he proposed that they all, he and his followers, as well as the leaders in the community, cease to ask any interest from their needy fellow-countrymen. At his command, the leaders of the people consented to restore at once the fields, the vineyards, and the houses which they had taken from their poorer brethren, and to remit all exactions. To insure the fulfilment of the promise, Nehemiah administered to them a solemn oath in the presence of the priests, and called down a curse of expatriation and divine judgment upon any one who should prove faithless to his covenant. " And all the congregation said,' Amen,' and praised the Lord." 173. Tims the radical reform, which was destined to transform the life of the community, began beside the half builded walls and under the direction of the patriot Nehemiah. The precedents which he then established, were later embodied in that collection of laws known as the Priestly Code (sect. 201). The earliest Israelitish law provided for the selling into slavery of a Hebrew son or daughter by the parent (Ex. xxi. 2-6). The Deuteronomic law reasserted the earlier, only extending more favorable terms to the male slave (xv. 12-18). The action of the leaders of the Judean community was, therefore, strictly legal, for Deuteronomy was still the code which governed them. Nehemiah and those who had returned from the dispersion were, however, beginning to recognize a higher principle of brotherly love. That principle and the precedent established by Nehemiah are expressed in the Priestly Code (Lev. xxv. 39-41), which emphatically enacts that no Hebrew shall be made a "bondservant." Similarly, in the older laws of Exodus xxii. 25 and Deuteronomy xxiii. 19-20, which were recognized by the community, it is forbidden to take interest on a loan to a fellow Israelite. According to their standards, the conduct of the leaders in demanding interest was indefensible; but Nehemiah and his followers, in accepting it on ordinary loans, were following the custom which, for practical reasons, was becoming common among the Jews of the disper- THE DANGER OF HEATHEN MARRIAGES 185 sion, and which was later adopted by those in Palestine (Matt. xxv. 27). What Nehemiah attacked was the exacting of interest from those in distress. This principle again is precisely what is emphasized in the Priestly Code (Lev. xxv. 35-37). The fact that it alone prohibits the taking of interest from "the brother who has become poor," implies that it was permitted in ordinary business relations. 174. In other matters, Nehemiah, imbued with the stricter ideals of the Jews of the Bast, proved the pioneer of that priestly reformation which ultimately revolutionized the character of Palestinian Judaism. The question of the attitude of the community toward the heathen and the half-heathen peoples, who pressed it closely on every side, was so vital and insistent that he could not ignore it. Already the little Judean state was divided over it into two bitterly contending parties. The ruling party, the rich, the nobles, and the priestly aristocracy, as we have seen (sect. 153), advocated alliances and intermarriage with their heathen neighbors, and consequently extended to them the courtesies of the temple (Neh. xiii. 4, 5), thereby virtually acknowledging the equality of the heathen religions with that of Jehovah. The danger of this position is obvious. If the unique revelation vouchsafed to the Jews was to be transmitted to mankind, it must be by members of the Jewish race. The temple and those who rallied about it were the keystone which preserved the integrity of the scattered people. Under the Persian rule, political distinctions meant little; the influences which kept intact the Judean community were those of common blood-kinship and of religion. If the former was weakened by intermarriage with foreigners, and the latter by the further introduction of heathen ideas and customs, the absorption of the weak group of Jews by the stronger and more aggressive communities about them was inevitable. Certainly the religious life of the Palestinian community was at too low an ebb to survive the assimilation of many more heathen elements. 175. Only a few enlightened men in Judah, the sturdy Puritans, appreciated the danger. As a matter of fact, the Jews of Palestine, who were subject to the temptation, did not realize its real significance nearly as clearly as did those of the dispersion. The constant horror of being absorbed into the great heathen world, in the midst of which they found themselves, led the latter to guard most jealously the purity of their blood and their religion. The peril was too great to admit of

a broad tolerance toward all mankind; therefore they devoted their energies to building about themselves a wall which would not only keep the Gentile out, but would also keep the Jew true to his race and his religion. Unattractive as was that high wall of separation, it undoubtedly saved Judaism from the mighty assaults of heathenism which were directed against it during the next four centuries. Like the great structures of the past, it was the work of many hands, and grew slowly through the ages. 176. Nehemiah's memoirs indicate the prominent part which he took in building this, as well as the wall of stone, which was required before exclusive measures could be instituted. It is suggestive that there is no evidence that, during the first period of his governorship, he directly opposed the practice of intermarrying, and of making alliance with the heathen people, which ATTITUDE TOWARD HEATHEN MARRIAGES 187 had become so common in Judah. They were distasteful to him simply because they weakened the loyalty of the nobles and priests, who were the chief culprits. If he had at first openly declared his opposition to the principle of foreign marriages, the friends of Tobiah the Ammonite would not have dared persistently to speak to him of the good deeds of this heathen prince. Their aim was clearly not to overrule the principles of the wise governor, but to remove the personal antipathy which he felt toward a treacherous enemy (Neh. vi. 17-19). Twelve years later, however, when Nehemiah again, in 532 B. c., returned to Jerusalem, his attitude toward foreign marriages was entirely different. He recognized more clearly than before the dangers of the practice, and the twelve years spent in contact with the stricter Jews of the East had crystallized his principles. The only events which he records in connection with his second sojourn in Judah, are the measures which he instituted with the aim of purifying the external religious life of the community. To his horror, he found that a large room, connected with the temple, in which consecrated offerings and sacred vessels had formerly been stored,

had been set aside by Eliashib the chief priest for the use of Tobiah the Ammonite, his relative by marriage. Indignantly the zealous governor threw out the possessions of the heathen prince. After the room had been cleansed, he caused the vessels and offerings to be restored to their place (Neh. xiii. 4-9). 177. He also discovered, during this visit or later, that many of the Jews (especially those living in the southwestern towns of Judah) had taken as wives women of Ashdod, Ammon, and Moab. The children who were born as the fruit of these mixed marriages naturally spoke a mixed dialect. This fact impressed upon Nehemiah's mind most forcibly the dangers of the practice. His usual energy and righteous anger found immediate expression. Personally he went to work to remove the evil. By expressive word and blow, after the manner of Orientals, he assailed the offenders, and made them swear by Jehovah that they would not allow their children to intermarry with foreigners. To impress upon them the danger of their course, he appealed to no law, but to the well-known disastrous effects of such acts upon the character of the great King Solomon. Nehemiah refused absolutely to listen to the defence of those who favored foreign marriages, and openly declared that it was a sin against God (xiii. 23-27). Undoubtedly, many and specious arguments were urged by the advocates of this lax practice. The story of Ruth the Moabitess, the ancestress of their illustrious King David, contained one of the many prominent precedents to which they were able to appeal. They also could point triumphantly to the example of their present rulers and priests. 178. Having put his hands to the plough, it was not Nehemiah's wont to turn back. The influence and position of some of the offenders did not daunt him. He did not hesitate to expel in time even the grandson of the high priest Eliashib from Jerusalem, because he had married the daughter of Sanballat (xiii. 28). Such a sweeping revolution as this represented, could not be permanently effected in a day, so that it is not surprising that to other hands was left the completion of the work; but only one man of this period was REFORMS IN SABBATH OBSERVANCE 189 strong enough to institute it, and that was Nehemiah. It is fortunate that the chronicler, whose natural tendency was to exalt the priest Ezra at the expense of the equally devout laymen, has preserved in his incomplete citations the record of this fact. The oath of the people at the Great Assembly, recorded in Nehemiah x., was an almost verbal reiteration of the one which they had made to Nehemiah (compare x. 30 and xiii. 25). 179. By other forcible acts this energetic pioneer of reform enforced in Judah the higher ideals of the Jews of the dispersion, and in so doing established precedents which became the basis of the great reformation. In Judah the institution of the Sabbath, which was so highly esteemed by the Jews of the exile (compare sect. 36), was laxly observed. In certain parts of the country the governor found the people doing their ordinary agricultural work on that day; the peasants also brought wine, grapes, figs, and different kinds of merchandise to Jerusalem. Traders from Tyre came with fish and other provisions on the Sabbath, that they might find a ready market for their goods, when the people were at leisure to buy. Nehemiah first reprimanded the rulers of Judah for allowing a state of affairs to continue which had brought divine vengeance upon their nation in the past, and which would again incur the displeasure of Jehovah. Having preached to them as a prophet, he gave command, as governor, that the gates be closed, as the evening of the Sabbath approached, and that they should not be opened until the day was past. Not trusting the local authorities, he sent some of his servants to see that no merchants were admitted into the city on that day. When certain hucksters came repeatedly and stayed during the night of the Sabbath just outside the "walls, the governor himself warned them away so effectually that they never came again. To insure the permanence of his reform, he commanded certain Levites to prepare themselves and go regularly to the gates, and prevent anything from entering to destroy the sanctity of the Sabbath (Neh. xiii. 15-22). By these enactments Nehemiah encircled the sacred city with another high wall, separating it from the heathen world without. The second obligation assumed by the people at the Great Assembly: " If the peoples of the land bring merchandise, or any provisions on the Sabbath day to sell, we will not buy of them on the Sabbath or on a holy day " (Neh. x. 31), was a formal acceptance of the principle enforced by him. 180. Nehemiah also gave his personal attention to purifying the services of the temple, and to rectifying those abuses which had brought the sanctuary into such ill repute (see sect. 151). He found that the Levites did not receive their appointed portions, so that they and the singers had been obliged to leave the temple in order to support themselves by tilling the soil. After denouncing the representatives of the people for allowing the service of the sanctuary to be thus neglected, he summoned all the Levites. At his command the people brought in the tithe of their corn and wine and oil to the place where they were stored. To secure their fair distribution, Nehemiah appointed four treasurers to take charge of them. Shelemiah, who was probably the father of the Hananiah who assisted in building the walls (iii. 30), represented the priests. The second member was Zadok the scribe, REFORMS IN THE TEMPLE ORGANIZATION 191 probably a priest (compare Neh. iii. 29; vii. 40), who belonged to that body of literati destined soon to become the most influential class in Jewish circles. Pediah seems to have represented the Levites proper, and Hanun, who, according to the chronicler, was one of the sons of Asaph (Neh. xi. 17; xii. 35), represented the singers. Upon these reliable men, Nehemiah laid the responsibility of distributing equably to their brethren the tithes which were brought for them. 181. This new regulation marked an important departure from the prevailing laws, the defects of which it was intended to remedy. Deuteronomy enacted that the people, taking the tithe of their corn and wine and oil, should come up to the temple and use it to provide a great feast, of which they and their households should partake. Generous charity to the poor Levite, especially every third year, was enjoined, but the amount of the gift depended entirely upon the liberality of the donor, and no provisions were made for the equal distribution of what was thus given (xiv. 22-28; xxvi. 12-15). Nehemiah's plan recognized the need of better regulations, but did not anticipate the enactments of the Priestly Code, which became the basis of the law adopted by the Great Assembly. According to the later system, the tithes were collected by the Levites and brought to the temple; then a tithe of the tithes was handed over by them to the priests, " the sons of Aaron " (Neh. x. 37-39; Num. xviii. 24-28). Nehemiah further adds, in the closing extract from his memoir, that he laid down specific rules respecting the distribution of the work of the priests and of the Levites. He also appointed certain times when the wood-offerings for the altar and the first fruits should be brought into the temple. Unfortunately, he gives no details, but there is little doubt that these much-needed regulations were the basis of the two corresponding articles in the covenant recorded in Nehemiah x. (verses 34, 35). 182. Thus the true relation of Nehemiah's work to the Great Assembly becomes clear. In the light of the facts already studied, it is hardly necessary to cite further evidence to show that the formation of the true " Israel " (" Israel" being the term employed in the later times to postulate the claim of the Jews to be the chosen people of Jehovah), and the acceptance of the solemn covenant by the congregation did not precede, but followed the reforms of Nehemiah. On the hypothesis that the Great Assembly preceded 532 B. c., Nehemiah's absolute silence respecting it is, to say the least, inexplicable. He knows nothing of the true " Israel " in Palestine, which was created by the fusion of the faithful who returned from the dispersion and those who separated themselves from the people of the land and subscribed to the new Priestly Law. If the Great Assembly preceded the events recorded in Nehemiah xiii., Nehemiah's regulations, and especially those respecting the distribution of the tithes to the Levites, were entirely unnecessary and even reactionary; or else the priestly reformation, usually associated with the names of Ezra and Nehemiah, and dated about 445 B. c., had proved a practical failure, a conclusion which is absolutely disproved by the character of later Judaism. On the other hand, as has been noted repeatedly, Nehemiah's acts all give the impression of being pioneer reform measures, constituting a most natural and necessary prelude to the HISTORICAL IMPORTANCE OF HEHEMIAH'S WORK 193 action of the Great Assembly. It is a striking fact that all but one of the articles subscribed to by that body, according to the record (Neh. x.), are suggested by Nchemiah's reforms. 183. Our study of the character of the Judean community has demonstrated conclusively that the chief impetus to reform must come from without. That it did actually come from the Jews of the East is confirmed by all the traditions relating to the subject. In the light of conditions in Judah before the advent of Nehemiah, however, it is impossible to believe that all that was necessary to influence the Jews of Palestine to give up customs and religious practices cherished for centuries, to reform fundamentally their social and religious practices, to expel from their homes many beloved wives and children, and to subscribe almost unanimously to a new code, was that a deputation of Jews from the East visit them with the new law in their hands, read it in their presence, and then forthwith convene a Great Assembly for the purpose of promulgating it. The herculean task was one which required, not a week, but years to accomplish. It called for the consecrated service, not of one man, but of many. There is abundant evidence that there were many faithful prophets and priests within and without the community who joined in the work (compare Isa. lvi. to Ixii. and Mai. i.-ii.); but the one who alone possessed at the same time the authority,

the prestige, the energy, the tact, and the devotion, was the illustrious layman, Nehemiah. Without his important services, it is difficult to conceive how the great transformation could have been accomplished. The tradition, preserved in the second Book of Maccabees (i. 18-36), that he, and not Ezra, restored the true service of the temple, is not without foundation. It is significant that, with the one exception of the tradition preserved by the chronicler, in the writings of the next two or three centuries the name of Nehemiah is immortalized, while that of Ezra is ignored. To the pioneer who conquers the soil, more than to the one who reaps the fruit, is rightly due the higher honor. When Nehemiah had completed his many sided work, the Judean community was for the first time in its history ready to give heed to the law book which Ezra and the consecrated Jews of the dispersion brought in their hands. THE DATE AND CHARACTER OF EZRA'S EXPEDITION 184. Radical reform measures always call for the formation of new laws, so as to insure the permanence of the new order. Tims the reformation of Josiah in 621 B. c. was sealed by the Book of the Covenant, preserved in our present Book of Deuteronomy. If the principles which guided the actors in that important movement had not been put into the form of written laws, they certainly would not have continued to influence the Jewish race as powerfully as they did, long after the exile had loosed all the moorings which bound it to its past. Similarly, Nehemiah's revolutionizing measures not only prepared the way for a new and revised code, but also made it absolutely necessary. While hitherto the Jews in Judah had contented themselves with the Deuteronomic law, new conditions, new experiences, and new revelations had led the Jews of the dispersion, like Ezekiel, freely to revise and extend the old system, so that a new, in the sense of an expanded, law was gradually taking form. How far Nehemiah was influenced in his reform work by a familiarity with the laws already formulated by the Jews in the East, and how far in turn the precedents which he es-

tablished, became the basis of the laws themselves, are questions which can never be answered with certainty. We do know that his attitude towards the conditions in Judah changed most radically during the decade spent in the Bast after his first visit to Jerusalem (compare sect. 176). On the other hand, most of his reforms were such as would be suggested to a fertile and devout mind by the conditions themselves. Evidently he was not attempting to introduce an esoteric system devised by priests who were ignorant of the needs with which they were dealing. The Priestly Code itself also reveals familiarity with conditions in Judah, as well as with the Jews in the dispersion. The most natural conclusion to be drawn from the facts is that Nehemiah took with him to Judah at least a knowledge of the principles and practices obtaining among his brethren in the East; and that, in turn, the reforms which he effected, guided those who gave the final form to the system of laws which was gradually being developed. 185. Unfortunately, the sources of information regarding the institution of the new, revised code are not nearly as detailed or reliable as those which record the building of the walls of Jerusalem. The tradition preserved by the chronicler associates it with the names of both Nehemiah and Ezra. As we have seen, the extracts in Ezra vii. to x. originally formed part of the same narrative which is contained in Nehemiah vii. 70 to x. 39, and their separation, and the assignment of Ezra's expedition to the seventh year of Artaxerxes, apparently represent an attempt on the part of the chronicler to give Ezra, the priest and scribe, the precedence before Nehemiah, the layman (sect. 96), and possibly also to convey the impression that the walls of Jerusalem were built largely by the hands of re- EVIDENCE THAT EZRA FOLLOWED NEHEMIAH 197 turned exiles, or else they are due to a later disarrangement of the text. In the light of the conditions in Judah before the building of the walla of Jerusalem by Nehemiah, and before his reforms begun in 432 B. c., the expedition of Ezra recorded in Ezra vii. to x. was not only highly improbable but practically impossible. Even those who continue to assign it to the year 458 B. c. are obliged to adduce the hypothesis that it was a complete failure, although the narrative itself states that it was the opposite. The entire absence of the slightest references in Nehemiah's memoirs, where they would surely be expected, to the expedition, and to the strenuous reform measures of Ezra, can be explained only on the hypothesis that they were later than 432 B. c. Not one of the prominent men who returned with Ezra (Ezra viii.) is mentioned by Nehemiah, although, if they were already in Jerusalem, they would naturally have been his most ardent supporters. After the institution of Ezra's exclusive measures, which were accepted almost unanimously by the community (Ezra ix.; x.), the practice of intermarrying with foreigners, which continued unrestricted until Nehemiah opposed it during his second visit to Jerusalem, is also inexplicable. 186. On the other hand, the evidence that Ezra's expedition took place at a period subsequent to 432 B. c. is cumulative and reasonably conclusive. In Ezra's prayer (Ezra ix. 9), he gives thanks that the wall of Jerusalem has been rebuilt and Judah's defences restored. He found the sacred city not depopulated, as Nehemiah found it in 445 B. c., but strong and blessed with many inhabitants. His surprise and horror that the people had not yet completely separated themselves from the foreign population presupposes Nehemiah's exclusive measures (Ezra ix. 1-3). The man who rebuilt their fallen walls, for the first time since the beginning of the exile, brought the Jews of Palestine into close and sympathetic touch with those of the dispersion, and paved the way for an expedition such as that led by Ezra. Nehemiah's work in fortifying their ruined capital, and again establishing their prestige, also for the first time, aroused in the hearts of the poor Palestinian Jews a feeling of deep gratitude toward their brothers in the East. His reforms likewise prepared them for still more sweeping ones emanating from the

same source. His work in turn aroused the interest of the Jews of the dispersion in their kindred in Judah. When Jerusalem was encircled by walls, it again became, for the first time since 586 B. c., a safe and attractive abode for its returning sons and daughters. The reforms which he introduced into the rude, shiftless, half-heathen community in Judah promised, if enforced, to convert it into a body with which the more cultured and devout Jews of the East could live in harmony. Judah presented at last an inviting missionary field, which appealed — when in time the real conditions became generally known — to the religious zeal, as well as to the patriotism, of the more favored Jews beyond its limits. The desire to re-establish the true Israel in the ancient territory, and about the sacred temple, grew so strong that it impelled many during the next half century to turn their faces toward Jerusalem, that by their presence, as well as their influence, they might support the cause of pure religion. Also during the earlier part of the reign of Artaxerxes I., the satrap Megabyzus was the DATE OF EZRA'S EXPEDITION 199 real ruler of Syria, and the province was regarded with great suspicion by the king (sect. 144); but, thanks to the diplomacy of Nehemiah, the attitude of the court at Susa toward the Jews had now changed. The manifest weakness and corruption of the great Persian empire also inspired many of them with the hope that in the time of its approaching dissolution the little Judean state might again attain to independence, if not to world-power (see Isa. xxiv. to xxvii.). 187. One of the first, largest, and most zealous of these bands of returning exiles was led by Ezra. The exact date of his expedition, and of the Great Assembly which followed in the next year, cannot be determined with certainty from the material at our command. It has been suggested that the statement of the chronicler in Ezra vii. 8, that Ezra made his expedition in the seventh year of Artaxerxes, is due to his desire to date Ezra before Nehemiah. Others maintain that it is simply a mistake commonly made by copyists, and that "

thirty" has dropped out, so that it originally read " the thirty-seventh year of the king," or 427 B. c. It has also been strongly urged by a conservative Dutch scholar (Van Hoonacker, *Nouvelles Utudes sur la Restauration Juive,* 270-277), that the reigning Artaxerxes was the second Persian ruler bearing that name, and that therefore " the seventh year of the king" was 398 B. c. Since the chronicler and the Jewish writers of the Greek period were ignorant even of the order of the Persian monarchs (see Ezra iv.; Dan. v. 31; ix. 1; x. 1), it was most natural that they should be unable to distinguish between different rulers of the same name. 188. The internal evidence which must determine the choice between these three possible hypotheses, is unfortunately not very definite. If the " Jehohanan the son of Eliashib " to whose room in the temple Ezra retired after addressing the people (Ezra x. 6) was the grandson of Eliashib, who was high priest in 445 and 432 B. c. (compare Neh. xii. 22, 28), and if, as is less certain, Jehohanan (or Johanan) was high priest when Ezra visited Jerusalem, the latest date (398 B. c.) is practically established. Furthermore, if the four treasurers (two priests and two Levites), to whom Ezra and his followers delivered the contributions which they bought for the temple, occupied the offices created by Nehemiah in 432 B. c. (sect. 180), the reference would also suggest the latest date for the expedition, for the men originally appointed by the governor had all been succeeded by others (Ezra viii. 33). At the head of the commission, however, was Mermoth, the son of Uriah, who was especially prominent in building the walls in 445 B. c. (Neh. iii. 4, 21). It is possible, but not probable, that he continued to occupy high positions in public life for half a century (398 B. c.), so that his appearance here strongly favors an earlier date than 398 B. c. Similarly, Malchijah of the tribe of Harim (as well as others whose identification is not so certain), who assisted in the work of 445 B. c. , was among those who covenanted after the arrival of Ezra to put away his wife (Ezra x. 31; Neh. iii. 11). The lax practices in regard to foreign marriages which aroused Ezra's astonishment and indignation, indicate on the other hand that several years at least had passed since Nehemiah instituted his first vigorous crusade against the more culpable offenders. The fact alone is established that some time during the latter part of the fifth SIGNIFICANCE OF EZRA'S EXPEDITION 201 or in the opening years of the fourth century B. c. (between 430 and 397), probably in 397, the new code was instituted in Judah which gave the community the distinctive character which it bore in later times. 189. In the light of the preceding studies, it is possible to appreciate the real significance of the expedition led by Ezra. It was the culmination of centuries of development. It represented the supreme contribution of the Jews of the East to their kinsmen in Palestine. Its aim was completely to bridge the gulf which hitherto had yawned between them, and to realize on the sacred soil of Judah the ideals of their earlier prophets and of their later priests. Its program was a law expressive of the ritualistic tendency of the age, and adapted to the new circumstances in which the Jewish race found itself. Its leader was representative of the movement. The chronicler traces his genealogy through the chief Judean priestly family back to Aaron, and describes him as " a ready scribe in the law of Moses which the Lord the God of Israel had given." During the earlier days of the Hebrew kingdom the " scribe" was the royal secretary or chancellor of state (I. 123). Before the exile, however, the term began to be applied to those who devoted themselves to studying and editing the earlier writings and especially the law. Jeremiah complained bitterly that his people were ignorant of the will of Jehovah, because " the false pen of the scribes had made of it falsehood" (viii. 7, 8). Amidst the peculiar conditions and needs of the dispersion, the priests, having no temple for which to care, became ministers of the law, carefully studying, arranging, and interpreting it. Their pent-up energies found expression in the zeal with which they guarded it, and insisted that

all their race should faithfully observe its injunctions. It was to them the final and complete expression of the divine will. To refuse to obey it was to defy Jehovah himself. So many of the roots of the law were found in the dim past, and so imperceptibly had the great structure grown, that the traditions which assigned it as a whole to the earliest days of their national history and to Moses, the greatest personality of that period, were accepted unquestioningly. Hence it enjoyed the sanction, not only of Jehovah, but of the hallowed past, whose authority was recognized in this later age as almost divine. To men like Ezra, the knowledge that the services of the temple at Jerusalem were not conducted in accordance with " the sacred law of Moses," and that Jehovah's holy shrine was constantly polluted by the presence of priests and laymen who were unclean according to the Priestly Code, was intolerable. 190. Since the aim of Ezra's expedition was not political, but religious, it was not difficult to secure royal permission to return to Jerusalem (Ezra vii. 27, 28). The potent influence of the loyal and sympathetic Nehemiah may have secured certain special concessions, as is suggested by the version of the royal decree preserved in Ezra vii. 11-26. There is no evidence, however, that in his reform work Ezra appealed to any other authority than that of the law which he bore in his hand. The leader himself came from the province of Babylon, the original centre of Judaism in the East; but the names borne by the different groups of Jews which followed him indicate that they were enlisted widely from the different lands of the dispersion. In view of the secondary position which was assigned to the Levites in HISTORY OF EZRA'S EXPEDITION 203 the Priestly Code, it is not strange that none at first rallied to his standard. Moreover, the priests of the temple at Jerusalem, not those of the ancient high places, were carried to Babylon by Nebuchadrezzar, so that there were probably few Levites in the East. Only thirty-eight could finally be found to return. In all, about fifteen hundred men, representing six or seven thousand souls,

joined Ezra at the assembling place beside the river Ahava, probably one of the small streams or canals flowing into the Euphrates about one hundred and twenty-five miles northwest of Babylon. The great majority of the Jews who could not themselves return shared in the restoration of " Israel" to Palestine by contributing rich presents to the temple. According to the Ezra narrative, the gifts of the Persian king and his court, together with those of the Jews, amounted to six hundred and fifty talents of silver, a hundred of gold, and a thousand darics, besides many large vessels of gold and silver. Since the value of the contributions aggregates over four million dollars, these numbers, like many handed down by the chronicler (compare especially those in the Books of Chronicles with the corresponding ones in the Books of Kings), may have grown in transmission. 191. When the returning patriots had fasted, after the custom of the faithful Jews of the dispersion, and besought Jehovah's protecting care, they set out about the first of April on their long wearisome march. Since the journey was made during the heat of summer, it was necessary to make an extensive detour to the north to avoid the Arabian desert, and to travel very slowly, so that four months and a half were required to traverse the eight or nine hundred miles. Jerusalem was reached in August, and, after a rest of three days, the rich gifts, which during the journey had been intrusted to a commission of prominent priests and Levites, were formally turned over to the treasurers of the temple. The returned exiles also presented appropriate offerings to Jehovah in behalf of " all Israel," which they had come back to restore; for their first task was to establish the services of the temple on a basis in keeping with its dignity as the central shrine of the nation, and in harmony with the more elaborate demands of the Priestly Law, which they recognized. In addition to the valuable gifts which the returning Jews brought with them, Nehemiah, as the representative of the Persian government (Neh. vii. 70; viii. 9), contributed for this purpose a thousand golden darics, fifty vessels, and five hundred and thirty priests' garments. Some of the heads of the tribes in the Judean community, emulating his example, gave liberally money, gold, and silver. Even the common people caught from the returned pilgrims the spirit of generosity and self-sacrifice in behalf of their religion, and swelled the endowment fund of the temple by their gifts of gold and silver and priests' garments. Their petty jealousies and meannesses were forgotten, as they mingled their gifts before Jehovah's altar. The sense of common blood, of common religion, and of common service again bound together the Jews of Judah and of the East, and prepared the way for the more revolutionary reform work. THE INSTITUTION OF THE PKIESTLY LAW 192. The first two months after the arrival of Ezra's expedition at Jerusalem were devoted to regulating the service, and to completing necessary repairs on the temple. Quarters were also assigned to the priests, the Levites, and the minor officials of the sanctuary who had returned. Many of them found homes in the towns outside Jerusalem (Neh. vii. 73). The laymen, with their families, also sought suitable places in which to settle. The external restoration of " all Israel" had begun. In the eyes of the priestly reformers, however, everything yet remained to be done. The character of the native community must be radically changed before a complete amalgamation could be effected. Probably these first two months were spent in studying conditions and in quiet missionary work among the people. The burning zeal of the six or seven thousand who had left their homes, and had come to Judah as the apostles of " the law of Moses," could not fail to communicate its leavening influence to their more ignorant and apathetic brethren. 193. On the feast of the new moon, the first day of the seventh month, celebrated ever after by the Jews as the feast of trumpets or day of holy convocation (Lev. xxiii. 23-25; Num. xxix. 1-6), the people were assembled from all parts of the laud to the open space near the water gate on the eastern side of Jerusalem. At

their request, Ezra brought " the book of the law of Moses." Taking his place on a wooden pulpit constructed for the purpose, and having given thanks, he publicly read the law to them, while attendant Levites explained it. When the native Jews understood the content of the new law, they were filled with dismay, and gave expression to their feelings in cries of lamentation; for they appreciated in part what sweeping changes it would introduce into their life, and how contrary to it were their present practices. Nehemiah appears to have actively co-operated in this movement which represented the culmination of his earlier work. If we had his complete memoirs, instead of an extract from a priestly narrative, the sympathies of which are all with Ezra, we would probably find that he took a prominent part in the great reformation. At this critical time, both he and Ezra wisely disarmed the fears of the people, and urged them to observe the day as they were wont, with feasting and by sending gifts to the needy in their midst (Deut. xvi. 14). 194. On the second day the leaders of the community and their priests and Levites came to Ezra for further instruction in regard to the details of the new law. Among other commands, they found one which enjoined that " the children of Israel should dwell in booths in the feast of the seventh month, and that they should publish and proclaim it in all their cities and in Jerusalem " (Neh. viii. 14, 15). The passage in question was evidently the twenty-third chapter of Leviticus. Following out its injunctions, the Feast of Tabernacles was faithfully observed, beginning with INTERPRETATION AND APPLICATION OF THE LAW 207 the fifteenth day of the month, and closing with the holy convocation on the twenty-second (Lev. xxiii. 38-39; Neh. viii. 18). Each day Ezra improved the favorable opportunity to read and to impress upon the people the commands of the new code; while those who had returned with him from the exile set an example before the native Jews as to how the feast should properly be observed (Neh. viii. 17). The entire assembly was moved by a deep reli-

gious enthusiasm. During those eight days it experienced a genuine revival. The self-sacrificing missionary zeal of the reformers bore fruit. At last the self-centred Jews of Palestine were also ready to make sacrifices. 195. When the preliminary work of instruction had been completed, and the conscience of the community had thus been aroused, certain of the leaders of the people came to Ezra and confessed that many of the people, and even some of their priests and Levites, had failed to hold themselves aloof, as the new law enjoined, from the contaminating influences of their heathen neighbors, "the people of the land" (Ezra ix. 1). Many of the leading men in Judah had committed the sin, against which Nehemiah had so earnestly warned them (Neh. xiii. 27), and had married heathen wives, and encouraged their sons to do the same. Nothing was more calculated to arouse the horror of a zealous Jew of the dispersion, like Ezra, than disclosures of this nature. He felt that the whole community and land were contaminated. Recognizing that the evil was one which must be absolutely eliminated, if "the true Israel was to be established," he opposed it with all the strength of his intense nature. Unlike Nehemiah, Ezra did not have the authority to cominand, but endeavored to appeal to the conscience of the people. His prayers and exhortations finally so impressed them that one of their number proposed that they all solemnly covenant to put away their foreign wives and the children born of these marriages. Assured of their support, Ezra first made the priests and Levites take the oath of separation. Then the nobles and elders proclaimed an assembly of the entire nation. Forfeiture of property and excommunication from the congregation was the penalty imposed for non-appearance. 196. By these radical methods, a general representation of the people was secured. On the twentieth day of the ninth month (January), they all assembled in the open space before the temple. To Ezra's demand that they separate themselves, and thus remove the burden of guilt which rested upon them, they acceded;

but the magnitude of the sacrifice involved, and the torrents of rain which deluged them, for it was the middle of the rainy season, dampened their enthusiasm. Since the measure was one which called for careful investigations, and demanded time, they proposed that all who had married foreign wives be required to come up to Jerusalem at appointed times, with the elders and judges of their respective towns, that their cases might be carefully considered. The proposal was accepted, and Ezra was appointed at the head of a commission to examine and superintend the matter. Beginning on the first day of the tenth mouth (late in January), they did not complete their work until the first day of the following year (March). Painful as must have been the details of the execution of this measure, which ruthlessly severed family ties, CALLING THE GREAT ASSEMBLY 209 it is probable that under the watchful direction of the stern Ezra it *was* faithfully enforced. One hundred and thirteen men, who were found guilty, and who submitted to the extreme penalty, are mentioned in the list given in Ezra x. 197. When this preliminary work was completed, and not before, was it possible publicly to institute the new Priestly Law. On the twenty-fourth day of the month in which the commission concluded its labors, when " the seed of Israel had separated themselves from all strangers " (Neh. ix. 1, 2.), Ezra and his fellow-reformers were permitted to behold the fruits of their year of unremitting toil. The way in which the new law was introduced was characteristic of the age. When Nehemiah wished to institute some reform, he called an assembly of all the people, and publicly presented the matter before them, and extracted a solemn oath of agreement (Neh. ii. 16-18; v. 7, 12, 13; xiii. 25). Similarly, Ezra repeatedly gathered all the people together (Neh. viii. 1; Ezra x. 7-9,12). At a later time, when Judah was threatened by a locust plague, the first thought of the prophet Joel was to call a solemn assembly (i. 14; ii. 15). The Jewish state was so small, and distances so short, that it was not a difficult matter to as-

semble the entire population. Three days were considered by the leaders of the community amply sufficient to convene all the men at Jerusalem (Ezra x. 9.) 198. The great reformation of Josiah, the influence of which was still paramount in Judah, undoubtedly established a precedent which guided the later reformers (II. Kings xxiii. 1-3). Since the power formerly vested in the monarchy now resided in the congregation of the people, the priestly reformation was necessarily much more democratic than that of 621 B. c., and probably for that reason was more permanent. The new law was not forced upon them by royal decree, but accepted by popular vote. The Great Assembly was opened by the reading of the more important sections of the law, and then followed by a popular confession of the sins of the community. The character of the service was closely analogous to that of the ordinary Jewish synagogue. This fact is emphasized by the tradition of the " Great Synagogue,-" which originally was the later Jewish account of the Great Assembly (compare Midrash to Kuth). According to the Septuagint version, the long prayer, preserved in Nehemiah ix., in which Jehovah's care and fidelity toward the people and their infidelity and sins are reviewed, was delivered by Ezra. It fittingly indicated the relation of the important act which they were about to perform to the past history of their race. As in the earlier prayer of Ezra (Ezra ix.), the conceptions of that history, and the point of view throughout, are those of the new priestly legislation. After the preliminary services had been completed, Nehemiah, the nobles and the representatives of the lay, the priestly and the Levitical clans solemnly covenanted to accept the new law, and, in token thereof, subscribed their names. Then the assembly as a whole, including those who had returned with Ezra, and all, whether of Jewish descent or not, " who had separated themselves from the peoples of the land unto the law of God," together with their families, took an oath, sealed by a curse upon the one who proved faithless to it, that they would observe " the law of

God which REGULATIONS ADOPTED AT THE GREAT ASSEMBLY 211 was given by Moses the servant of God " (Neh. x. 28, 29). 199. The chief articles in that law, as reported in Nehemiah x., are: (1) To abstain from all intermarriage with heathen peoples; (2) to abstain from buying and selling on the Sabbath or on a holy day; (3) to observe the commands respecting the Sabbatical year; (4) to pay a poll tax of one third of a shekel to support the services at the temple; (5) to provide wood for the sacrifices at the temple in accordance with the decision of the lot; (6) to bring the first-fruits and the first-born, as commanded, to the temple for the support of the priests; (7) to deliver the tithes of the ground to the Levites, who in turn were to distribute them according to the law; and (8), in general, not to neglect to provide for the needs of the temple service. 200. The trustworthiness of this brief report is strikingly confirmed by the fact that each regulation was intended to correct evils in the Judean community with which we have already become familiar through the memoirs of Nehemiah and the writings of contemporary prophets. There is good ground for believing that the reformation affected the inner spiritual as well as the external life of the community; but it was natural that a tradition, probably preserved among the records of the temple, should refer only to objective reforms. The articles subscribed to at the Great Assembly became at once the constitution, both of Judaism and of the new temple service. The first regulation was intended to separate the Jews from the rest of mankind; the second, in enforcing the strict observance of the Sabbath, emphasized the same distinction; the third aimed to improve the social organization of the community; while the remaining five relate entirely to the sanctuary, and their aim is to make its services more elaborate and impressive, and, with this end in view, to secure for the temple aiid its ministers an increased and definite income. 201. The account of their work leaves no doubt that Ezra and his fellow-reformers were guided by the body of laws found chiefly in Exodus xxv. to xxxi.; xxxiv. 29 to xl. 38, and the Books of Leviticus and Numbers, which is usually designated as the Priestly or Levitical Code. In general, the prominence given to the services of the temple, the accent placed upon the written law, and the custom of reading the law at the Feast of Tabernacles (see Lev. xxiii. 33-36) are all marked characteristics of this system. Five out of the eight regulations, while unknown to the earlier Deuteronomic, are based upon the Priestly Code. The Pentateuch contains no detailed enactments respecting the provision of wood for the sacrifices. The reference in Nehemiah *x.* 34, "As it is written in the law," is, therefore, to a section in the Priestly Code which has been lost, or to the traditional usage of the temple, based perhaps upon Nehemiah's ruling (Neh. xiii. 31). 202. There is, on the other hand, evidence that at the time of the Great Assembly the Priestly Code was not quite complete. For example, the poll tax of one-third of a shekel for the support of the temple service was increased to one-half of a temple shekel (Ex. xxx. 11-16; xxxviii. 26; so in New Testament times). In the covenant of the Great Assembly, reference is made only to the tithe of the ground (Neh. x. 37; compare CHARACTER OF THE NEW CODE 213 also xiii. 5), which, as in Deuteronomy xiv. 22-29, included only the produce of the field; but, according to the later priestly legislation of Leviticus xxvii. 30-33, the people were commanded to bring not only the tithe of the field, but also the tithe of the herd and of the flock. Similarly, in Ezra's time, the day of atonement was evidently not celebrated on the tenth day of the memorable seventh month described in Nehemiah viii.; but, according to the law in Leviticus xvi., and the usage of later Judaism, this day (the tenth of the seventh month) was set aside for national confession and atoning sacrifice. It soon became one of the most important days in the religious calendar. Thus the account of the Great Assembly introduces us to the Jewish law still in the course of formation. The long process, however, was nearly complete, for the position given

to the written torah at that time soon led to the closing of the canon of the law. 203. The new expanded code, like the system devised by Ezekiel, aimed to make objective the principles of the prophets. The majority of the Jews of Palestine were so ignorant that, if they were to be led into the way of holiness, that way must be very plain and the guide-posts many. The old Hebrew prophets were obliged to be content if a mere handful of disciples listened to their message, while the mass of their nation went on unheeding. The apostles of the expanded law of Moses aimed to reach all, and to transform the community. They succeeded where the prophets had failed, partially because conditions were more favorable. The political ambitions which distracted those to whom the earlier prophets spoke, were, under the rule of Persia, impossible; the community which the apostles of the law addressed, was a compact social unit, not a large and heterogeneous nation; they were also powerfully supported by the influence and gifts of the great body of faithful Jews outside of Judah; and the tendency of the age, without as well as within Judaism, was toward a ritualistic type of religion. They succeeded also because the law which they presented, was itself " a schoolmaster " to whom the people had already learned to listen as authoritative, and whose teachings were definite and explicit. While the new code exalted the sanctuary, and centred about it all the life of the community, it also encircled the " true Israel," which included all who subscribed to it, with impassable walls of separation, imparting to the little hierarchy that consistency which made it an immovable rock where all about was chaos. By the act of the Great Assembly, the union of all faithful Jews, whether in Palestine or in the distant lands of the dispersion, was effected. They now acknowledged one system of laws, and felt that they all had a part in the service of their common sanctuary. At this time also the real centre of Jewish religious thought was transferred from the East to Judah. Henceforth the chief influences which

moulded Judaism came not from the Jews of the dispersion but from those of Palestine. At last " the restoration " was a reality. THE SAMARITAN TEMPLE ON MOUNT GEKIZIM 204. Two great monuments arose to commemorate the success of the priestly reformation instituted under the direction of Nehemiah and Ezra: The one was the Jewish hierarchy; and the other was the Samaritan temple on Mount Gerizim, with the religious community which grew up about it. The schism between the two closely related communities was consummated when the Priestly Law was adopted at Jerusalem, but the action of the Great Assembly only precipitated differences which were nearly as old as the race. It was merely a reassertion on a religious basis of the same ancient rivalry and mutual antagonism which led to the division of the united Hebrew kingdom after the death of Solomon (II. sects. 18-21). During the centuries of their independent national existence, the Israelites and the Judeans had been subjected to different influences and experiences which had only widened the gulf that separated them. The infusion of heathen blood which came through the colonists introduced into the province of Samaria after 722 B. c. by the Assyrian kings (II. sect. 105), extended it still farther: for, although the immigrants accepted the religion of the land, they communicated to the native Israelites many of their idolatrous customs. 205. Josiah's conquests and reform crusade left a lasting impression upon the Samaritan people (II. Kings xxiii. 15-20); henceforth Deuteronomy was the law book of the northerners as well as of the Judeans, and Jerusalem the one accredited sanctuary (Jer. xli. 5; Zech. vii. 2); but many heathen ideas and customs survived in the north, despite the sword of the zealous reformer. There is evidence that in the evangelistic spirit of the Deuteronomic reformation, the Jews endeavored, in the age of Nehemiah, to complete the conversion of their northern kinsmen. In the account which the chronicler gives of the reformation of Josiah (II. Chrs. xxx. 10,11), he probably has in mind the history of this later proselyting movement: " The messengers passed from city to city through the country of Ephraim and Manasseh, even unto Zebulun; but they laughed them to scorn, and mocked them. Nevertheless certain ones of Asher and of Manasseh and of Zebulun humbled themselves and came to Jerusalem." A psalmist of the period mentions the princes of Zebulun and Naphtali, together with those of Judah and Benjamin (Ixviii. 27). Gradually and quietly, during the last century of the Persian, and during the opening years of the Greek period, was consummated that religious union between Galilee and Judea which was destined to prove such an important factor in determining the faith of humanity. Isaiah Ixv. 1, 2, apparently refers to the failure of the same proselyting movement in Samaria. In the name of Jehovah, the prophet declares: " I allowed myself to be consulted by those who asked not after me; I was ready to be inquired of by those who sought me not; I said, Here am I, here am I, to a nation which called not upon my name. I CAUSES OP THE SAMARITAN SCHISM 217 spread out my hands to a rebellious people who walk after their own purposes in the way which is not good " (compare also Ixvi. 4). 206. The spirit of love, which conquers all things, was not strong enough in the hearts of the Judeans, and the religious customs of the Samaritans presented too great variations to make a fusion of the two peoples possible in an age when great stress was laid upon the externals of religion. The Judean prophet accuses the northerners of sacrificing as of old in groves, of burning incense upon bricks, of tarrying among the rock-cut graves, probably that they might thereby have inspired dreams, of eating swine's flesh and other unclean meats, and of paying homage to the Syrian gods, Fortune and Destiny (Ixv. 2-4, 11; Ixvi. 3; compare sect. 146). The spirit of self-righteous Pharisaism also was not confined to the Jews, for through the words of the same prophet we can hear the Samaritans exclaiming: " Keep by yourself, do not come near me, for I am holier than you " (Ixv. 5). Before Nehemiah and Ezra

inspired a deeper piety within the Jews of Palestine, they were little better than their northern brethren. It is not strange that the Samaritans refused to abandon their form of religion for that of the despised Jews. According to the logic of numbers and strength, it was natural to expect that the weaker would be absorbed by the stronger. Before Nehemiah arrived, this solution of their political and religious differences was by no means impossible. He recognized, when he reached Jerusalem, that the Jews, who were both morally and physically weak, were not capable of assimilating the larger and more influential community. He, accordingly, at once threw down the gauntlet, by declaring that hereafter Sanballat and his followers " should have no portion, nor right, nor memorial in Jerusalem" (Neh. ii. 20), and aroused thereby their bitter opposition to his enterprise. He it was, who, on personal and religious grounds, hastened the schism. 207. The history of the detailed steps which led to the final rupture is only obscurely written. Nehemiah's memoirs indicate that Sanballat, the leader of the Samaritans, made repeated and strenuous efforts to renew their former relations with the Jews, and that there were many prominent men in Jerusalem, including both priests and prophets, who favored such a union. Nehemiah, however, would listen to no compromise, and the influence of the Jews of the dispersion supported him in his position. In their eyes, the Samaritans were hopelessly unclean. As that influence became more potent in Palestine, the possibilities of union diminished. The expulsion from Jerusalem by Nehemiah of the grandson of Eliashib the high priest, because he would not put away his wife, the daughter of Sanballat, marks an advanced stage in the controversy (Neh. xiii. 28). Henceforth, it was characterized — as are most contentions which concern the externals of religion — by the greatest bitterness on both sides. In Isaiah Ixv., the unknown prophet intersperses his promises of future blessedness for "Jehovah's servants, they of Judah," with dire predictions of destruction and misfortune to

fall upon " them who forget Jehovah's holy mountain " (verses 8-15). 208. When the Jewish community solemnly accepted the new Priestly Code as its law, the Samaritans FOUNDING OF THE SAMARITAN TEMPLE 219 recognized that they were forever excluded from the Jerusalem temple, toward which the Book of Deuteronomy directed them as the one sacred site where Jehovah could rightly be worshipped. Their condition was in some respects analogous to that of their ancestors after their separation from the Judeans in 937 B. c. The precedent then established guided them now. The old sanctuaries at Dan and Bethel had been desecrated, and neither were easily accessible to the Samaritans. Therefore, they selected a site closely associated in their traditions with the memory of their earliest and most revered ancestors. Mount Gerizim, although not the highest, is one of the two most prominent peaks in the territory of Samaria. Its location, overhanging the ancient northern capital, Shechem, gave it a position of great importance. Probably, since the earliest period of Semitic settlement in Canaan, a sacred shrine was to be found crowning the fertile plateau on its eastern brow. There the Samaritan people reared the temple which became the centre of their religious life, and which soon rivalled the older one at Jerusalem. Although the original structure was destroyed by John Hyrcanus about 130 B. c., the Samaritans have continued, even down to the present day, to worship Jehovah on their holy mountain. 209. According to Josephus (Ant. xi. 8, 2), the original Samaritan temple on Mount Gerizim was built by Sanballat, that his son-in-law Manasseh, who had been expelled from Jerusalem because of his marriage to Nicaso, the daughter of the Samaritan prince, might have a temple in which to minister. While the tradition, which preserves the names of the chief actors in this important event, is probably historical. Josephus, aa is often his wont, because of his intense antipathy to the Samaritans, has given a wrong setting to his data. The priestly noble, Manasseh, was without doubt the son-in-law of

Sanballat, and the grandson of the high priest Eliashib whom Xeheiniah drove from Judah. He was the son of Joiada, and therefore the brother of Johanan the high priest, and not of Jaddua who succeeded Johanan (Xeh. xii. 22), as Josephus asserts. This late Jewish historian also makes Sanballat a contemporary of Darius Codomau-nus (336-330 B. c.) and of Alexander the Great, thus dating the building of the Samaritan temple during the last two decades of the Persian period. His testimony, of course, has little weight when it is so flatly contradicted by that of the contemporary record preserved in Nehemiah's memoirs. That Josephus is manipulating his material is clearly indicated, not only by the inconsistencies apparent in his story, but also by the fact that, in his brief summary of Nehemiah's narrative, he always omits the name of Sanballat (Ant. xi. 5, 6-8). Inasmuch as he placed Nehemiah's activity in the reign of Xerxes, he was keen enough to realize that, although he made Sanballat die in a ripe old age, the Samaritan prince could not have been living both in the earlier part of the fifth and also in the latter part of the fourth century B. c. 210. If the source for Josephus' statement, that Sanballat was given permission to build the Samaritan temple by Darius, is reliable, the Persian king in question was not the last, but the second who bore that name and who reigned from 424 to 404 B. c. Possibly DATE OF THE SAMARITAN TEMPLE 221 the error of Josephus arose because he made the common mistake of confusing these two monarchs. Johanan, the brother of Manasseh, was probably the same into whose room in the temple Ezra retired when the final exclusive measures were introduced (Ezra x. 6). This reference confirms the conclusion that the building of the Samaritan temple followed very soon after the Great Assembly. Joiada, the father of the exiled priest, was high priest during the last quarter of the fifth century. Nehe-miah, at the most, could not have lived long after the close of that century, so that his expulsion of Manasseh, and the building of the Samaritan temple, must be dated

not far from 400 B. c., possibly during the closing years of the reign of Darius II. (424-404 B. c.) or immediately after 397 B. c. 211. In connection with his reference to the driving away of Manasseh, Nehemiah calls down a curse upon certain ones, " because they had defiled the priesthood and the covenant of the priesthood and of the Levites." From this reference it is evident that Manasseh was by no means the only one from the ranks of the Jerusalem priests and Levites who offended against the strict Priestly Law, which forbade marriages with foreigners. Ezra also found many such offenders (Ezra x. 18-23). That they all consented to put away their foreign wives is, on *a priori* grounds, improbable, and Josephus confirms this conclusion, for he states that " many of the priests and Levites of Jerusalem were entangled in such marriages; for they all revolted to Manasseh; and Sanballat gave them money and divided among them land to cultivate, and also provided them with habitations" (Ant. xi. 8, 2). This defection probably assumed larger proportions than either Nehemiah or Josephus were willing to admit. In a sense, both the Jewish and Samaritan communities were benefited by it. Delivered from the uncongenial and opposing elements within its midst, the " true Israel " was free to devote all its energies to living in accord with the new Priestly Law. Emulation of their southern rivals, and the building of the temple on Mount Gerizim, also aroused a new religious zeal among the Samaritans. Although, at certain points and on personal grounds, at variance with the dominant party in Jerusalem, Manasseh and his fellow-exiles had caught the spirit of reform and appear to have been as ardent champions of the revised Jewish code as were Nehemiah and Ezra. The result was that the Samaritans, instead of reverting to heathenism, under the influence of their new priesthood, at once, or soon, adopted as their law the completed Jewish code, practically in the form in which we have it to-day in the Pentateuch. This, together with an abbreviated edition of the Book of Joshua, has

continued until the present to be their sacred scriptures. It certainly is a source for regret that we are acquainted with the work of these early Samaritan reformers only through the chance references of hostile Jewish historians. In the unprejudiced eyes of the great Prophet of Nazareth, the type of religion which they introduced, compared by no means unfavorably with that which was found under the shadow of the Jerusalem temple. In the bitter contest waged during the succeeding centuries between the Jews and Samaritans, it is certain that right was not entirely with either side. Much of the intolerance and acer- RELIGION AND CHARACTER OF THE SAMARITANS 223 bity which disfigured the character of later Judaism was the result of these fierce struggles. Henceforth, the worshippers on Mount Gerizim possess for the student of Jewish history a powerful but negative interest. XII THE LAST CENTTJRY OF PERSIAN KTJLE 212. The years which immediately followed the Great Assembly were undoubtedly the happiest which the Jews of Palestine had known since the destruction of Jerusalem in 586 B. c. While the institution of strict, exclusive measures rendered their relations with their neighbors more bitter than ever before, new hopes filled their hearts. The consciousness that they were faithfully observing the law of Jehovah, gave them renewed confidence. They regarded the unwonted prosperity which they enjoyed as unquestionable evidence of his favor and an earnest of still greater blessings. The same prophet who was so bitter in his denunciations of the Samaritans, voiced, in the name of Jehovah, the expectations which inspired his hearers: " I will rejoice in Jerusalem, and joy in my people: and the voice of weeping shall be no more heard in her, nor the voice of crying. They shall not build, and another inhabit; they shall not plant, and another eat: for as the days of a tree shall be the days of my people, and mine elect shall long enjoy the work of their hands. They shall not labor in vain, nor bring forth for sudden trouble; for they are a seed blessed of Jehovah, and their offspring shall remain with them "

(Isa. Ixv. 18, 22, 23). EVIDENCE OF A GENERAL RETURN TO JUDAH 225 213. A subsequent passage, probably from the same author, refers to the birth of the " true Israel " and to the return of the scattered Jews: " Who has heard such a thing? Who has seen such a thing? Shall a country be born in a day, or a nation be brought forth at once? As soon as Zion travailed, she brought forth her children" (Isa. Ixvi. 8). There is evidence that Ezra's expedition represents but one of several groups of exiles who returned at this time. If the rebuilding of the walls of Jerusalem and the preliminary reform of Nehemiah sufficed to attract six or seven thousand Jews of the dispersion, the added knowledge that " Zion had travailed," that the Priestly Law had been proclaimed, and solemnly accepted in Judah, must have attracted thousands more. At last the religious atmosphere of Palestine was congenial to the stricter Jews of the Bast, and the uninhabited spaces within and without the walls of Jerusalem invited colonists. The exclusive spirit which drove Manasseh and his fellow-exiles from Jerusalem, drew many zealous priests and laymen in their stead. Long years of preparation had preceded, but, when the final moment came, a " nation indeed was born in a day." 214. In the census, preserved in Ezra ii. and Nehemiah vii., of " the children of the province who went up out of captivity," the names of the majority follow those of Nehemiah and Ezra (in Ezra ii. 2, Seraiah). Since the names of the first four stand in their relative chronological order, it is at least reasonable to conclude that the same is true of the rest; in which case these lists also testify that a majority of those who returned did so after the Great Assembly. Since it seems probable that only a comparatively small number returned with Zerubbabel, Joshua, and Nehemiah, and about six thousand with Ezra, at least three-fourths of the varying totals given in the different versions returned with the eight other leaders. The names borne by some of the clans, as, for example, " the children of Pahath-Moab " (children of the governor of Moab),

suggests that not all represented in the census returned from Babylon. The lists may even comprise all in Judah who accepted the new Priestly Law, which had been brought by those " who went up out of captivity," irrespective of whether or not they or their ancestors had ever left Palestine. This may be the significance of the general title, "children of the province," which is used instead of the " children of the captivity," by which the chronicler always distinguishes the returned from resident Jews (Ezra iv. 1; viii. 35). 215. An index of the date of this census is found in the fact that many of " the children of the province " were settled in towns which were not held by the Jews when Nehemiah went to Judah in 444 B. c. (see map opposite page 158). The extension of Jewish territory thus indicated, is toward the north and northwest, and includes such debatable towns as Geba, Michmash, Bethel, Ai, Kiriath-jearim, Chephira, Lydda, Hadid, and Ono, lying on the southern borders of Samaria. This extension corresponds exactly with that which Josephus and the first Book of Maccabees declare took place during the years following the advent of Nehemiah and Ezra. By the beginning of the Macca-bean period, Bethel, Beth-horon, and Timnath Pharathon are no longer Samaritan but Judean cities (I. Mac. ix. 50; Jos. Ant. xiii. 1, 3). The Jewish population on CONDITIONS FAVORABLE FOR A RETURN 227 the plain of Ono (compare Neh. vi. 2) had also increased to such an extent that in 145 B. c. the Jews demanded that the toparchy of Lydda, as well as those of Apharema (Ephraim) and Ramathaim, be transferred to them by the Syrian king (I. Mac. xi. 28, 34; Jos. Ant. xiii. 4, 9). 216. During the closing years of the Persian period, and under the rule of the Ptolemies, the Jews in Palestine were oppressed, and large numbers of them were deported, especially to Egypt; but during the long reign of Artaxerxes II. (Mnemon, 404-58 B. c.), the central government was.so pitiably weak and inert that the different states under its nominal control were free to do very much as they pleased without fear of in-

terference. Hence the period of Judah's expansion must have been, as already inferred on other grounds, during the first half of the fourth century. Its cause was evidently the return of large numbers of Jews from the dispersion; for the strict policy of separation which was adopted at the Great Assembly tended to diminish rather than increase the native Jewish population. From this half century, therefore, in all probability, came the census of the lay population introduced by the chronicler in Ezra ii. and Nehemiah vii. Then the influence of " the returned " became dominant in Judah; while the mixed population which had remained in the land began to fall into ill-repute, as their previous record and laxer practices were viewed from the stricter point of view of the Priestly Law; so that then, for the first time,there was a strong motive for taking and preserving such a census. The same tendency to disparage the resident and to assign all that was good to the returned Jews continued to develop until, as in the case of the chronicler, it distorted all the later conceptions of earlier post-exilic history. The actual return of a few thousand evidently inspired in the hearts of the Palestinian Jews hopes of a complete restoration of their race. Fervently and often they prayed:

Save us, 0 Lord our God,
And gather us from among the nations,
To give thanks unto thy holy name,
And to find our pride in thy praise.

Another psalmist, looking back upon this bright epoch from out of the shadows which darkened the succeeding years, exclaimed:

When the Lord brought back those that returned to Zion,

We were like unto them that dream.

Then were our mouths filled with laughter,

And our tongues with singing:

Then said they among the nations,

The Lord hath done a great thing for them.

The Lord hath done a great thing for us;

We are glad. 217. During the long reign of Artaxerxes II., the supine weakness of the Persian rule, which had given the Jews their opportunity for expansion, brought upon them a new danger. As so often in the history of the Hebrew people, it came from the land of the Nile. Tachos, the native king of Egypt, which had for nearly half a century successfully defied the authority of the Great King, about 361 B. c. advanced into Syria on his Ps. cvi. 47. Ps. cxxvi. 1-3.

REIGN OF ARTAXERXES III. (OCHUS) 229 way to attack Artaxerxes. The Phoenicians had joined his cause, and he had begun the siege of certain Syrian towns, when he was suddenly obliged to return to Egypt to put down threatening insurrections. Meantime, the aged Artaxerxes died in the year 358 B. c., nnd the Persian throne was seized by his younger son Ochus, who is known as Artaxerxes III. He proved as shrewd and energetic as he was unscrupulous and cruel. His reign was the bloodiest in Persian history. His accession was marked by the wholesale murder of all the members of the royal family who might in any way endanger the continuance of his rule. At the same time, he did more to revive the tottering empire than any other monarch since Darius I. Instead of trusting to his generals, he in person conducted the more important campaigns. Egypt naturally demanded his first attention. The reigning Egyptian king Nectanebus, however, with the aid of Greek generals and mercenaries, about 350 B. c., completely defeated the vast army of Ochus. 218. This signal defeat early in his reign encouraged the subjects of Ochus in many parts of the empire to revolt. Probably at the instigation of the Egyptians, the Phoenicians, led by the town of Sidon, also raised the standard of rebellion. The Persian soldiers within their territory were massacred. Insurrections in other parts of his empire prevented Ochus from immediately crushing the uprising, so that it soon assumed large proportions. Tennes, the Sidonian king, supported by a large body of Greek mercenaries sent by his ally, the victorious king of Egypt, defeated two of the Persian satraps sent against him, and for a time delivered the province of Syria from Persian rule.

By 346 B. c. Oclms succeeded in collecting another large army (estimated *by* the Greek historians at 330,000) and advanced against Sidon. Its king, thereupon, betrayed his city and allies into the hands of the Persians. In keeping with his usual treacherous policy, Ochus repaid the perfidy of Tennes by murdering him, and by slaying the principal citizens of Sidon who came to plead for clemency. The remainder, preferring death by their own hands to the mercy of this bloodthirsty Oriental despot, shut themselves within their homes, and then burned them over their heads. It is reported that in this manner forty thousand perished. After having reduced to ruins the centre of rebellion in Syria, Ochus advanced with his main army to the conquest of Egypt, which he completed by 343 B. c. 219. The part which the Jews took in this great uprising, and the fate which overtook them, like certain other unpleasant events in their history, are only obscurely recorded by their historians. The narrative of the chronicler stops abruptly with the institution of the Priestly Law, and Josephus is almost equally silent. He does, however, associate with the name of " Bagoas, the general of another Artaxerxes," an enslavement of the Jewish people and a pollution of their temple (Ant. xi. 7,1). This general was evidently identical with the eunuch Bagoses, one of the three Persian commanders of Ochus (Artaxerxes III.) in the great Syro-Bgyptian campaign. He it was who later slew his master and became the virtual ruler of the empire. The cause which Josephus assigns for the severe visitation upon the Jews, was the murder by the high priest John (Johanan of Nehemiah xii. 22, 23), of his brother Jesus, for whom the Persian courtier had promised to REBELLION OF THE JEWS AJSID ITS PUNISHMENT 231 secure the high-priesthood. Since the crime was committed within the sacred precincts of the temple, Josephus traces the misfortunes which overtook his race at this time to the divine displeasure aroused by the act. The characters of the high priests of the period were such that the story is by no means incredible; but the

judgment which the Persians visited upon the Jewish community was out of all proportion to the cause assigned. The tradition related by Josephus preserves the facts that the Jews were enslaved, that their temple was polluted, that their punishment continued through many years (seven according to Ant. xi. 7,1), that Bagoses was a prominent agent in inflicting it, and that it was regarded as a divine judgment for sins which had been committed. 220. Certain independent references in the writings of the non-Jewish historians supplement the writings of Josephus, and suggest the true cause of the calamities which befell the Jewish community. They present few details. The fact, however, is established that the Jews were involved in the rebellion against the Persians, and that they were the victims of the same bloody vengeance that Ochus visited upon the Phoenicians and Egyptians. It is also recorded that Jericho was captured and destroyed, and that a part of the Jewish people were transported to the province of Hyrcania, located on the south of the Caspian sea (Solinus xxxv. 6; Syncellus i. 486). The basis of the Book of Judith is not improbably also a late tradition, concerning the suppression of the Syrian insurrection by Ochus. The name of Holofernes, the leader of the hostile forces in this grotesquely distorted tale, may be identified with that of Olophernes, one of the generals who figured prominently in the same Syro-Bgyptian campaign (Diodorus xxxi. 19, 28). In referring to the same period, the author of the ninetieth chapter of the Book of Enoch (verses 74, 75), declares, in his quaint symbolism, that" the eyes of the sheep Jews were blinded so that they saw not. As a consequence, they were given over in large numbers for destruction, and were trampled underfoot and devoured. And the Lord of the sheep remained unmoved until all the sheep were dispersed over the field and mingled with the beasts " (their heathen foes). 221. The actual course of events suggested by these general, but mutually confirmatory allusions seemsto have been as follows: during the first half of the ftrwt century B. C. the Jewish community grew to such an extent, both in numbers and strength, that its insignificance no longer delivered it from threatening political complications. The old aspirations for independence and world-wide rule were also again kindled in the hearts of the Jews. The brutal cruelty and tyranny of Ochus destroyed all gratitude which they may have felt toward the Persians, and instead aroused only intense hatred and loathing. In their eyes, the Persian monarch and his equally unprincipled advisers represented the arch enemies of Jehovah and of his kingdom. On the other hand, the Jews felt, even as King Josiah when he attacked the mighty host of Necho on the disastrous field of Megiddo (II. sect. 190), that, by their zealous reforms and faithful service, they had won Jehovah's favor, and that he was under obligation not to allow them to fall before their enemies. The third chapter of the Book of Joel, which comes from this period of peace and prosperity, expresses this feel- FALSE HOPES OF THE JEWS 233 ing: " Proclaim this among the nations; sanctify war; stir up the mighty men; let all the men of war draw near, let them come up. Beat your ploughshares into swords, and your pruning-hooks into spears: let the weak say, I am strong" (verses 9 and 10). The prophet then challenges the mighty nations to advance to the conflict. He has no doubt of the issue. Jehovah will judge the nations, and use his omnipotent power to punish their guilt, while " he will be a refuge unto his people and a stronghold to the children of Israel." When this day of Jehovah, which the prophet's contemporaries hoped was near, arrived, Jerusalem would be recognized by all as holy, and "there should no strangers pass through her any more." With these expectations before their eyes, it is easy to appreciate the reasons which led the Jews to join in defying Persia. To have refused also might have meant destruction at the hands of their more powerful neighbors in Palestine. 222. The entire province of Syria appears to have been compromised, and when the common cause was betrayed and lost the Jews

shared the consequences. What these were may be learned from a study of the awful vengeance which Ochus visited upon the Phoenicians and Egyptians. Thousands were slain, cities destroyed, temples spoiled, and mercy shown to none. Since many of the Jews were deported, it is evident that the wrath of Ochus rested as heavily upon them as upon their neighbors. Although the historians refer only to the capture of Jericho, Jerusalem must have suffered a still worse fate, for, like Sennacherib, centuries before (II. sect. 152), Ochus, as he advanced to conquer Egypt, would never have left such a natural stronghold to be a menace in his rear. There is little doubt, in the light of the independent but confirmatory evidence, that at this, the time of their second captivity, the holy city and its sanctuary were again despoiled and nearly destroyed. Whether the one detailed to accomplish this work was Olophernes or Bagoses, we may be assured that it was characterized by the greatest cruelty and vindictiveness. 223. While the biblical historians pass over these events with a silence which is exceedingly suggestive, the prophets and psalmists, who experienced their horrors, frequently refer to them. Isaiah lxiii. 7 to lxiv. 12, as has been shown (sect. 102), without much doubt come from this trying epoch. The first part of the section consists of a review of the crises in Israel's past history when Jehovah delivered his people and concludes with a cry almost of reproach, because he has " made them to err from his ways" and because he apparently pays no heed to the overwhelming misfortunes which have befallen them. " His sanctuary, which his holy people (a term begotten by the Great Assembly) possessed but a little while, their adversaries have trodden down" (lxiii. 18). They bitterly complain that " Zion has become a wilderness, Jerusalem a desolation. Our holy and beautiful house, where our fathers praised thee, is burned with fire; and all our pleasant things are laid waste " (lxiv. 10,11). The entire passage is wonderfully suggestive of what the feelings of the community were in the presence

of the great calamity. Most painful of all was the sense of having been forsaken by Jehovah. They had trusted that he would deliver them, but they had been disappointed. Their woes they regarded as evidence that THE POLLUTION OF THE TEMPLE 235 they had sinned in his sight. They who had prided themselves upon the strict observance of his laws were polluted and unclean. The old problem of the Book of Job was now the problem, not merely of a few faithful ones, but of the community as a whole. Like the hero of that great drama, they besought Jehovah by some miraculous interference to deliver them from their calamities and to vindicate their innocence. 224. The seventy-fourth and seventy-ninth psalms, which reflect precisely the same historical background as the passages in Isaiah, complete these pictures of disaster and despair. Since Judah at this time was pre-eminently a religious community, and since the motives which prompted its revolt against Ochus were also chiefly religious, the wrath of the Persians was visited especially upon the temple and the places of worship. In the light of these psalms it is possible to follow the dissolute and pitiless soldiers of Ochus as they entered the solemn assembly of the Jewish people, uttering rude jeers and heaping insults upon the gathered worshippers. Within the precincts of the temple, they set up their hated standards, and then with axes and hammers began the work of demolition. Soon the highly prized carving and ornaments of the sacred structure were in ruins. By fire they completed its destruction (lxxiv. 3—7). Not content with polluting the holy shrine with their vile presence, they strewed it and Jerusalem with the dead bodies of the faithful. Truly could it be said of the mercenaries of Ochus, that " they shed blood like water " (lxxix. 2, 3). After the temple and Jerusalem had been laid waste, they turned their attention to the synagogues of the land. Without exception, they were burned to the ground (lxxiv. 8; compare Isa. lxiv. 10). Through the same psalms, we can hear the sigh of the prisoners, some condemned to death, and some to deportation to a distant land (lxxix. 11). 225. The psalmists, as well as the prophets, were overwhelmed with fear that " Jehovah had cast off his people " (lxxiv. 1). Their sense of being deserted was intensified by the "scorn and derision of those who were round about" (lxxix. 4). Not only did they pray for vengeance upon their persecutors, but also that " the revenging of the blood of Jehovah's servants which is shed might be known among the heathen" (lxxix. 10). The reproach of their neighbors was even harder to bear than actual persecution (lxxix. 12,13). The loyal work of Nehemiah in reviving their national strength seemed undone. Again the Jews were the prey of their ever-present foes, whose hostility had been intensified by the exclusive attitude of the Jerusalem community. The Jewish literature of the few remaining years of the Persian period is filled with passionate prayers for a speedy deliverance from oppression and wrong, and for vengeance upon their merciless foes (compare Ps. xciv.; Isa. xxiv. to xxvii.). In all probability the main sections of the Book of Job (iii. to xxxi. and xxxviii. 1 to xlii. 6) were written at this time. Taking the familiar story of Job (Ezek. xiv. 14; Job i., ii., and xlii. 4-17) which taught the time-honored dogma that righteousness, after it had been tested and found true, will bring its speedy and proportionate reward, the author presented in the experiences of the hero the new and more painful aspects of the old problem. The questions which he thus treats, are of universal human interest; but no Jew of the MESSAGE OF THE BOOK OF JOB 237 period would fail to recognize in the revised story of the patriarch Job the portrait of the true Israel, created by the reformation of Nehemiah and Ezra. Although observing most punctiliously all the demands of Jehovah's law, the Jewish community, like the Job of the poetical sections, had been overtaken, for some unknown reason, by a series of overwhelming calamities, which had stripped it of all that it held dear: material prosperity, physical wellbeing, and beloved children. While conscious of its own inno-

cence, it was the object of the taunts of its neighbors, who, like all the members of that ancient world, could see in misfortune only the punishment of sin (compare even John ix. 1-3). Faithfully and dramatically, the great prophet-sage presents, in the dialogue between Job and his friends, all the anguish and doubts that distracted the heart of Judaism at this crisis in its history. Sometimes he uses almost the very words of contemporary prophets and psalmists. He does not stop, however, with merely presenting the problem in its new aspect, and with showing that the old doctrine of proportionate rewards is sometimes false. He has a positive message, and this he reveals in chapters xxxviii. to xlii. 6. In its first anguish, and as it considered its own woes, the nation doubted Jehovah's justice and love. The prophet-sage can adduce no conclusive proof of that which he believes, but with inspired tact he urges his nation to take a broader view of Jehovah's rule in the universe, to recognize how circumscribed is man's outlook, to note what infinite power and wisdom is revealed in the realm of nature, and, having done this, to be silent in the presence of the Eternal and to trust his wisdom and justice. 226. The messages of such inspired teachers as the author of the Book of Job saved the faith of Judaism at this great crisis; but it is not surprising that they welcomed the prospect of the speedy dissolution of the corrupt Persian empire (Jos. Against Ap. i. 22), and that they hoped that the victorious advance of Alexander represented the beginning of the era in which Jehovah would " turn the world upside down " and punish the arrogant foes of his people and vindicate his righteous ones (Isa. xxiv.). When the Greek rule brought little relief, many Palestinian Jews improved the opportunity to turn their backs upon Judah, with all its discomforts, and to find new homes in Egypt and northern Syria (sects. 271, 272); but the faithful who remained behind were still inspired with hopes of final deliverance and national exaltation. Meantime they clung to the law of Jehovah, which was the source both of their

persecution and their joy, with the energy of despair. The temple and its services were the loadstone which attracted and held them.

A day in thy courts is better than a thousand.

I had rather be a doorkeeper in the house of the Lord

Than dwell in the tents of wickedness, expressed the feeling of those zealots who remained in the land of Palestine. Thus the last century of Persian rule witnessed the return to Palestine of many faithful Jews, the institution of the Priestly Law, the temporary realization of long cherished hopes, the second great overthrow of the Jewish state, and the pollution of the temple. During this period, usually regarded as uneventful, both Samaritanism and Judaism were born and nearly attained to their full stature.

lxxxiv. 10. THE ORIGIN AND ORGANIZATION OP PRE-

HELLENISTIC JUDAISM

227. In the light of the peculiar conditions and experiences which were the lot of the Jewish race during the Persian period and the short half century preceding, it is possible to understand the unique politico-religious organism which is designated as Judaism. An historical review of this period is also the key to the intelligent appreciation of that miracle of succeeding ages which we behold with our own eyes in the Jews of to-day; for the character of the Jewish church, which so stoutly resisted the alien influences following in the train of Alexander's conquests, has been only slightly modified during the intervening centuries. Although the fact is often ignored, nothing is more obvious than that the type of religious and social life which centred about the second temple was radically different from that which was to be found in the land of Canaan in the days of Isaiah the son of Amoz. Ancient Hebrew life was free and joyous; the sense of Jehovah's immediate presence was strong. In the petty things of daily existence, as well as in matters of national concern, he was constantly consulted through prophets and priests; sacrifice offered in person

by the worshippers at the many local shrines scattered throughout the land *was* a common method of communing with him; while he himself was popularly regarded as a tribal God, well pleased with his chosen people. 228. With Judaism all was changed. The reform of Josiah, based on the Book of Deuteronomy, marked the beginning of that transformation; for it declared that the nation had sinned grievously against Jehovah, and presented a written law as a divine guide-book for the people. The tendency which produced Judaism—the tendency to embody Jehovah's revelation of his will in a system of precepts intended to regulate both belief and conduct, and so to make religion a law — was strongly developed before the exile. The principles and the purposes also which actuated the men who were instrumental in forming Judaism, were those of the pre-exilic prophets; but the remarkable conditions which favored, indeed forced its growth, appear in the two centuries and a half which followed the first destruction of Jerusalem. They may with profit be briefly recapitulated. The overthrow of the Judean state, not only left the Jews free for four centuries to devote all their time and energies to religion, but also made it necessary for them radically to reconstruct the external form of their religious life so that it might exist without the political organization which hitherto had been its main support. The literary habits and above all the intense religious zeal of their conquerors, the Babylonians, undoubtedly influenced them. The dazzling spectacle of lordly temples and of a wealthy influential priesthood also could not have failed, indirectly at least, to foster the tendency toward ritualism, already strong within INFLUENCES WHICH CREATED JUDAISM 241 the hearts of the exiles. At the same time the feelings of doubt and uncertainty which seized them, as they viewed the ruins of their beloved city and nation, and recognized that many of the articles of popular faith which they had accepted uuquestioningly must be abandoned, led them to turn as a final refuge to the externals of religion. To them, as to many

tried souls in all ages, it was a great relief to be able to follow implicitly the dictates of a system which with authority pointed out plainly and in detail the way of duty. If the ignorant masses of the Jewish race were to be delivered from the temptations presented by the heathen cults with which they were thrown into close contact, religion must be made objective. Especially was this true of the Jews who remained behind in Judah. The Priestly Code represented the efforts of faithful priests and scribes to meet the varied needs of their race. The smallness and compactness of the Jewish community in Palestine, the liberal religious policy of the Persians, and the noble work of Nehemiah, all favored the efforts of the zealous reformers who instituted the new system. The malignant opposition of their neighbors forced the Jews to draw together the more closely. The sympathy, the reverence, and the contributions of their loyal brothers beyond the bounds of Judah upheld and encouraged them. The dissenting Samaritan community drew away all who were not ready to swear allegiance to the written law. Persecutions only intensified the loyalty of the Jews to a system for which many of their number had died. The furnace of affliction in which Judaism was cast, burned so fiercely and long that it is not strange that it has successfully resisted the many disintegrating forces to which it has been subjected. 229. When Nebuchadrezzar dealt the final blow to the tottering Hebrew monarchy, he prepared the way for the growth of the Jewish hierarchy. Hitherto the priesthood had been dependent upon the throne for patronage and support; but henceforth the little political authority retained by the Jews was gradually transferred to the priesthood. True, Ezekiel introduced a civil ruler into his ideal state, but the power of his prince was limited to collecting the revenues necessary for the support of the temple. Jews, like Zerubbabel and Nehemiah, occasionally appointed by the Persian monarchs as governors of Judah, were only shadowy spectres of the ancient Hebrew king. Many who claimed direct

descent from David and the ancient Judean kings were found, but there is no evidence that their birth gave them a position of prestige (I. Chrs. iii.). In the first half of the Persian period, the heads of the different tribal and town organizations still regulated the local affairs of the community. Nehemiah also recognized in them the leaders of the commonwealth, but side by side with them he found a priestly aristocracy which was beginning to overshadow them. As the prestige of the temple grew, the influence of the priesthood increased proportionally; while that of the civil nobility waned. After the establishment of the hierarchy through the institution of the Priestly Code, both religious and civil functions were again wholly centred in one person, only now the priest had absorbed all remnants of the power once exercised by his royal patron; while in ancient Israel the king, as head of the nation, was THE FUNCTIONS OF THE HIGH PRIEST 243 originally its high priest as well. Then the state was the church; now the church was the state. 230. Whether or not the Persian government recognized the authority of the Jewish high priest is uncertain. A passage in Josephus suggests that it did (Ant. xi. 8, 3). According to the Priestly Code, he was to be given complete control of the people. By the beginning of the Greek period, the only limitations to his power were the dictates of the foreign rulers to whom the Jews were subject, and the will of the masses to whom the high priest usually deferred. Like the kings of old, he was anointed, wore the purple and a crown, and enjoyed royal honors; while the representatives of the old secular nobility were assigned a humble place in his petty ecclesiastical court. Also like the ancient Israelitish kings, he represented the nation before Jehovah. He alone entered the holy of holies. He alone of all the priests wore the ephod with the Urim and Thummim, and he it was who offered the great sin-offering of the people before the Lord on the day of atonement (Lev. xvi.). 231. Under the high priest was a carefully graded corps of temple ministers whose respective duties are minutely denned in the Priestly Code. Naturally, the members of his family not only shared the honors of their head, but were also assigned the most desirable offices, so that they soon constituted the ruling aristocracy, and in time coalesced into a distinct party, known in later times as that of the Sadducees, the descendants of Zadok who was placed by Solomon in charge of the Jerusalem temple (I. sect. 142). Following the tendency which first found clear expression in the writings of Ezekiel (see sect. 47), the Priestly Code drew a sharp line of distinction between the priests and the Levites. It traced the lineage of those priests whom it recognized as legitimate back to the family of Aaron. As an historical fact, they were the direct or traditional descendants of "the priests, the Levites, the sons of Zadok " (Ezek. xliv. 15) who ministered at the pre-exilic Jerusalem temple. By the beginning of the Greek period, they were divided into twenty-four classes or courses. At a later time, at least each class in rotation served at the temple for one week. According to the chronicler, the priests constituted a large proportion of the total population of the community. In the census contained in Ezra ii., they numbered four thousand, two hundred and eighty-nine. 232. The chief duties of the priests consisted in presenting before Jehovah the various offerings which constituted the essential part of the temple ritual, for they alone were qualified according to the Priestly Code to perform this service. In their life and person, they were under obligation to exemplify the sanctity of their task and the holiness of the God whom they served. Any physical infirmity permanently disqualified them. As they entered upon the office (probably at the age of twenty), they were solemnly consecrated for their work by means of ablutions, sacrifices and public anointing. Henceforth, the tasting of wine, shaving their head or beard, or the doing of any act which would render them ceremonially unclean, was absolutely forbidden them. Obviously the idea that the entire nation was a holy nation of priests (Ex. xix. 6) underlies the institu-

tion of the priesthood, but in time holiness was so strictly defined POSITION AND DUTIES OF THE LEVITES 245 in the terms of ceremonial cleanliness that the mass of the people, in consequence of their ordinary occupations, were disqualified. Hence the priests were required worthily to represent the people before Jehovah, and at the same time to guard his sanctuary from profanation. 233. In the hierarchy, the Levites were the servants of the priests and of the sanctuary. According to the Priestly Code, they were given to the priests as a possession by the people in exchange for the first born of each Israelitish family, who belonged to Jehovah (Num. iii.). As a matter of fact, in earlier times priests and Levites together constituted the tribe of Levi. Those who were later designated as Levites were the descendants of the priests who had ministered at the high places outside Jerusalem, which were discountenanced and destroyed at the time of Josiah's reformation. Ezekiel plainly declared that although they shall be given a place at the Jerusalem temple, their position shall be a menial one, because in the past they encouraged the people in what he and his generation regarded as gross apostasy (xliv. 10-14). In this respect his program was carried out. They were strictly excluded from the first positions of honor and responsibility; they were not allowed to enter the inner sanctuary nor to approach the altar. The more unpleasant tasks were assigned to them, such as cleaning the temple, caring for the sacred vessels, preparation of the showbread, and the opening and closing of the doors. Before the preliminary reforms of Nehemiah were instituted (Neh. xiii. 10-14), their means of support were very uncertain. It is not surprising that at first very few Levites reported at the temple. Only with much difficulty did Ezra persuade thirty-eight to return with him in his expedition. In the census contained in Ezra ii., there are found only seventy-four, as compared with over four thousand priests. Nehemiah's reforms and the institution of the Priestly Code insured to the Levites a definite income and certain

rights and privileges, so that from that time on their numbers appear to have rapidly increased, especially as the singers and doorkeepers were later added to their ranks. 234. The chronicler distinguished three distinct classes of Levites: (1) those who were assigned to the general service of the temple; (2) the singers or temple-musicians; and (3) the doorkeepers (I. Chrs. ix. 24—26; xxiii. 5). It is interesting to note that early in the Greek period, the temple-singers were classified as Levites. Although there are references to song and music in connection with the ritual before the exile, there is no direct evidence that it was given over to an order distinct from the general body of worshippers. Song, to the accompaniment of instruments played by the singers, constituted such an essential part of the ritual of the second temple that a special class of officials gradually grew up who attained to an even more prominent position than the regular Levites. The chronicler considered them so important a part of the temple corps that ho attributed their original appointment to Samuel and David. According to him, they were divided into three tribes or guilds, bearing the names of Asaph, Heman, Jeduthun or Ethan (I. Chrs. xvi. 41; xxv. 1, 6; II. Chrs. v. 12; xx. 19). In the older census of Ezra ii., only one guild, that of Asaph, is mentioned; while in the succeeding century THE DUTIES OF THE TEMPLE-SINGERS 247 the temple-choirs were greatly increased. The superscriptions of certain psalms suggest that, like all minstrels of antiquity, they not only sang but often composed the words of their songs. Thus, for example, Psalms I. and lxxix. are assigned to the sons of Asaph, lxxxix. to Ethan, and xliv. to xlix. to the sons of Korah. The latter guild appears to have been subordinated by the chronicler in his general classification to that of Heman (I. Chrs. vi. 33-37). He further states that the singers received fixed salaries (N"eh. xi. 23), and, like the priests, were divided by lot into twenty-four courses, each bearing assumed names like, " I have magnified " and " I have exalted help " (I. Chrs. xxv.

8—31). These groups probably in turn participated in the public service, uniting on the great feast days or whenever the psalms (of which several examples have been preserved in the Psalter), containing strophies and autistrophies, were chanted. The general body of worshippers appears also, as of old, to have participated in the song-service (Ps. xxvii. 6). 235. Repeated references in the Books of Ezra and Nehemiah indicate that at the close of the Persian period still another group of servants were associated with the temple. They are designated as the Nethinim, " the given," and the children of Solomon's servants (Ezra ii. 43-58). Three hundred and ninety-two are represented in the census of Ezra ii. As their names suggest, and as later tradition asserts, they were probably the descendants of slaves who had originally been presented to the temple (compare Ezek. xliv. 7-9). To them were undoubtedly assigned the most menial duties. Being virtually possessions of the temple, they occupied permanent quarters close to the sacred precincts (Nch. iii. 26, 31; xi. 21). 236. The same conditions which moulded Judaism called into existence a new type of religions teachers, the scribes. Their influence steadily increased as that of the prophets waned, so that at the close of the Persian period they were rapidly becoming the dominant intellectual leaders in the Jewish church. By the beginning of the Greek period, they were organized into guilds for the pursuit of their work (I. Chrs. ii. 55). To them were due, not only the development of the Priestly Code, and the final editing of the Hexateuch and the prophetical writings, but also the interpretation and further expansion of the ceremonial system by means of the traditional oral law. Theirs was the work which is recognized in the comparatively late tradition respecting the " Great Synagogue." Their activity did not cease with editing, interpreting, and expanding the law; since their aim was to influence their fellow Jews, they also devoted their attention to its practical application. They proved far more zealous champions of it than the priests

themselves. The scribes first began the general education of the masses. Under their thorough tutelage, the Jewish race as a whole became intimately acquainted with the details of their law. 237. The work of the scribes was greatly facilitated by the institution of the synagogue. As has been noted, it grew out of the practical needs of the Jews in the dispersion (sect. 37); but with the institution of the Priestly Code, it became an absolute necessity in Judah also. Without its popular instruction respecting the detailed demands of the law, the success of the ORIGIN AND AIM OF THE SYNAGOGUE SERVICE 249 sweeping reforms introduced by Nehemiah and Ezra would have been impossible. Deprived of the privilege of personally participating even in private sacrifices, the common people also required some other channel through which to give individual expression to their religious feelings. The synagogue belonged to them, and its service was as democratic as that of the temple was exclusive. Instruction, however, not worship, was the main aim in its organization. Popular ignorance of the law was no longer tolerated; hence just such opportunities as it offered were demanded. The collections of the sacred writings by the scribes furnished the material for use in the synagogue, and the prevailingly reverential attitude toward the teachings of the past provided the incentive for study. Although the chronicler does not use the word synagogue in the account which he gives of the preliminaries of the institution of the Priestly Code, he presents a picture of a synagogue service which is remarkably similar to those of later times. It included prayer, reading of the law and its interpretation. Thus it is not only extremely probable but practically certain that the large body of zealous Jews who returned to Palestine in the wake of the reformation of Nehemiah and Ezra, brought with them from the lands of the dispersion the institution of the synagogue. This conclusion is further confirmed by the reference in Psalm lxxiv. 8: " They have burned up the synagogues of God in the land," which finds its background in

the cruel revenge visited upon the Jews by the bloodthirsty soldiers of Ochus. 238. Obviously, life under the law during the centuries immediately following the great priestly reformation was not, as is sometimes considered, a burden, but a joy. The early scribes were not the enslavers of the people, but instead consecrated, zealous, efficient teachers who by their faithful instruction pointed out to the masses the way of righteousness, and gave to the forms of worship a meaning which they had never before possessed. The new demands made by the law upon the time and resources of the Jews only gave to their life, which would otherwise have been exceedingly barren, a definite content. The temple with its solemn worship, its songs, and its impressive sacrifices to atone for the sins of the nation, the frequently recurring feasts, commemorating important national and religious events in their past history, and the democratic atmosphere of the synagogue, with its free discussion and constant instruction, imparted to their religious life a variety which was most welcome. While the Jews were ruled by foreign masters, the law had no rival; hence it was able to command all their energies. At the same time it gave the glad assurance to its devotees that they could by their efforts attain to righteousness. Thus the oppressive sense of national sin, which since the beginning of the Babylonian exile had saddened and crushed the faithful members of the race, at last was partially removed, and the nation and individual rejoiced in the possibility of winning God's favor. The deep popular love for the law finds joyous expression in many of the psalms:

How lovely are thy tabernacles, O Lord of Hosts!

My soul longs, yea, even pines for the courts of the

Lord.

lxxxiv. 1, 2.

POPULAR LOVE FOB THE L.W 251

Blessed are they whose way is blameless,

Who walk in the law of the Lord.

Give me understanding that I may keep thy law,

That I may observe it with my whole heart.

Make me to go in the path of thy commandments,

For therein do I delight.

Oh how love I thy law,

It is my meditation all the day.

To the great majority, the observation of the corn-mauds of the law was a glad privilege, and in faithful obedience to that which to them was the will of God, they doubtless enjoyed a rich blessing. cxix. 1, 34,35,97. XIV THE INNER LIFE AND FAITH OF JUDAISM 239. The psalms reveal the real depth and breadth of the religious life of pre-Hellenistic Judaism. In them, as well as in the law, the great truths proclaimed by the earlier prophets lived and moulded the character and faith of the race. They also show how intimate was the communion between the individual and Jehovah. If the ordinary Jew could not sacrifice upon the great altar at Jerusalem, he could at any time present before the divine throne his offering of praise and his fervent petitions for forgiveness or help. Both public and private prayer were exceedingly common. In the presence of an impending calamity, the prophet Joel urges the priests to " weep between the porch and the altar," and to pray that Jehovah will spare and deliver his people (Joel ii. 17). Psalm xxvi. 12 speaks of publicly praising God in the congregations (probably in the synagogue services). The Psalter contains prayers voicing both the supplications of the community and of the individual. Although debarred from performing certain rites in the temple, it is obvious that in the Jewish church the individual enjoyed a prominence unknown before the exile. His responsibilities were also increased, as his knowledge of the demands and content of the law expanded. The com- INFLUENCE OF FOREIGN RELIGIONS 253 bination of stately ritual, of song-service, of public and private prayer, and of the thorough instruction of the synagogue produced on the whole a healthful and attractive type of religious life; at least it was far in advance of that which it superseded in Judah. 240. In considering the peculiar forms and tenets of Judaism, the question naturally arises, How far were they the result of foreign influences? The opportunities for the exertion of those influences were legion. Judaism gradually assumed form during the centuries when the most intelligent and active members of the race were brought into personal and continued contact with the dominant peoples of the age. From the Jews of the dispersion also came the movement which culminated in the establishment of the hierarchy and the rule of the law. Since in every other respect, their habits were moulded and transformed by their new environment, it would have been strange indeed if their religious life was entirely unaffected. The first two sources of possible influence, Egypt and Babylonia, have already been partially considered. Their most important effect upon the faith of the Jews was negative; their gross polytheism confirmed the monotheistic tendencies of those who were loyal to their religion. At the same time their highly developed ritualism and their priestly hierarchies must have unconsciously influenced the exiles in both the East and the West to regard ceremonialism as the natural and true expression of religion. 241. The most powerful external religious influences, however, came from the Persians. The fact that the great prophet of the exile hailed Cyrus as Jehovah's Messiah suggests the attitude of the more advanced Jewish leaders toward the conquerors of Babylon and the liberators of the Jews. The chronicler represents the earlier Persian kings as recognizing Jehovah (Ezra i. 2). Certainly there were more striking resemblances between the religious beliefs of the Persians and of the Jews than between those of any other ancient peoples. Both were originally proclaimed by prophets, and both laid emphasis on moral acts; both declared one God to be the supreme object of worship; according to both it was unlawful to make an image of the deity; both grew more and more intolerant toward the gods of other peoples. In their development, the two cults presented striking points of similarity. While both were originally prophetic, at about the same date they became ecclesiastical religions, with a complex priestly code which was regarded as given verbally to the respective founders of the two faiths, Zarathustra (Zoroaster of the Greek historians) and Moses. In many details the two systems were similar. For example, ceremonial cleanliness was arbitrarily defined; contact with certain animals or with a dead body brought defilement, and one of the most strenuous commands of the law was to avoid all such ceremonial impurity. These tendencies certainly cannot be fairly claimed to have been imparted directly from one religion to the other, because they were found in germ in both long before the two came into contact. At the same time, it is reasonable to believe that the example of their Persian masters, whom the Jews at first esteemed so highly and with whom those in the East came into intimate relations (for example, the great reformer Nehcmiah), fostered and, possibly in certain details, guided the development of the move- GROWTH OF THE BELIEF IN IMMORTALITY 255 ment which produced Judaism. Similarly, the custom of meeting at different places for the reading of sacred books, for prayer, and for the singing of songs, which among the Jews grew into the synagogue service, was common among the followers of Zarathustra. 242. Some of the characteristic tenets of Judaism have been traced by certain scholars directly to the Persian religion. It is an established fact that the belief in the resurrection and future rewards for the righteous and wicked was generally accepted by the generation to whom Zarathustra preached. Among the Jews, it did not find expression until after the exile and at first only sporadically. Persian influence, in all probability, favored its growth; but the destruction of the ancient Hebrew state, the immortality of which had contented earlier generations, and the new prominence thereby given to the individual opened the religious consciousness of the Jewish race to this great truth. The author of the Book of Malachi speaks of " a book of remembrance which was written before the Lord for them that feared him and thought upon his name" (iii. 16). The author of the Book of Job was eagerly groping in this direction, and had almost found the clear light (xiv. 12-15; xix. 25-27). A prophet, probably writing near the close of the Persian period, and speaking of the saints in the Jewish community, boldly declares: " Your dead shall live . *my* dead bodies shall rise. Awake and sing, 0 dwellers in the dust: for a dew of light is your dew and the earth shall produce the shades " (Tsa. xxvi. 19). Certain of the psalmists avow the same faith; but its general acceptance did not come all at once nor in one century, as might be expected if it were a direct importation from Persia, but gradually. By the beginning of the Maccabean period, many — perhaps the majority — of the Jews believed in the resurrection of the dead, but even then, as is well known, the conservative Sadducean party continued stubbornly to reject it. 243. It is also a suggestive fact that their conception of the functions and character of the angelic messengers rapidly enlarged during the period when the Jews came into closest contact with the Persians, whose religion postulated the existence of a host of heavenly beings who carried out the will of the deity. Again, the Persian influence was probably only indirect, for the Hebrew belief in angels long antedated the exile. The added prominence given to them in the writings of such prophets as Ezekiel and Zechariah was undoubtedly due to the fact that, as Jehovah was then regarded as more exalted and farther removed from man, messengers were required to perform his will on earth and to communicate between him and his people. Later Judaism conceived of a highly developed hierarchy of angels (compare the beginning of the conception in the Book of Zechariah and its full development in Daniel and Enoch). Although the names given to these heavenly beings are of Hebrew origin, the many close points of similarity to the Persian system suggest a more direct influence. Especially is this conclusion confirmed when we find that one of the names of an evil an-

gel (Asmodeus—*shma-dcevd)* has been adopted from the Persian into Jewish thought (Book of Tobit). 244. Still another striking illustration of the truth that " germs which lay hidden in Judaism were fertil- GROWTH OF THE BELIEF IN SATAN 257 ized by contact with the Persian religion " is found in the growing belief in a personal spirit of evil who is hostile to Jehovah and, to a certain extent, independent of him. This represented a wide departure from early Hebrew thought. Such a late writer as the great prophet of the exile distinctly asserted in the name of Jehovah: " I form the light and create darkness: I make peace and create evil: I am the Lord that doeth all these things" (Isa. xlv. 7). Heretofore the teachers of his race had assumed this truth. Its assertion suggests that it had been called in question either by contact with the Persians, who saw in the universe a constant struggle between Ahura Mazda (Ormuzd), the spirit of good, and Angra-Mainyus (Ahriman), the spirit of evil, and their hosts of followers, divine and human, or else the prophet found the idea in the minds of his fellow-exiles. Such an explanation of evil was most natural, and the belief in evil as well as good spirits was common in early Semitic religions. The Hebrew germ is found in I. Kings xxii. 19-23, where a prophet in the days of Ahab vividly presents a scene from the councils of Jehovah, in which a certain spirit volunteers and is commissioned to be a lying spirit in the mouth of Ahab's prophets, that thereby the king may be deceived. In the vision of Zechariah contained in the third chapter of his prophecy, there appears to accuse Joshua, the high priest, an angel who bears for the first time in Jewish literature the title, " Satan," the "Adversary." He is obviously a regularly accredited official of heaven whose duty it is to present before Jehovah's tribunal the charges against mankind; but, as his title and Jehovah's rebuke suggest, he is, if not actually hostile toward mankind, at least lacking in the divine spirit of charity. In the dramatic prologue to the Book of Job, " Satan " is still the title of a trusted official; but

his attitude is more clearly antagonistic toward mankind, for he skilfully devises methods whereby the righteous Job may be led to commit sin. The adversary has become a tempter. The chronicler strikingly illustrates the remarkable development of this belief in the personification of evil, for in his reproduction of the original passage in II. Samuel xxiv. 1, which reads: " Again the anger of the Lord was kindled against Israel and he moved David against them, saying, Go, number Israel and Judah," he reads: " Satan stood up against Israel and moved David to number Israel" (I. Chrs. xxi. 1). When Satan next emerges into prominence in Jewish literature, he is a distinct personality, at enmity with Jehovah and righteousness, gifted with power almost equal to that of God himself, and surrounded by a hierarchy of evil spirits, corresponding to the spirits of light who do the will of the Lord. 245. The defects and evils in Judaism were plainly revealed in later times, when they were exaggerated, and especially when they were brought into strong contrast with the teachings of Jesus of Nazareth. The tendency to substitute ceremonial for genuine righteousness, and to ask, not what is right, but what does the law say, was by no means a new one in Israel's history (compare Am. iv. 4, 5; v. 22-24; Mi. vi. 6-8). Some of the apparently meaningless distinctions between animals clean and unclean represent survivals from the heathen past. Certain of the laws of ceremonial purity were both absurd and harmful, for they branded as unclean SPIRITUAL LIFE REFLECTED IN THE PSALMS 259 the humble toilers of Judah; while those who possessed wealth and leisure, so that they could live in strict accord with the demands of the law, gained a false and odious sense of their own righteousness. This in many cases became mere hypocrisy. The great privileges and income granted to the priestly class by the law often tended to make them all the more grasping. The words with which Jeremiah condemned the corrupt priesthood of his day, in time became doubly appropriate: " Is this house which is called by my name become a den of robbers in your eyes?" (vii. 11). 246. The psalms which voice the better conscience of Judaism indicate, however, that there were many who retained a true estimate of the relative importance of moral and ceremonial righteousness. Through them the messages of the prophets live again. Since the prophecies were regularly read in the synagogues, extreme ceremonialism could never sweep all before it. Beautifully the author of Psalm xv. indicates the true requirements for admission to Jehovah's holy temple: upright conduct, purity of purpose, freedom from such vices as slander and treachery, antagonism to evil, love of the right, unswerving integrity, generosity toward the needy, and impartial justice. Repeatedly the psalmists emphasize the truth so subversive to extreme ritualism:

For thou delightest not in sacrifice, —
  Else would I offer it;
  Thou hast no pleasure in burnt offerings.
  The sacrifices of God are a broken spirit,
  A broken and a contrite heart, 0 God, thou dost not despise. li. 16, 17; compare xl. G.

The breadth of vision of the author of Psalm I., who evidently lived when formalism was beginning to chill the heart of Judaism, is amazing:

I do not reproach you for your sacrifices;
  Nor for your burnt offerings,
  Which are continually before me.
  I wish no bullocks out of your house,
  Nor he-goats out of your folds.
  For every beast of the forest is mine,
  And the cattle upon a thousand hills.
  Whoso offers the sacrifice of thanksgiving
  Glorifies me;
  And to him who orders his way aright
  Will I show the salvation of God.
247. With these songs on their lips, the Jews could never be entirely lulled to sleep by a ritual. Glorious hopes of national vindication and exaltation also inspired and united them. The psalms and prophecies of the period are full of Messianic predictions; but the real danger

was that their national ideals would become selfish and sordid. The great prophet of the exile had proclaimed that they had been chosen by Jehovah that they might be his witnesses to the world. Plainly he showed them that their true glory was to be found in voluntary self-sacrifice. The moment they recognized that Jehovah was not merely a tribal God, but the supreme Ruler of the universe, their responsibility to the nations of the world confronted them. " There is but one God and Israel is his prophet" was the logical watchword of Judaism. Not only the great prophet of the exile, but also his immediate successors 1 1. 8-10, 23.

THE JEWISH ATTITUDE TOWARD FOREIGNERS 261 appreciated the missionary responsibilities of their race. Zechariah declared: " Many nations shall join themselves to the Lord in that day, and shall be my people " (ii. ll). In one of his latest sermons, he announced the divine purpose still more plainly: " It shall come to pass that as you were a curse among the nations, 0 house of Judah and house of Israel, so will I save you and you shall be a blessing" (viii. 13). His closing words proclaim that " many peoples and strong nations shall come to seek the Lord of hosts in Jerusalem and to entreat the favor of the Lord. Thus saith the Lord of hosts: ' In those days ten men shall take hold, out of all the languages of the nations, shall even take hold of the skirt of him that is a Jew, saying, We will go with you, for we have heard that God is with you'" (viii. 22, 23). The psalms contain many passages in which the universal character of Jehovah's kingdom is plainly declared (for example, Ixvii.; Ixxxvi. 9; Ixxxvii. 4, 6; cii. 15-22). There is clear evidence that during the first century of the Persian period the Jewish community received many foreigners into its midst. The author of Isaiah lvi. 3— 8 undoubtedly expresses the attitude of at least the more progressive Jews of Palestine. He assures the strangers who had united with the community that they need not fear that Jehovah would separate them from his people. All who love the Lord, faithfully serve him, observe

the Sabbath and the terms of his covenant, shall be freely admitted to the services of the temple, and their offerings accepted, since Jehovah's " house shall be called a house of prayer for all peoples." He adds that it is Jehovah's purpose to gather others to him besides his own that are gathered. 248. The reasons why this early proselyting movement ended abruptly have already been considered (sects. 206). The trouble was primarily with the Judean community itself; it was not able to assimilate many heathen elements with impunity. Contrary to their later attitude, the Jews of the dispersion during the Persian period were much more strenuously opposed to admitting foreigners into their ranks than those in Palestine. The result was that, when their influence became dominant in Judah through the institution of the Priestly Code, the rest of the world was practically excluded by the high wall of separation which was reared. The door of Judaism, however, was not entirely closed to the outside world. The clause in the older Deuteronomic law which admitted the descendants of the Egyptians in the third generation, and even the hated Edomites, was not erased (xxiii. 7, 8). In the Priestly Code " the strangers who sojourn among them" are subject to the same laws and enjoy the same social and religious privileges as the Jews themselves (Lev. xvii. 8, 10, 12, 13; Num. ix. 14). Evidently in all these passages the reference is to the proselytes who have conformed to all the requirements of the Jewish law, and have in turn been fully adopted by the community. Exodus xii. 48 plainly states that all such, who submit to the rite of circumcision, shall be on a perfect equality with the native born Jews. Through this narrow door came the thousands of proselytes who were attracted to Judaism during the Roman period. 249. During the two centuries following the institution of the Priestly Code, any earlier impulses toward proselyting were stifled. Within their high wall of THE MESSAGE OF THE BOOK OF JONAH 263 separation, the Jews, intent on following the details of their law, almost forgot that Jehovah was God not merely of their nation, but of the nations. Hatred, begotten by the wrongs which they had suffered from the heathen, took the place of missionary zeal. When they thought of their neighbors, it was to pray for their speedy destruction rather than for their salvation. Self-righteous, because they considered that they alone were observing the law of God, they regarded the rest of the human family as unclean. The bitter struggles of those trying centuries were not calculated to arouse a deep love for the peoples with whom they came into contact. 250. Only a few inspired souls kept before their eyes the real mission of their race and the true character of the kingdom of God. Occasionally, a psalmist echoed the noble ideals of the earlier prophets; but the author of the marvellous little Book of Jonah alone fully appreciated and clearly pointed out to his race how inconsistent and contemptible was their attitude toward the rest of mankind, who like themselves were the objects of Jehovah's unbounded love. He appears to have taken the outlines of a popular story, associated with the name of Jonah the son of Amittai, a prophet who during the reign of Jeroboam II. predicted Israel's victory over her foes (II. sect. 79), to illustrate his inspired, but to his contemporaries exceedingly unpalatable message. He also employs the imagery of a well-known Semitic myth of a great sea-monster which in Hebrew prophetic typology represents the world-powers which prey upon the weaker nations, and especially upon Israel (Isa. xxvii. 1). Like the Great Teacher, the prophet freely recasts these elements, gleaned from the popular consciousness, into the form of a parable, replete with deep spiritual truth. Its application is obvious, and was doubly so to his contemporaries, who were familiar with its imagery. 251. Jonah is a perfect type of narrow Judaism during the period under consideration. Perversely blind is Jehovah's servant whom he has sent. He is ready to do anything rather then execute Jehovah's command to preach to the enemies of his race. As he clearly declares, his reason for fleeing from the

land of Israel was not because he feared the Ninevites, but because he was afraid that they would listen to his message of warning. If they did so, he knew that Jehovah was " a gracious God and full of compassion, slow to anger and plenteous in mercy," and that when they repented he would not destroy them (iv. 2). Like the Jewish race, he stood in a unique relation to Jehovah, and in unfavorable contrast to the representatives of heathendom, who according to their light are pictured as faithfully serving the gods whom they knew. The repentance of the Ninevites and their forgiveness by Jehovah recall the words of the author of the Book of Malachi, who, in condemning the meanness of the Jews toward their God, declared that "from the east to the west Jehovah's name was great among the Gentiles, and that in every place incense and a pure oblation are offered to his name" (i. 11). To a Jew, the manner in which Jonah turned from Jehovah, and sought refuge from him on the troubled sea, would suggest the mad, perverse conduct of his Hebrew forefathers, who likewise turned from Jehovah and sought to escape his inexorable command on the perilous sea of Oriental politics. Similarly, the great fish which THE PARABLE OF JONAH 265 rose out of that sea to devour, and at the same time, in God's providence, to preserve his servant, "would at once recall their experiences in Babylon. A prophet of the exile had already employed the same figure in referring to the fate of his people: " Nebuchadrezzar the king of Babylon has devoured me and crushed me... he has swallowed me up like a great sea-monster, filling his maw from my delights, he has cast me out" (Jer. li. 34). In the following verses (44, 45), Jehovah replies to the lament of the exiled nation: " I will punish Bel in Babylon, and I will bring out of his mouth that which he has swallowed.... My people, go out of the midst of her." Like Jonah, the Jews, disciplined and instructed by their experience, recognized (as the words of the great prophet of the exile indicate) Jehovah's call to proclaim his message to the heathen world. Jonah's brief words of warning, presented under

compulsion, and his contemptible complaining, because Jehovah had spared the foes of his race, and because some petty discomforts had come to him, complete this uniquely remarkable sketch of Hebrew and Jewish history. 252. With the Jews, the parable was a favorite method of presenting truth, but in simplicity, in graphicness, and in fidelity to human character and motives, the picture painted by the unknown author of this little book is comparable only to those flashed before the eyes of the humble Galileans by him who " spoke in parables." The prophecy abounds in rich truths which only those who have stumbled over the miraculous coloring of the story have failed to appreciate. The more important are: (1) God is infinitely more loving and compassionate than his people would make him; (2) He is ready to pardon all, irrespective of race, who sincerely crave his mercy; (3) the Jewish people were trained and commissioned to proclaim his will to the nations; (4) refusal to carry out his divine purpose will bring certain judgment, although he will ever be ready to forgive and restore his prophet-nation, whenever defiance is changed to penitence. The subsequent history of the Jews strikingly illustrates this last principle. Too late, they awoke to their duty and opportunity. Race-pride, unbending ceremonialism, narrowness, and inertness in many of its parts, made the earnest and in many ways noble attempt of Judaism in the Roman period to proselyte the world a tragic failure, except that it prepared the way for the conquests of Christianity. 253. The characteristic of pre-Hellenistic Judaism which most impresses itself is its many-sidedness. The whole was a strange bundle of contradictions. While the Jews c&nceived of Jehovah as a universal God, they acted as though he was only a tribal deity, jealously guarding their race, and hostile to the rest of mankind; while they declared that he was the Creator and Ruler of the whole universe, and God of the heavens, they proclaimed that sacrifice could be presented to him only on the sacred temple mount; while they sang, " Thou hast no pleasure in burnt offering," they devoted their best energies to keeping up an elaborate sacrificial system; while they taught that Jehovah was morally righteous, and demanded the same quality in his people, they gave their chief attention to observing the often grotesque laws of ceremonialism; while they regarded him as the source alike of all good and evil, they entertained a growTHE INCONSISTENCIES OF JUDAISM 267 ing belief in a personal prince of evil, antagonistic to Jehovah and in a sense independent of him; while they believed that God's richest blessings were moral and spiritual, the chief hopes which they cherished, were that they might behold the overthrow of their foes and the establishment of a temporal kingdom in which they themselves would rule over the nations. These striking inconsistencies were the natural consequence of the fact that Judaism drew its ideas from many different sources and ages, and was itself the product of a great variety of forces. It was the repository of much heathen rubbish, as well as of the most precious religious truth revealed to the human race. The crying need of Judaism and of mankind was not for the temporal Messiah of popular expectation, but for one divinely gifted and commissioned to bring order out of this chaos, to distinguish between the gold and the dross, to unite the true and the eternal into a consistent system, and, above all, to impart to the whole the breath of life. Until, in God's good providence, that Anointed One was sent, Judaism, sometimes at the cost of its life blood, faithfully guarded the treasures intrusted to its keeping. PART III THE GREEK PERIOD OF JEWISH HISTORY THE HISTORICAL SOURCES AND LITERATURE 254. The conquest of Palestine by Alexander in 332 B. c., inaugurated the Greek period of Jewish history; but its close is not so definitely marked. If it be made to include those centuries when Greek language, customs, and ideas were the dominant foreign influences in Jewish life, it would extend beyond the beginning of the Christian century. If its limit be decided on political grounds, there is still oppor-

tunity for a difference of opinion, for the Jews did not all at once and finally throw off the yoke of Alexander's successors. The year 165 B. c., which marks the third great victory of the Jews over their former Syrian masters, and the rededication of the temple, has been adopted as the limit of the Greek and the beginning of the Maccabean period. Many times later, the Jews fell a prey to Syrian armies, and were forced temporarily to acknowledge the rule of the Seleucids; but the victories of 165 B. c. secured for them permanently the most coveted fruits of independence, and turned back the wave of Greek influence, which hitherto had threatened to engulf everything distinctively Jewish. Henceforth, there was never wanting a well-organized native party in Judah which defied, by force of arms and with increasing success, the claims of Syria. In 165 B. c., the Maccabean kingdom was born, and therefore then the Maccabean period properly begins. 255. Respecting the first century and a half of the Greek period, the Jewish historians are almost silent. Josephus alone has preserved a few traditions. The inner life and thought of the Judean community is reflected in three distinctly different types of Old Testament books. It was during this period that the chronicler (between 300 and 250 B. c., compare sects. 88, 89) wrote his ecclesiastical history of the Hebrew nation contained in I. and II. Chronicles and Ezra-Nehemiah. If he naively read into the earlier epochs the conditions and current traditions of his own times, his work thereby becomes a most valuable historical source for this period regarding which light is so much needed. The desire to deceive was so foreign to him that he leaves no doubt respecting his late point of view. For example, in describing Solomon's sanctuary, he often has in mind the second temple. Its services are far more elaborate than those of the shrine described in Samuel-Kings. One of its gates even bears the Persian name " *Parlar* " (I. Chrs. xxvi. 18). It is interesting to note that in his earnest zeal to trace to the sacred past the origin of those institutions which he

and his generation cherished and revered so highly, he performed a far greater service than if he had merely realized his ideal to write a second history of ancient Israel. His significant omissions, as well as his revision of the older histories contained in Samuel-Kings, also vividly reveal the different standards of the later age in which he lived. 256. The marked differences in language, ideas, and DATE OF ZECHARIAH IX. TO XIV. 273 allusions between the first eight and the last six chapters of the book which at present bears the name of the Zechariah who with Haggai encouraged his countrymen to rebuild their ruined temple, have led scholars generally to recognize in them the work of different hands. The date of the unknown writer, or possibly writers, of the last six chapters is one of the complicated problems of the Old Testament. At first glance, the references to Ephraim, Damascus, Assyria, and Egypt (ix.) point to some period before the exile when these kingdoms still existed. Certainly the centuries of Babylonian and Persian rule furnish no satisfactory background. After the division of Alexander's empire, however, Judah became the bone of contention between the Ptolemies of Egypt and the Seleucids of Syria. By the Jews, who in the later days lived so much in the past, the names of the old foes of their race, Egypt and Assyria, were used to designate these, their new oppressors (compare Isa. xxvii. 13; Ps. lxxxiii. 8). Similarly, Ephraim and Israel were the terms applied to the Jewish community, " the true Israel," which represented the old Hebrew state. The many direct and indirect quotations from the pre-exilic and exilic prophets indicate that the present chapters were written in the late Jewish period, when the Jews began to study closely their sacred scriptures. The promise in ix. 8, that " no oppressor shall pass through them any more," recalls the same promise in Joel iii. 17. The vagueness and apocalyptic tone of the predictions are also characteristic of the declining days of prophecy. The distinct reference to the Greeks, not as a distant nation, as in the Book of Joel, but as foes already in conflict with the Jews (ix. 13), confirms the conclusion that the wars and dissensions alluded to in these chapters were those which came to the Jews between the years 320 and 240 B. c., when the Ptolemies and Seleucids were each fighting for the rulership over the distracted Jewish community. Our ignorance of the details of these contests makes it impossible to identify the historical allusions. The sections, however, are sad and undoubtedly true revelations of the intense hatred and scorn with which the Jews regarded the degenerate foes who destroyed their peace. The fact that they are found in the collection of the prophecies and not, like the Book of Daniel, among " the Sacred Writings," fixes their date before 200 B. c. 257. The same hostile attitude toward the Gentiles, and the same joy at the thought of their destruction, are reflected in the Book of Esther. Although the historical background of the story which it contains is the Persian, it probably comes from some Jew, living in the latter part of the Greek (or possibly the Maccabean) period. He is dependent upon later tradition for his knowledge of conditions in the Persian empire. He is unfamiliar with the fact that in the Persian court the reigning queen was always chosen from one of six noble families. Between the seventh and twelfth years of the reign of Xerxes, according to Herodotus, Amestris was queen. The marked dramatic character of the narrative, the surprisingly large numbers slain by the Jews during a period when the attitude of the Persians toward them was conspicuously friendly (compare the later expeditions of Nehemiah and Ezra), and the evident aim to glorify the Jews has led many to classify this book as one of HISTORICAL VALUE OF THE BOOK OF ESTHER 275 the romances, like the Books of Tobit and Judith, with which later Jewish writers delighted and inspired their countrymen. Ezra ii. 1 refers to a certain Mordecai, who led back to Palestine, after Nehemiah, a band of faithful Jews. It is exceedingly probable that the story rests upon certain historical facts which have been exaggerated or distorted in transmission.

The chronicler and the son of Sirach ignore the events related in the book. Its great popularity with later Jews is due to its intense nationalistic feeling, and to the fact that it gives the traditional origin of the most secular of the Jewish feasts, that of Purim. This feast is first mentioned in II. Maccabees xv. 36, as the day of Mordecai, in connection with the victory of the Jews over Nicanor. Although the authority is late, the natural inference is that the feast of Purim was known at least early in the Maccabean period, and its origin was traced to the incidents related in the Book of Esther. If this be true, the latter part of the Greek period is reasonably well established as its date. 258. From the same period, probably, comes the strange mingling of Jewish and Greek thought known as the Book of Ecclesiastes. Its peculiar vocabulary and awkward, broken constructions proclaim that it was written when Hebrew was becoming an unfamiliar tongue to the Jews. The implication in the opening chapter, that it is the work of Solomon, is but one of the many illustrations of the tendency of later Judaism to attribute all literary productions to famous characters who lived centuries before (compare the very late " Wisdom of Solomon " and the " Psalter of Solomon "). The book shows many marks of later revision. The author of the original sections was evidently born and educated as a Jew, but had lost the strong faith of earlier generations, and had none of the enthusiasm for the law which filled the hearts of his race in the century or two following the institution of the Priestly Code. The fragments of Greek philosophy which he had absorbed, had fundamentally altered his original beliefs. The dispiriting influences of the age in which he lived, and his own experiences, had driven him to the pessimistical conclusion that" all is vanity." Like the Sadducean party, to which he would undoubtedly have belonged if it had already taken definite form in his day, his creed consisted chiefly in negations. Unfortunately, his indefinite historical allusions do not establish his exact date. Certainly he could not have lived before Greek

thought had for a considerable period exerted its powerful influence upon the intensely conservative Jewish mind. Hence a date earlier than about 250 B. c. is impossible. The closing years of the rule of the Ptolemies in many ways furnish the most satisfactory background. The other possible period is the reign of Herod the Great (which has recently been strongly urged by Professor Cheyne in his " Jewish Religious Life after the Exile"). It must, however, be seriously questioned whether or not such a late book could have gained admission into the canon of the Old Testament, and especially a book of the character of Ecclesiastes. Still more time was required for the repeated revisions to which it has obviously been subjected, and these must have antedated its formal approval as canonical, near the close of the first Christian century (Mishna, ladaini iii. 5). 259. From the same school of wisdom-thought, but from a much more hopeful point of view, comes the THE PROVERBS OF THE SON OF SIRACH 277 apocryphal book, Ecclesiasticus or the Wisdom of Sirach. It is the only book of this period which is definitely dated. The superscription states that the present complete Greek version was translated by the author's grandson, who came to Egypt in the thirty-eighth year of Euergetes, who must be the second ruler of Egypt to bear that name, since the first reigned only twenty-five years. This was therefore in 132 B. c., and Jesus the son of Sirach, the grandfather, must have written between 200 and 175 B. c. In I. 1, Sirach speaks of Simeon, the son of Onias, who is probably to be identified with Simeon II., high priest during the first part of the second century B. c. Ecently, a large fragment of the original Hebrew edition, corresponding to chapters xxxix. 15 to xlix. 1 of the Greek, has been discovered, and made accessible to Hebrew students (Cowley and Neubauer — The Original Hebrew of a Portion of Ecclesiasticus). The discovery is undoubtedly the most important which has been made for years in the Old Testament field. It shows, in the first place, that the Greek translation was very free. The original Hebrew approximates closely to the classical models of which the author was a careful student. He was familiar with the Pentateuch and both the " earlier" and the " later " prophets, from Joshua to Malachi. This gives definite grounds for concluding that the prophetic canon was completed as early as 200 B. c. Naturally the son of Sirach quotes most from the kindred wisdom-books: Job and Proverbs. His style closely resembles certain of the psalms, and his book closes with a psalm. The general testimony of the work is, not that the Psalter was then complete, but rather still in the process of formation. Several of the psalms themselves contain internal evidence that they come from the Greek period, and therefore may be counted as one of its historical sources. 260. The merciless persecutions of Antiochus Epiphanes, and the valiant and successful resistance of the Jews, which filled the closing years of the Greek period with stirring events, called forth a large volume of literature. The apocalyptic type, which was exceedingly popular with the later Jews, was the most common. The prophets, who wished to encourage and strengthen their afflicted countrymen, no longer preached to them by word of mouth and simple direct statement, as did Isaiah and Jeremiah, but presented their messages in the form of visions and predictions, abounding in mysterious figures and symbolism, and usually placed in the mouth of some saint of the past. The number of these writings which have been preserved out of the undoubtedly greater body which has been lost, is surprisingly large. They all testify that if the prophets had not altogether been " expelled from the land," they had at least begun to be " ashamed every one of his vision when he prophesied " (Zech. xiii. 2,4), and to seek to give it authority by associating it with a name revered by his generation. 261. The noblest representative of this different type of prophecy is the Book of Daniel. Its position in the latest group of the Hebrew canon, " the Sacred Writings," at once suggests that it was written too late

to find a place in the prophetic canon. Its omission in the otherwise complete list of the prophetic books given by the son of Sirach, is equally significant. This external evidence that it was written after 200 B. c. DATE OF THE BOOK OF DANIEL 279 is confirmed by the testimony of the language, part of it (ii. 4 to vii. 28) even being written in Aramaic. The Aramaic also is not that employed by the Jews in the East, as would naturally be expected in the light of the narrative, but the peculiar type in use in Palestine. In the passages which purport to antedate the establishment of the empire of Cyrus, a large number of Persian words is found; while at least three of Greek origin appear in the book. The point of view of the author is not that of the Babylonian, nor of the Persian, but of the Greek period. For example, Belshazzar, who must historically be identified with Belsharuzur, the son of the usurper Nabonidus, the last ruler of Babylon, is designated as the last king of Babylon and the son of Nebuchadrezzar (v. 2, 11, 13, 18, 22). Darius, who organized the Persian empire, and not Cyrus, is regarded as the successor of Belshazzar and the first conqueror of Babylon (v. 31; vi.; ix. 1; xi. 1). This confusion in regard to the perplexing details of early Babylonian and Persian history is exactly parallel to what has already been noted in other writers of the Greek period (sect. 89). Other minor inconsistencies are found, and possess a positive value because they assist in fixing the true historical setting of this wonderful book. Its theological ideas likewise point to a date late in the Greek period. The exact circumstances of its composition may be determined with reasonable certainty. The predictions focus the attention not upon the return from Babylon, nor upon any of the important events which characterize the Persian and the earlier part of the Greek period, but upon the crises in the reign of Antiochus Epiphanes. He is evidently represented by the little horn of chapter eight. Chapter eleven, after giving a brief summary of the events following the conquest of Alexander, devotes verses 21 to 45 to a minute description

of the reign of Antiochus. The persecutions which the Jews experienced at his hands are also the background of the promises contained in chapter twelve (compare verses 7, 11-13). The history presented in the Book of Daniel in the form of prediction, becomes more and more detailed as it advances to these persecutions, and after their horrors are fully described, it suddenly ceases, and certain general Messianic promises alone are given, which it is impossible to identify with any known historical events. These facts all point to the conclusion that the book, with its examples of heroic and successful defiance to the commands of tyrannical human potentates, when they were contrary to those of Jehovah, with its glorious promises of divine deliverance for the persecuted and discouraged people, was written when the persecutions were at their height. There are no definite references to armed resistance, nor to the dedication of the temple; Jehovah is expected personally to deliver his people, and forthwith to institute his Messianic kingdom. Therefore it is not probable that the book was written after the great victories of Judas, and the establishment of the temple service in December, 165 B. c. The period between 167 and the beginning of 165 B. c. is consequently established with considerable certainty as its date (compare sect. 308). This conclusion at once gives to the great messages of the book a new significance, and a supreme historical value, for its testimony respecting the closing years of the Greek period is that of a contemporary. At the same time, the probability THE EARLIER SECTIONS OF THE BOOK OF ENOCH 281 is not precluded that the narratives of the first six chapters rest upon a traditional basis, and that Daniel was an historical personage, and not the pure creation of Jewish imagination. 262. Closely related in character and content to the Book of Daniel is the Book of Enoch. Both are frequently quoted by the New Testament writers and the Church Fathers. The Book of Enoch consists of a collection of apocalyptic writings coming from different dates and authors. These represent fragments of a voluminous literature which was put forth during the Greek, Maccabean, and Roman periods in the name of the antediluvian of whom tradition. declared: " He walked with God." In later Jewish thought, Enoch became the father of the apocalyptic, as did Moses of the legal literature. The present book was probably not edited until about the beginning of the Christian era; but two sections, chapters i. to xxxvi. and Ixxxiii. to xc., reflect the Jewish thought of the latter part of the Greek period. In Ixxxiii. to xc., the general point of view is that of the author of the Book of Daniel. It refers symbolically to the persecutions of Antiochus; but is a little later than the Book of Daniel, for it speaks of the armed and successful resistance of the Maccabean family (xc. 6). It also anticipates after these victories the speedy establishment of the Messianic kingdom. Its date, therefore, is about 165 B. c. These chapters make use of the other section i. to xxxvi.; but the latter knows nothing of the persecutions of Antiochus, and are written from a different point of view; hence their date must be somewhat earlier than 168 B. c. 263. The events of the last decade of the Greek period (175-165 B. c.) are described in detail in the first four chapters of I. Maccabees. From certain references, it is evident that the author of this remarkably vivid and on the whole exact history wrote during the earlier part of the first century B. c. He was therefore removed only two or three generations from the events recorded. He probably also had before him short notices written not long after the great uprising. His interests are those of orthodox Judaism; but in his temperate statements, in his careful chronological and geographical notes, and in his attention to details, he exhibits for almost the first time in Jewish history the true instincts of a modern historian. In all these respects, his history is much superior to that contained in II. Maccabees, which covers the period from 175 to 160 B. c. When the order of events differs, that of the first book must in general be regarded as the more reliable. The interest in II. Maccabees

is religious rather than purely historical, and the supernatural element is much more prominent. As is definitely stated in ii. 24-32, it is an epitomization (with the exception of the letters in chapters i. and ii.) of a much earlier work written by Jason of Gyrene, who probably lived about 160 B. c., had access to earlier authorities, and apparently was not acquainted with I. Maccabees. The two books, therefore, represent independent sources and furnish many mutually supplemental facts. 264. In his " Antiquities," Josephus has preserved certain later and largely legendary traditions respecting Alexander's relations to the Jews. The impossible account of the translation of the Hebrew scriptures into Greek purports to be a direct citation from the writings of Aristeas, a Greek official of Ptolemy II. THE WRITINGS OF JOSEPHUS 283 (Philadelphus). The real author, however, must have been a Jew who probably lived during the closing years of the rule of the Ptolemies. The clear picture which he incidentally gives of conditions in Judah and Jerusalem, is intended to glorify his nation. It is nevertheless valuable because it is largely the result of personal observation. In his polemical treatise " Against Apion," he likewise quotes from a writing purporting to come from the Alexandrian Greek philosopher and historian, Hecataeus, who was a contemporary of Alexander the Great. In reality, its author was probably a Jew, living in the third century B. C., who employed as the basis of his tract the statements of Hecataeus. The incidental historical data thus presented may, therefore, be regarded as partially reliable. In his treatment of the reign of Antiochus Epiphanes, Josephus depends almost entirely upon I. Maccabees. His meagre history of the Greek period is supplemented by those of the Greek writers. Polybius in book xxvi. and Diodorus in book xix. of their histories vividly describe the character and reign of the arch persecutor of the Jews. In the histories which record the conquests of Alexander, and the reigns of his successors, is presented in detail the setting of the picture of the Greek period which it

is possible to reconstruct with the varied but not altogether satisfactory materials at our command. II THE CONQUESTS OF ALEXANDER AND THE KTTLE OF THE PTOLEMIES AND SELETJCIDS

' 265. At last the longed-for upheaval came, and the vast Persian empire, which in the period of its decay had become the object of Jewish hatred (compare Isa. xxiv. to xxvii.), fell in ruins before the victorious armies of Alexander. To the Jews, who were ignorant of the real weakness of Persia and of the careful preparations which had long been going on in Macedonia under the sagacious guidance of Philip, the appearance of Alexander was a most marvellous spectacle. A year of active campaigning in Asia Minor, culminating in the sweeping victory over Darius at Issus in 833 B. c., and, lo, he was knocking loudly at the gates of Syria. Triumphantly, he swept down the eastern coast of the Mediterranean, conquering northern Syria without serious opposition, gathering fabulous spoils from the rich city of Damascus, and meeting his first serious opposition at the great trading city of Tyre. Since his first purpose was to secure the commercial and naval command of the Mediterranean, he did not pass on until he had captured this well-nigh impregnable fortress, even though it required an active siege of seven months. The only other formidable opposition came from the city of Gaza, which fell after making a most stubborn defence.

THE VICTORIOUS ADVANCE OF ALEXANDER 285 266. The traditions preserved by Josephus indicate that the Samaritans, in keeping with their usual policy, hastened to pay homage to Alexander while he was besieging Tyre (Ant. xi. 8, 4). Soon after he sent to the high priest at Jerusalem a demand for auxiliaries, provisions, tribute, and allegiance. Remembering the awful judgment which had followed their recent defection from Persia (sect. 221), the Jews were naturally very slow to acknowledge another master. Although the short section contained in Zechariah ix. 1-8 may possibly come from a slightly later date, it finds its most satisfactory setting at this time. It pictures exactly Alexander's victorious advance down the valley of the Orontes, the capture of Damascus, the submission of the coast cities, and predicts, as did the old Hebrew prophets when the Assyrian armies advanced along the same route, the conquest and destruction of Tyre, who " has built her a fortress, and heaped up silver like dust, and gold like the dirt of the streets." It also predicts the downfall of the Philistine cities, and closes with the assurance that Jehovah " will encamp as a guard about his house, so that none shall pass by or return." 267. The capture of Gaza and the other cities of the Philistine plain influenced the Jews to accede to the demands of Alexander, and to swear a ready allegiance to him. The tradition that he visited Jerusalem at this time, and was miraculously influenced by a dream to spare the Jews, and to grant them many special privileges, reveals all the characteristics of a late tale intended to glorify the Jewish race (Ant. xi. 8, 4, 5). His ambitions and plans for the conquest of Egypt left him no time to turn aside for such an insignificant community as that at Jerusalem. Even the conquest of au important city like Damascus he deputed to one of his generals. Jerusalem probably at this time, as in the earlier days of its history, escaped by simply submitting, because the conqueror was eager to advance into Egypt. The slowness of the Jews in throwing off the Persian yoke commended rather tha.n condemned them in the eyes of Alexander. The original demands for provisions, auxiliaries, and the same tribute as had been paid to Persia were doubtless enforced. Repeated references in the writings of Josephus (Against Ap. i. 22) suggest that henceforth Jews were regularly found in Alexander's armies. This confirms the statement that many accompanied him in his wars (Jos. Ant. xi. 8, 5). They can, however, hardly have been enrolled from the better classes. The fact that large numbers of the Jewish race were scattered throughout the lands which Alexander hoped to conquer, and that, while industrious and intelligent, they felt no attachment to

the existing governments, may well have influenced him to grant them certain religious privileges, even as he did the Egyptians and Babylonians, with a view to securing their loyal support. Certainly in Alexandria, where his policy found clearest expression, he conceded to them special civil and religious rights. The suggestion has also been made that because of their close connection with each other, he wished to employ them as guides and informers in the lands which he hoped to conquer. 268. Under Alexander, there was little immediate change in the life of the Jewish community in Palestine. It made no difference to the Jews whether they paid tribute to Persia or Macedonia. Jaddua the THE CITY OF ALEXANDRIA 287 high priest continued to direct local affairs, subject to the Greek governor who resided at Samaria. While Alexander was in Egypt, Andromachus, whom he placed over the province of Coslo-Syria, was murdered by the Samaritans (Quintus Curtius iv. 5, 8). In punishment, a part of their territory (according to a late tradition) was given to their foes the Jews, who were thus enabled to extend their narrow limits northward. A Macedonian colony was established at Samaria, many of the inhabitants of which had been either slain or banished for their crime. 269. The subjugation of Egypt was easily and quickly accomplished by Alexander, since he found there no genuine attachment to Persia. His great work during his brief sojourn in Egypt was the founding of the city which bore his name. The destruction of Tyre prepared the way for Alexandria's commercial greatness. Located on the sea, with Lake Mareotis in its rear, it was easily defended. Provided with a superb harbor, connected with the Nile by a canal, and without a formidable rival, it enjoyed a practical monopoly of the trade of the East. It was laid out by the architect of the temple of Diana. Built at royal expense, it was one of the most beautiful cities of antiquity. Its population consisted of Egyptians, Greeks, and Jews. Each occupied separate quarters. The Jews lived together in the northeastern part of the city, and

their quarter was surrounded with walls. Within these, they lived in accordance with their peculiar laws, and were ruled and represented by one of their number who bore the title of Alabarch. Alexander's wise policy soon attracted many there, and under the Ptolemies their numbers were still further increased, so that Alexandria soon became the second greatest Jewish centre in the world. 270. From Egypt, Alexander set out in 331 B. c. to complete the conquest of the Persian empire. At Arbela, he fought in the same year the decisive battle which broke forever the power of Darius. During the next seven years, he extended his rule to the Oxus and Indus. Before he had consolidated his vast empire, he died in 323 B. c., leaving no heir to succeed him. Perhaps the most remarkable fact in his marvellous history is the permanence of his suddenly acquired conquests. The explanation is found in the superiority of Greek valor, arms, and culture to that of the East, in the servile attitude of the peoples conquered, in the military ability of the generals who succeeded Alexander, in the fact that, instead of destroying the nations which he vanquished, he endeavored by liberal concessions to win their loyalty, and above all because he built Greek cities and introduced Greek colonists and customs throughout the entire empire. The Orient is naturally imitative; and Hellenistic culture became fashionable. The result was that it transfused and transformed the life of the peoples of southwestern Asia and Egypt. Greece was transported to the East, and each Hellenistic city exerted a wide leavening influence. Palestine was powerfully affected. The coast cities of Gaza, Ashdod, Askelon, Joppa, Appolonia, and Ptolemais soon became centres of Greek population and rule. In addition to Samaria, many of the east-Jordan towns — Hippos, Gadara, Pella, Gerasa, and Philadelphia — were colonized and Hellenized by Alexander's veterans. Thus, from the beginning of the Greek period, the Jewish community in Palestine waa THE CAPTURE OF JERUSALEM BY PTOLEMY 289 closely encircled by a ring of Hellenistic towns.

The conquests of Alexander suddenly brought the two great currents of ancient thought and culture into closest contact. The real history of human civilization during the succeeding centuries is the record of the conflicts and the final fusion of the permanent elements in each. 271. The successors of Alexander inherited his inordinate ambitions and weaknesses, but few of his redeeming virtues. The fusion of eastern and western blood and civilization magnified the vices of both. The subject peoples were the prey of the conflicts which soon sprang up between Alexander's generals. Palestine, being the main highway between Asia and Africa, again became the bone of contention between the great powers of the East and the West. Peace was not to be secured even by servile submission. The first attack was made about 320 B. c., by Ptolemy I. (Soter), son of Lagus, who after the death of Alexander had established his rule over Egypt. Apparently at this time, according to the tradition preserved by Josephus (Ant. xii. 1; Against Ap. i. 22), Jerusalem was captured by a sudden attack on the Sabbath, because the Jews refused to fight on that day. The resistance of the Jews and Samaritans gave Ptolemy an excuse for carrying many of them to Egypt. They were taken from the country districts, as well as from the larger towns. Special inducements were also held out by him which attracted still others. 272. Compared with the barren hills of Judah, exposed to constant attack from relentless, treacherous foes, Egypt under the rule of Ptolemy, with its rich opportunities for the enjoyment of peace and wealth, offered attractions which were well-nigh irresistible. In the Greek period, "the flesh pots of Egypt" were a sore temptation to the Jews, and became the stronger as the Jewish colony there grew larger and more influential. Ptolemy on the other hand, assisted by only comparatively few Greeks, and confronted with the problem of maintaining the rule over his rebellious Egyptian subjects, wisely recognized in the Jews and Samaritans his best allies. They were so thoroughly denationalized that they were influenced by no political motives other than loyalty to the master who would treat them most generously. Their personal interests all led them to unite with the Greeks, rather than with the native Egyptians. In that age when fidelity was a rare virtue, they could be trusted. Their ambitions were modest. They were industrious, and possessed a rare facility for adapting themselves to their environment. In the great commercial centres of Egypt, their genius for trade found complete expression. Their exceptional morality secured for them many positions of trust. They soon became the strongest pillar of the Ptolemaic state; and as the individual rulers became weak and corrupt, the Jews came more and more into prominence. Their lot, however, was not altogether a peaceful one. The special favors which they enjoyed, made them an object of intense hatred to the native population. They were also thrown into close relations with the Samaritan colonists. The result was that their racial antipathies found there more bitter expression than in Palestine itself (Jos. Ant. xii. 1). Frequent were the conflicts between the advocates of Mount Zion and of Mount Gerizim. CONTESTS FOR THE POSSESSION OF PALESTINE 291 273. During the closing years of the fourth century, the rule of Palestine was hotly contested between Ptolemy and his powerful rival Antigonus. About 315, the latter seized and held it, until, in a battle near Gaza in 312 B. c., his son Demetrius was defeated by the Egyptian forces. Josephus states, on the authority of pseudo-Hecataeus (Against Ap. i. 22), that at this time Ptolemy visited Jerusalem and persuaded many Jews to go with him to Egypt. Among others, there was a certain Hezekiah, a member of the high priestly family, who enjoyed great respect among his people. Palestine, however, was ceded on the following year to Antigonus. After 306, when he assumed the title of king, Ptolemy endeavored again to reconquer southern Syria, but without much success, until Antigonus was slain in the battle of Ipsus in 301 B. c. Then he gained possession of Palestine, and his successors maintained their authority, with only a few lapses, for nearly a century. About 297 B. c., Demetrius invaded Palestine, but his conquest was brief. The Seleucids, however, who succeeded to the empire of Antigonus, never ceased to assert their claim to it whenever they were especially strong or the Ptolemies weak. Between the years 264 and 248 B. c. , the tide of war seems to have rolled back and forth through Palestine, bringing its horrors to the Jews; but history has preserved few details. Daniel xi. 7-9 contains veiled allusions to these conflicts. On the whole, the eagerness of the Ptolemies and Seleucids to possess Palestine led each to court the Jews. Seleucus I., who founded Antioch about 300 B. c., extended many privileges to them with a view to attracting them to his new capital. According to Josephus (Ant. xii. 3, 1), he granted them equal rights with the Macedonians and Greeks. That many availed themselves of these opportunities is evinced by the number of Jews found in later times in Antioch and the cities of Asia Minor. 274. The first three Ptolemies proved, on the whole, active and efficient rulers. They gradually extended the bounds and influence of Egypt until, at the death of Ptolemy III. (Euergetes) in 222 B. c., it included not only Palestine and Coelo-Syria but also the more important cities on the coast of the eastern Mediterranean. Their rule was much more popular with the Jews than that of the Seleucids. Ptolemy II. (Phila-delphus) figures in Jewish tradition as the patron of their temple and the ruler under whose direction their scriptures were translated into Greek, as well as the liberator of all Jewish captives in his realm (Jos. Ant. xii. 2). His successor Euergetes is also accredited, after a successful campaign in Syria, with having offered rich sacrifices at the temple in Jerusalem (Jos. Against Ap. ii. 5). The tribute demanded by the Ptolemies does not appear to have been exorbitant; and, when it was regularly paid, the peoples of Palestine were left free to manage their own affairs. This freedom exposed the Jews to the attacks of their hostile neighbors. Josephus states that " at this time the Samaritans w-erc in a flourishing condition, and much distressed the Jews, cutting off parts of their land and carrying off slaves " (Ant. xii. 4,1). A passing reference of the son of Sirach indicates that the ancient feud with the Samaritans and Philistines was as bitter as ever (Ecclus. I. 25, 26.) 275. The story told by Josephus respecting Joseph the tax-collector, sheds much light upon conditions THE STORY OF JOSEPH THE TAX-COLLECTOR 293 within the Jewish community in Palestine. About 230 B. c., Onias II. the high priest refused for some reason — probably at the instigation of the rival Syrian power—to pay the annual tribute to Egypt. From the account, it appears that this was surprisingly small, being only twenty talents, while that of all Syria and Phoenicia was eight thousand and later twice that amount. Its collection also was left to the Jews themselves, the high priest being held responsible for the whole. The refusal of Onias brought an ambassador of Ptolemy Euergetes to Jerusalem. His presence and the threat that Judah might be settled with Egyptian veterans naturally alarmed the Jews. Joseph, the crafty and unscrupulous nephew of the high priest, improved the opportunity to secure his appointment to represent them at the Egyptian court. By simple effrontery and intrigue, he ingratiated himself, first with the Egyptian ambassador, and then with the king and queen. Later, when the right of farming the taxes of Ptolemy's Asiatic provinces was sold, as was customary, at public auction, he bid twice as much as the princes of Syria and Phoenicia. Although he had no security to offer, his daring action and words so appealed to Euergetes that it was sold to him, and he departed with an army of two thousand Egyptian soldiers to assist him in collecting the revenues. At first the demands of this Jewish upstart were scornfully refused; but after he had put to death and confiscated the property of certain of the leading men of Askelon and Scythopolis who had resisted his authority, the different provinces humbly submitted. For twenty-three years, by force and intrigue, he held the position of chief tax-collector, and as such was the virtual gov- ernor of Syria and Phoenicia. His extortions were so notorious that the saying, " Joseph is stripping the flesh from Syria and is leaving only the bones," became one of the jokes of the Ptolemaic court. While he brought wealth to the Jews, his influence was most pernicious. He himself was immoral, and readily abandoned the faith of his fathers for the corrupt practices of the Greeks. His sons followed in his footsteps, and used their inherited wealth and influence for the basest ends. His unjust extortions kindled anew the antipathies of their neighbors toward the Jews, and ultimately brought upon them a long train of disasters. 276. The political decline of the Ptolemies began with the accession of Ptolemy IV. (Philopator), at the age of twenty-four. From the first, he led his profligate and effeminate court in all excesses. He manifested a supreme disregard for his own interests and those of his subjects, and was ruled by intriguing courtiers. The result was that Egypt's great prestige suddenly vanished. Ptolemy's rival was Antiochus III., rightly designated " the Great," who came to the throne of the Seleucids at the age of twenty-one (224 B. c.). In him to a certain degree the ambitions and energy of the great Alexander lived again. Confronted by formidable conspiracies within his capital, he at once turned his back upon them, and advanced to the conquest of Syria and Palestine, which he must acquire before his kingdom could be secure and complete. He met with little opposition, except from some of the walled cities like Gaza. Aided by the treachery of Ptolemy's general, who betrayed the cities and forces under his command, Antiochus, by 218 B. c., was mas- CONQUEST OF PALESTINE BY ANTIOCHUS 295 ter of Syria and Palestine. In the following year, however, Philopator inflicted upon him a crushing defeat (Dan. xi. 12) at Raphia on the borders of Egypt, and kept him out of Palestine for the next fifteen years. After this victory, Philopator is said to have visited Jerusalem, and to have attempted to enter the temple. He was probably de- terred by the outcries of the people. The third Book of Maccabees associates with his name the story of an attempt to exterminate his Jewish subjects in Egypt. It is at least evident that he alienated the affection of the Jews just at the time when their fidelity was destined to be most severely tested. 277. As soon as Philopator died in 205 B. c., leaving his throne to his son, a child of five years, Antiochus advanced into Palestine, and in 202 B. c. reconquered it. An Egyptian army was sent under Scopas to maintain the authority of Ptolemy; but in a battle near Paneion at the foot of Mount Hermon, it was finally defeated in 198 B. c. by the forces of Antiochus. The sufferings of the Jews at this time were extreme, for they were the prey of both armies. Josephus compares their lot to that of a ship tossed by the waves on both sides (Ant. xii. 3, 3). Many were carried off as slaves, and many more took refuge in flight (Jos. Ant. xii. 3, 3-4). Some of them from the first embraced the cause of Antiochus, possibly hoping thereby to secure greater independence; but they were doomed to disappointment, for Antiochus seized Palestine " with destruction in his hand " (Dan. xi. 14-16). 278. In return, however, for the provision which they furnished for his army and for their assistance in expelling the Egyptian garrison from Jerusalem, Antiochus undoubtedly granted them special privileges. Josephus states that, inasmuch as Jerusalem had been greatly depopulated by the ravages to which it had been recently subjected, Antiochus offered certain inducements intended to draw back those who had been scattered abroad. Liberal appropriations were made to defray the expenses of the temple service, and to rebuild the sacred structure. The public officials of the nation and the temple ministers were exempted from the poll-tax, and the Judean community as a whole relieved of all taxation for three years, until it should recover its former population and resources, and after that period wns freed from one-third of its former taxes. Freedom and restoration to their former possessions were granted to all who had been sold into slavery;

full religious liberty was also guaranteed to the Jews, and the execution of the strict Jewish law within Jerusalem was enforced by royal decree (Ant. xii. 3, 3, 4). While the generosity of some of these concessions arouses the suspicion that the Jewish historian has idealized the facts, the statements accord so closely with the situation to which they are assigned that they must rest upon some authentic data. It was certainly for the interests of Antiochus to win at any cost the loyalty of the Jews. He also did not manifest in his other acts the extremely mercenary spirit of his successors, which would have made many of the more important concessions impossible. Some such acts as these alone explain the favor which he enjoyed in the eyes of later Jews. He is also said to have deported two thousand families of Jews from Mesopotamia and Babylon, and to have settled them in the rebellious provinces of Phrygia and Lydia to THE RULE OF THE SELEUCIDS 297 guard the royal interests. Lands, and the remission of all taxes for ten years, and grain for seed, and food sufficient to supply their immediate needs, were granted them. Their civil and religious freedom was also carefully guarded. Evidently the Seleucids found the Jews as useful subjects as did the Ptolemies. 279. Henceforth, Palestine never reverted to Egypt. In 193 B. c., Antiochus nominally gave the taxes of Coslo-Syria and Palestine as a dowry to his daughter on her marriage to Ptolemy V. (Epiphanes); but this territory itself was firmly held by Syrian governors and garrisons. In their change of masters, the Jews gained little permanent advantage. Antiochus aimed to build up an empire which would effectually check the advance of the Romans in the East; but at the great battle of Magnesia in 190 B. c., he himself was forced to bow before the new world-conquerors. Soon after, while vainly endeavoring to replenish his treasury by plundering the temple of Belus in Elymais, he was slain (Dan. xi. 18,19). The ambitions of his son and successor Seleucus IV. (Philopator) were not for glory and conquest, but for the means wherewith to

gratify his luxurious tastes, and to pay the tribute demanded by Rome, whose powerful influence henceforth shaped the politics of southwestern Asia. 280. His character and needs lend credence to the story in II. Maccabees iii. concerning his attempt to rob the temple at Jerusalem. He was incited to do so by a traitorous Jew by the name of Simon, who had once been the guardian of the temple, but had quarrelled with Onias III. the high priest. In spite, he informed Seleucus, through his governor Apollonius, that the treasury in Jerusalem was full of untold sums of money. The possibility of securing it led the king to despatch his chancellor Heliodorus to Judea with orders to remove it. Although the high priest asserted, in response to the inquiries of Heliodorus, that the treasure was not great, and that it represented the deposits of private individuals, its surrender was demanded. The possibility that the sanctity of their temple would be violated, called forth from the entire populace the most passionate protests. When Heliodorus entered the sanctuary to seize its treasures, he was confronted by an apparition which led him to turn back in fright. Corrupt as were the Greeks at this time, they had not learned to pillage temples without experiencing a feeling of terror. The memory of the fate of Antiochus the Great was still fresh. The attitude of the excitable Jews, who would endure anything except an affront to their religion, was enough to intimidate braver men than were found in this degenerate age. That Seleucus Philopator made some such attempt to rob the Jews is confirmed by the fact that the author of the Book of Daniel, who must have been then living, refers to him as " one who shall cause an exactor to pass through the glory of the kingdom." The temple treasure was also saved from spoliation at this time as the story in II. Maccabees states, for it was carried off later by Antiochus Epiph-anes, who succeeded Seleucus in 176 B. c. His accession marks the beginning of the end of the Greek period, for just when tyranny, injustice, treachery, and degenerate heathenism seemed to have attained a

complete triumph, the best and bravest elements in Judaism, which hitherto had remained silent, arose and asserted themselves. JEWISH LIFE IN EGYPT AND PALESTINE 281. The closing decade of the Greek period marks the transition to a new era; but the life and thought of the preceding century and a half constitute a unit, and may best be studied as such. The Persian period witnessed the birth and development of Judaism, and the Greek its testing. The one was comparatively peaceful, the other was disturbed by frequent and devastating wars. Under Greek rule, great numbers of the Jews were again dragged from the seclusion which many of them had found in Palestine, and projected into the main currents of the world's life. The tendency toward centralization, which had been so strong during the last century of the Persian period, was completely reversed. By force and free choice the Jews were scattered more widely than before, so that soon colonies of them were found from the Indus almost to the Pillars of Hercules, and from the Indian Ocean to the Black Sea. Those in the East almost disappeared from history for a few centuries; while the new emigrants to Egypt, uniting with those already there, in numbers probably exceeded the Jews who remained behind in Palestine. 282. The Egyptian Jews of course took with them copies of their sacred writings, and especially the law, which they studied faithfully in their synagogues established in the lands of the dispersion. They were so near Jerusalem, that under the Ptolemies many of them made frequent pilgrimages to Jerusalem to celebrate the great religious feasts. Each had the privilege of contributing his yearly tax of about thirty cents for the support of the temple. Although connection with their kinsmen in Judah was exceedingly close, their different pursuits, and the active intellectual atmosphere, especially of Alexandria, where the majority of them were found, and their intimate contact with Greek life and thought, powerfully affected them, and produced a much broader type of Judaism. Engaged as they were in trade, they naturally adopted its language, which was a dialect known as Hellenistic Greek. A familiarity with this new tongue, which was a modified and simplified form of classical Greek, opened to the Jews for the first time the literary treasures of Hellas. Before long in Egypt this new language completely supplanted the ancient Hebrew, which even in Palestine had almost ceased to be spoken. Consequently, a century or two after the conquest of Alexander, the demand for a translation of the Jewish scriptures into Hellenistic Greek became imperative. 283. According to the late tradition associated with the name of Aristeas, and recounted by Josephus (Ant. xii. 2), it was made under the patronage of Ptolemy II. (Philadelphus), who wished thereby to show his favor to the Jews, and to secure a copy of their sacred writings for the great library at Alexandria. The story states that he first purchased at an enormous expense the freedom of all the Jewish slaves in Egypt, and then that, at his request, Eleazer the high priest at Jerusalem sent to him seventy-two learned Jews, six from THE TRANSLATION OF THE SEPTUAGINT 301 each of the twelve tribes. On their arrival, every facility was granted them for their work. After seventy-two days they presented to the king a translation which was admired alike by him and by the Jewish people. The improbabilities of the tale are obvious. A complete translation within the time given was practically impossible. The scribes, not of Jerusalem, but of Alexandria would at that date alone be familiar with the Greek language. The translation itself, which bears the title "The Septuagint" ("the seventy"), testifies by its peculiarities that it is the work of Alexandrian Jews. Different books were evidently translated by different men, and probably at different times. The books of the law, which naturally received the first attention, were translated much more literally and carefully than those of the prophets. In some cases, the translators did not grasp the meaning of the original Hebrew, in others they employed a different Hebrew text from the one now accepted, and in

others they translated freely, introducing variations; while to such late books as Esther and Daniel they added long sections. The tradition, which assigns the beginning of the work of translation to the reign of Ptolemy II. (Philadelphus) about 250 B. c. is undoubtedly historical. Many of the Old Testament books were not composed until much later, so that probably all were not translated before the middle of the next century at least. In 132 B. c., the grandson of Jesus the son of Sirach was acquainted with a Greek version of " the law, the prophets, and the other writings." The law may well have appeared in Greek before the close of the reign of Philadelphus. This broad-minded king may also have encouraged the Jews in the task, the accomplishment of which was so essential to the contentment of a large and important body of his subjects. 284. As the variations between the original Hebrew and the Greek text indicate, the translation was made, not only for the use of the Jews, but also to commend the Jewish race and religion to the Greek world. Anthropomorphisms in the Hebrew original are often eliminated. Many inconsistent dates and numbers are altered, and an effort is made to explain obscurities. The success and influence enjoyed by the Jews of Egypt made them the object of bitter attack both by Greek and native Egyptian writers. The modern anti-Semitic movement may be traced back to the Greek period, and to the same real causes, commercial, political, and religious, which produce it to-day. In his long history of Egypt, written in Greek, the Egyptian priest Manetho, who lived during the reign of Philadelphus, introduced certain legends concerning the origin and early history of the Jews which placed them in an unfavorable light before the heathen world. Many other writers followed the example of Manetho. The Jews replied by counter-statements. The translation of their histories and laws may have primarily been intended to refute the false charges brought against them. A certain Hellenistic Jew, Demetrius by name, about 215 B. c., also wrote a detailed history of the Jewish

kings. Others issued fantastic tales respecting their ancestors. Then, when their foes rejected all writings obviously of Jewish origin, they appealed to the earlier heathen historians who had referred to them. 285. As the contest grew more heated, in order to defend themselves and to give currency to their ideas, APOLOGETIC LITERATURE OF THE JEWS 303 the Jews took the liberty of expanding the original writings of Greek historians, like Hecataeus (sect. 264), who had spoken of them favorably. The deception in some cases must have succeeded, for they issued a great number of such writings, even putting verses into the mouths of the most famous Greek poets, like Jilschylus, Sophocles, and Meander. Often the forgeries were very skilful, genuine and spurious verses being artfully intermingled. Later, they even introduced a Jewish prophecy into the mouth of the heathen Sybil. These devices, although not justified by the low standards of the age, indicate to what an extent the Jews of the dispersion became acquainted with Greek literature, and were influenced by contact with its thought. Their eagerness to commend their faith to the Greek world foreshadowed the important proselyting movement which found in Alexandria its chief centre. Their forgeries were a practical admission that Jehovah spoke through the great heathen poets as well as through their prophets. Thus, as they were brought into more intimate relations, the Jew and the Greek learned to appreciate what was best in their respective religions, and the way was prepared for their ultimate fusion in Christianity. But before that fusion could be consummated, Judaism must save itself from being engulfed by its more powerful rival. 286. Jerusalem was the natural stronghold of Judaism, and conditions there were entirely different from those in its great outpost, Alexandria. The loose rule of the Greeks, which left dependent states to rule themselves, favored the extension of the civil authority of the high priests. As local princes, they ruled over the Judean community, imposed taxes, made public improvements, and represented the Jews at the courts of Alexandria and Antioch. The needs of the situation, and the commands of the law, gave them great influence. That many of them misused their power is plainly indicated both by the proverbs and by the stories coming from the period. The exceptions receive especial notice. Several lists of the names of the different high priests have been preserved, but the duration of their rule cannot be definitely determined, since the testimony of the sources differs (Chronicon Paschale; G. Syncellus, Chronogr. and Canon). Jaddua, who was high priest when Alexander conquered Palestine, lived until about 330 B. c., Onias I., his successor, ruled until about 300, Simeon I. until about 285, and his brother Bleazer until about 265. Manasseh and the brother of Simeon held the office until about 240, when Simeon's son Onias II. became high priest. About 225, he was succeeded by Simeon II., who ruled until about 195. 287. He is probably the famous Simon the Just, who figures in Rabbinical tradition as a great teacher and benefactor of his race. To him was attributed the saying: " The world rests upon three things: the law, worship, and good works" (Pirke-Aboth i. 2). His contemporary, the son of Sirach, informs us that he repaired the foundations and fortified the temple. He also improved its water-supply, and fortified the city of Jerusalem (Ecclus. I. 1-4). These repairs were undoubtedly much needed after Jerusalem had been subjected to repeated sieges and assaults during the destructive wars waged between the Seleucids and the Ptolemies from 220 to 198 B. c. The work of Simon II. was possible because of the concessions THE WOKK OF SIMON THE JUST 305 which Josephus reports were granted to the Jews by Antiochus the Great after the final conquest of Palestine in 198 B. c. (sect. 278). The liberal policy of Antiochus, supported by the wise, energetic action of Simon, seems to have revived the fortunes of the Jewish community, and to have drawn back many who had fled during the two preceding decades. Simon himself was the object of popular affection

and gratitude, for "he took thought for his people that they should not fall" (Ecclus. I. 4). Jesus the son of Sirach can hardly find language strong enough to describe his commanding mien as he performed his high priestly duties, clad in his " robe of glory," attended by the priests; while all the people " fell down upon the earth on their faces " and " the singers praised Jehovah with their voices, until in the whole house there was made sweet melody" (1. 5-18). We can also behold the people " in prayer before him that is merciful," and the beloved high priest, with outstretched hands, blessing the assembled " congregation of the children of Israel" (I.19-21). From such passages as this it is possible to understand why their religion and ritual had so great a hold upon the hearts of the Jews as it did, and why the influence of the high priests was as strong as it was. 288. In connection with the concessions granted by Antiochus the Great, the first reference is made to the Gerousia, or council of the elders (Jos. Ant. xii. 3, 3). Undoubtedly heretofore each high priest had consulted the heads of the families and prominent men of the community before taking important action; but henceforth they constitute an organized and recognized body, the legislative and executive powers of which were constantly increased. At this time also the scribes of the temple and the sacred singers were recognized as public officials, side by side with the senators and priests, and as such exempted from taxation. The genial son of Sirach, whose keen observations marvellously reveal the life of his age, remarks that:
The wisdom of the scribe comes by opportunity of leisure: And he that has little business shall become wise.

He regards the other professions as necessary, but that of the scribe by far the most honorable. The scribes are the ones that are sought for in the council of the people, they occupy the honorable seats in the public assemblies, they act as judges and expound the law, they are the teachers of the people, and they utter wise parables (xxxviii. 24-34).
289. The same writer refers to the dif-

ferent professions and occupations open to his fellow Jews who did not possess the leisure and ability to become scholars. Physicians are found, but they are evidently regarded with suspicion by many. The advice offered in regard to them by the son of Sirach is as amusing as it is profound:

Honor your physician according to your need of him with the honors due him; For verily the Lord hath created him. The skill of a physician shall lift up his head; And in the sight of great men he shall be admired. The Lord created medicines out of the earth; And a prudent man will have no disgust at them. He that sins before his Maker, Let him fall into the hands of the physician. xxxviii. 24. xxxviii. 1, 3, 4, 15.
OCCUPATIONS OF THE PALESTINIAN JEWS 307
Apothecaries were also found to put up the prescriptions of the men of medicine (xxxviii. 8). Among those " who maintain the fabric of the world, whose prayer is the handiwork of their craft" (xxxviii. 25-34) are mentioned those who hold the plough whose " wakefulness is to give their heifers their fodder," artificers, master-workmen, engravers of signets, smiths who " wrestle in the heat of their furnaces," and potters who " are always anxiously sitting at their work." While many other ancient nations despised manual labor the Jews honored it.

Hate not laborious work:

Neither husbandry which the Most High hath ordained, was the motto in accordance with which they won a living in barren Judah. In the Greek period the truth of the statement that,

A merchant shall hardly keep from wrong-doing;
And a huckster shall not be acquitted of sin,
cannot be questioned.
290. Many of the old democratic ideas still obtained in Palestine. The assembly of the people for the consideration of public questions was still common. Joseph the tax-collector was authorized by such an assembly to represent the high priest and the Jewish community at the court of the Ptolemies (sect. 275).

The son of Sirach repeatedly advises the rulers to patronize the multitude that they may secure their favor (iv. 7; xxxi. 23, 24). Even such a worthy man as he did not entirely resist the great temptations of his age to pander to the rich and influential (iv. 7). Gold was potent in Judah, as well as in corrupt Alexandria, and " presents and gifts blinded the eyes of the wise " (viii. 2; xx. 29). As in the days before the exile, judges perverted justice, and there was no court of appeal. " Poor men were a pasture for the rich" (xiii. 2-20). It was a selfish, grasping age, when might too often made right, and the cause of the oppressed had few champions. rii. 15. xxvi. 29.
Bread, discipline, and work for a servant;

Yoke and thong will bow the neck;

And for an evil servant there are racks and torture voiced the prevailing spirit of the day rather than: If you have a servant treat him as yourself.

Judaism continued to present the most glaring contrasts both in individual character and teaching. It produced such different types as Simon the Just and Joseph the unprincipled tax-collector. On the one hand, it had before its eyes the noble teachings and examples of the past, and on the other the corruption, the greed, and the injustice of its Greek masters. Under the rule of the law, which emphasized ritual rather than personal conduct, the most shameless deeds were often tolerated. Prophets of the ancient type were no longer found to denounce them, and thereby to furnish the true corrective to the teachings of the priests.
291. The pictures of Jewish home life which the son of Sirach also gives, are certainly realistic. xxxiii. 24, 26,31. DOMESTIC RELATIONS OF THE JEWS 309
Men who were themselves ruled by an uncompromising law naturally ruled their families with a rod of iron. " Stripes and correction are wisdom at every season" (xxii. 6). Children were brought up on the same principle that horses were broken to the harness (xxx. 8). The frank comradeship between father and son, which is one of the charms of the Christian home, was regarded as

dangerous:

Play with your son, and he will grieve you,

Laugh not with him, lest you have sorrow with him.

Give him no liberty in his youth

And beat him on his sides while he is a child,

Lest he grow stubborn, and be disobedient toward you.

One wonders who deserves the most pity, the father who is compelled by a false doctrine ever to play the tyrant, or the child who is the victim. Daughters are regarded as a constant care (xlii. 9-11). Happy, trustful relations are known between husband and wife, but not equality (xxvi. 1-4). " The beauty of a good wife is the ordering of her husband's house " (xxvi. 16). Evil wives are kept under lock and key (xlii. 6). When a man was tired of his wife, he could divorce her (xxv. 26). The majority of the women with whom the son of Sirach was acquainted, appear to have been quarrelsome, jealous of each other, given to gossip, and in some cases addicted to drink and unchaste, — the inevitable consequence of a false social system (xxv. 16-26; xxvi. 5-12). As in the East to-day, man was regarded as the only important member of society, and women, children, and slaves, his chattels. Consequently, men found their real companionship in each other's society. With so little in their political and domestic life to help and inspire them, it is not strange that the period produced so few noble characters. Their national memories, their law, their sacred writings, and their temple service were the only forces which upheld and inspired them.
xxx. 9-12. DIPFEBBNT CURRENTS OF JEWISH THOUGHT 292. Even the dull monotony and the dreary outlook of the Greek period did not entirely quench the perennial hopefulness of the Jews. The national expectations, however, which found expression were influenced by the narrowing, degenerate influences of the age. The broad tolerance of the author of the Book of Jonah found few apostles. Stung to fury by the contempt and violence of the heathen, with whom

they had been brought into painful contact, they longed for the destruction of their foes. The author of Zechariah ix. to xiv. rejoices in the prospect of their overthrow, which he regards as the necessary premise to the exaltation of Jehovah's people. In the day of judgment, which he hopes is near, the Jews, he declares, instead of being the prey of the nations, will divide the spoil. By his omnipotent power, Jehovah will establish his rule over the world. Then the flesh of the nations, which have warred against Jerusalem, shall rot away as they stand, — their eyes in their sockets and their tongues in their mouths. The few who survive, shall, like the Jews of the dispersion, make annual pilgrimages to Jerusalem, and faithfully observe the law. Plagues shall smite those who go not up to keep the feast of tabernacles. A greater contrast could not be imagined than is found between these gory predictions, and the ideal of the suffering servant of Jehovah who finds his true life in the service of mankind. It is the difference between the earlier prophetic teaching, and that of the prophet Jonah, who is represented as sitting outside of Nineveh complaining of God's mercy in sparing the ignorant Ninevites (Jon. iv.). It finds expression in certain psalms. It represents the attitude of perhaps a majority of the Jewish race toward the hostile Gentile world during the succeeding centuries. It voiced the feelings and hopes of the nationalistic party who longed for the day when Jehovah would " stir up your sons, 0 Zion, against your sons, 0 Greece, and make his people as the sword of a mighty man," that they might drink the blood of their nation's enemies (Zech. ix. 13, 15). They were the ones who rallied about the sons of Mattathias and were not content until, not only religious, but also political liberty was secured. 293. The character and writings of the chronicler reveal another and brighter side of Hellenistic Judaism. Living in the glorious past of his nation, and intent only upon the institutions of the ritual, he cared little what the heathen might do, provided the temple service was not interrupted. Life for him consisted in conforming to the varied demands of the law and in the worship of the sanctuary. To him ceremonial details were much more important than the rise and fall of the nations. He undoubtedly represented a large class in Judah. Their ideals were indeed narrow and temporal, and their conception of ' religion by no means attractive; but it must be noted that their faith was sincere, and that they were char- THE WORK OF THE WISE MEN Or ISRAEL 313 acterized by an intense moral earnestness and by a complete consecration to their conception of duty. It was not the dreamers who waited with folded hands for Jehovah, by some miraculous act, to destroy the foes of the true religion, but the type represented by the chronicler, who firmly met and overcame the repeated shocks and temptations which assailed their nation during the Greek period. They were the stern Puritans of their age, the lineal descendants of the followers of Ezra, who stood unmoved while many of broader culture bowed down before the gods of Hellas. 294. Another distinct current of Jewish thought is represented by Jesus the son of Sirach. He, like the author of Ecclesiastes, belonged to that unobtrusive but influential group of teachers known as the wise. Already they were a familiar figure in Israel's history (I. sect. 7). Side by side with the prophets and priests, they had faithfully labored in their peculiar way for the uplifting of the race (Jer. xviii. 18). The Book of Proverbs, which has preserved many of their most characteristic teachings, is the best testimonial to their work. Not the nation but the individual, questions not of public, but of private interest, commanded their entire attention. While they lacked the inspiration and exalted ideals of the prophets, they came closer to the daily life of the people. When the prophetic voices began to become indistinct, they continued to break the bread of truth to the masses who came to them for advice. They were the pastors and familiar advisers of the community. Their method of teaching by proverbs and parables was exceedingly acceptable to the Oriental mind. The exhortation:

Neglect not the discourse of the wise,
And be conversant with their proverbs;
For of them you shall learn instruction,
And how to minister to great men,

was undoubtedly heeded by the majority of the Jews. Not without reason did the son of Sirach declare:

The wise man shall inherit confidence among his people, And his name shall live forever.

The universality of their teaching was a valuable corrective to the narrowing tendencies of Judaism. In many of their utterances, as well as in their method and' point of view, the wise anticipated the " One greater than Solomon." Even though the son of Sirach was greatly influenced by the spirit of his age he taught that:

The mercy of man is upon his neighbor;
But the mercy of the Lord is upon all flesh.

He also prays Jehovah to send his fear upon all the nations,

And let them know thee, as we also know thee,
That there is no God but only thou, 0 God.

Like the author of Zechariah ix. to xiv., however, he regards the destruction of the enemies of his race as necessary before Jehovah's universal kingdom can be established (xxxvi. 7-10). 295. The son of Sirach lived when the wise man was becoming a scribe. His use of proverbs, his broad Ecclus. viii. 8. xviii. 13. xxxvii. 26. xxxvi. 2, 5. THE FUSION OF WISE MAN AND SCRIBE 315 outlook, and his consideration of the commonplace affairs of life are all characteristic of the earlier wise; but the emphasis which he places upon the observation of the Jewish ceremonial law, is an element foreign to the old wisdom-school which practically ignored it. The law had reduced the successors of those valiant defenders of personal righteousness, the prophets, to a position of vassalage. It was not to be expected that the wise would be able to withstand its imperious demands. Jesus the son of Sirach, perhaps referring to the struggles of the past between the champions of practical and ceremonial righteous-

ness, declares:

A wise man will not hate the law;
But he who is a hypocrite therein is as a ship in a storm.
A man of understanding will put his trust in the law;
And the law is faithful unto him, as when one asks at the oracle.

Like the prophets and scribes of his day, he holds up the hands of the priests:

Fear the Lord and glorify his priest;
And give him his portion, even as it is commanded you;
The first fruits of the trespass offering and the gift of the shoulders, And the sacrifice of sanctification, and the first fruits of holy things.

In his advice, he reveals the fusion of wise man and scribe:

Let your converse be with the man of understanding;
And let all your discourse be in the law of the Most High.
xxxiii. 2, 3. vii. 31. ix. 15.

He even identifies wisdom with, the law:

All wisdom is the fear of the Lord;
And in all wisdom is the doings of the law.

In keeping with the tendency of his age, he makes Moses the father of wisdom, as well as of the law (xxiv.). The ultimate victory of the scribe is foreshadowed, for he does not hesitate to state that wisdom is of less value than compliance with the law:

Better is one who has small understanding and fears, Than who has much prudence and transgresses the law.

Although in his writings the two fundamentally different types of teaching appear, he evidently regarded the identification of the wise man with the scribe as complete:

The wisdom of the scribe comes by opportunity of leisure: And he who has little business shall become wise.

In the following verses (xxxviii. 33; xxxix. 1-11), he presents a composite picture of the wise man-scribe who enjoys the seat of honor in the public assembly, who speaks in parables, who meditates on the law of the Most High, and who at the same time investigates the wisdom of all the ancients:

He will seek out the hidden meaning of proverbs,

And be conversant in dark sayings of parables.

He will show forth the instruction which he has been taught, And will glory in the law of the covenant of the Lord. xix. 20. xxxviii. 24.

xix. 24, xxxix. 3, 8. ETHICAL STANDARDS OF THE SON OF SIRACH 317 Since the law was regarded by later Judaism as a complete rule for human conduct, it was inevitable that the wise man should become a scribe. Scribism was greatly enriched by the fusion. Scattered through all its later literature are fables, proverbs, and epigram-matical sayings, the characteristic products, not of the legal, but of the wisdom school.

296. The son of Sirach voices the aspirations of the industrious middle class. Like his auditors, he looks up to the rich and the rulers, and down upon the poorer victims of the rich; and withal is contented with his lot (xxxi.). His morality is of the temperate type. His altruism is not a prominent quality. He, however, emphasizes the necessity of being faithful at any cost to the demands of friendship. Almsgiving is a duty (iv. 1-6). Deeds of mercy toward those in need are enjoined (xxix.). Several of his precepts recall those of the author of Ecclesiastes:

Defraud not yourself of a good day;

And let not the portion of a good desire pass you *by.*

Give, and take and beguile your soul;

For there is no seeking of luxury in the grave.

His love for banquets, with the accompaniment of wine and music, is strong (xxxii. 3-5); but he urges, on very utilitarian grounds, the necessity of strict moderation, both in eating and drinking (xxxi. 19-30). On the whole, he was a quiet, law-abiding citizen, a good neighbor, and an honorable business man. The aspirations of the nationalistic party did not appeal to him strongly. With the chronicler, he revered the law, not blindly, however, but because he recognized the reasonableness of its demands. His faith was

that of orthodox Judaism, for he draws the articles of hia creed from the past rather than the present. The doctrine of rewards corresponding to conduct, he reiterates (ii. 8; xi. 17). The belief in Satan and personal immortality has not been introduced into his confession. Such was Jesus the son of Sirach: a man of keen perception, of considerable learning, of broad culture, of strict integrity, and of a genuine, though narrow religious faith, — a worthy representative of the orthodox wisdom-school.

xiv. 14, 16. 297. It was impossible that, during the long, discouraging period of testing, all the disciples of Judaism should retain the old faith intact. During a corresponding season of depression preceding the advent of Nehemiah and Ezra, scepticism had first found open expression (sect. 152). The repeated calamities which overtook the Jews in the Greek period shook their faith in many of the fundamental doctrines of their religion. The direct and indirect influence of the philosophical thought of their Greek masters intensified the same tendency. It was also natural that the wise, whose outlook was the broadest, should be the most susceptible to this influence. The Old Testament has preserved some of the cries of doubt that escaped at this trying time from Jewish hearts. In the late appendix to the Book of Proverbs are found the " Words of Agur the son of Jakeh," in which he sadly confesses that he has earnestly but unavailingly sought for God. With a touch of irony, he complains that he must be more obtuse than other men who profess to be so well informed about the heavenly hierarchy. While ho doubts their claims, he longs to be able to question THE SCEPTICAL WISDOM SCHOOL 319 some one gifted with divine omniscience who can answer with authority all his inquiries respecting the real character of God (xxx. 1-4). The voice is that of honest scepticism, which the orthodox wise man who added the verses immediately following was not able to satisfy or silence. 298. Under the implication of Solomonic authorship, or at least by taking Solomon as its hero, a book representing the heretical wisdom-

school ultimately found a place in the Old Testament canon. Later writers also endeavored to make him a teacher of current orthodoxy; but the sceptical tendency of the original author of the Book of Ecclesiastes is unmistakable. He has not lost all faith, for he still believes that there is a God in the universe; but he questions almost everything else that the earlier Hebrews had held dear. The God of whom he conceives is omnipotent, inscrutable, far removed from the daily life of man, and one who rules the universe according to an unchanging, preordained plan (vi. 10; vii. 14; viii. 17). Like the Greek philosophers whose influence his writings reveal, he forms his conception of the deity from a study of human life and of natural phenomena. If his age had not been utterly selfish and sordid, his conclusions might have been different. As it was, he found little evidence of divine love, and much in the life which he studied in Palestine and Egypt that suggested only injustice. The time-honored dogma of proportionate rewards upon this earth, he completely rejected. He saw the righteous man dying in his righteousness, and an evil man living to a ripe old age, apparently enjoying heaven's highest favor (vii. 15; viii. 10). The new doctrine of rewards after death also brought no relief to his perplexity, for, like the son of Sirach, he did not accept it. " Man has no pre-eminence over the beasts. Who knows whether the spirit of the sons of men goes upward and whether the spirit of the beast goes downward" (iii. 20, 21). Even the law and the temple service gave him no joy. He urged conformity to the demands of the law, lest God should be angry and avenge the neglect (v. 4, 6). No Messianic hope inspired and comforted him. " Vanity, all is vanity " voiced his conclusions respecting human existence. With such a cold, barren faith, it is not strange that he had no higher advice to offer than to fear God and live a temperate life, enjoying the few fleeting pleasures which it afforded (iii. 12, 13; ix. 7-9) The possibility of obtaining true happiness by losing one's life in service for others had never occurred to him. When we consider, however, the atmosphere in which he lived, our attitude toward him, and the heretical wisdom-school which he represented, is that of pity rather than of condemnation. It is also easy to see through his eyes how little there was to hold, not only the more worldly Jews, but also the keener minds who recognized the futility of mere ceremonialism from absolute scepticism, or, worse still, from shameless hypocrisy. 299. During the comparatively quiet rule of the Ptolemies, Greek ideas, customs, and morality had been making peaceful conquests in Palestine. Their own inherent attractiveness, and the fact that they were supported by the authority of the dominant race, cast a glamour about them which made the severe religion of Jehovah, the simple customs and the strict morality of the Jews, seem barren and provincial. HELLENISTIC TENDENCIES IN JUDAISM 321 All the other peoples of Palestine, including the Samaritans, had set the example by imitating their conquerors. Hellenistic Greek was the language of commerce and polite society. Greek literature was widely studied. Greek manners were the standard throughout southeastern Palestine. The conservative sou of Sirach speaks in high terms of a " concert of music at a banquet of wine" (xxxii. 5, 6), which reveals to what an extent Greek customs had been adopted in Jerusalem itself. He also alludes to the graver of signets who " sets his heart to preserve likeness in portraiture " (xxxviii. 27), showing that Greek art was intrenched under the very shadow of the temple, for from the context it is clear that the artisans to whom he refers, were not foreigners but Jews. 300. The danger that the Jews would be completely Hellenized was the greater because only by adopting Greek habits and ideas could one hope to secure great wealth or political preferment. The story of Joseph the tax-collector furnishes a good illustration of this fact. His rapid rise in royal favor would have been impossible had he not abandoned the traditions of his race, and surpassed the courtiers of Alexandria in intrigues. Later, whenever at the court, he was a

favorite guest at the drunken orgies of the reigning Ptolemy, and was deterred by no scruples from participating in the shameless debauches. At one of these he is said to have contracted a violent passion for a certain dancing girl (Jos. Ant. xii. 4, 6). Jewish tradition also reports that he introduced at Jerusalem a modified form of the feast in honor of the Greek god of wine, Dionysus. The warnings of the son of Sirach against the seductions of public singers and harlots indicate that the corrupting influence of Greek life had in his day penetrated the sacred city (ix. 2-9). He also exhorts his disciples to prepare their souls for temptation, and denounces those who are of fearful hearts and who are trying "to go two ways" (ii. 1, 12). At the end of the Greek period, the number who were trying " to go two ways" was great. It included many who clung to the faith of their fathers, but who were eager to embrace Greek ideas and customs. Many of the members of the high priestly family were found in the ranks of this Hellenizing party. It also naturally included the growing body of apostates who were ready to abandon their religion entirely, and eager to conceal their Jewish antecedents in order that they might plunge into the dissipations of Greek life. The wealthy and influential descendants of Joseph (the Tobiadte) became the leaders of this powerful party, which soon became strong enough to contest for the rule of the community (Jos. Ant. xii. 5,1). They appear to have carried on an active propaganda, urging that the best interests of the community demanded the tearing down of the wall of separation between them and the nations (I. Mac. i. 11). They might in time have been successful, if at this crisis a great danger from without had not united in its defence all true lovers of the law, irrespective of their peculiar interests or affiliations. Out of the din and conflict of the next few decades rose two or three great parties which embodied in permanent form the different currents of thought which found expression in the Greek period. THE SUPREME CRISIS OF JUDAISM 301. Antiochus Epiphanes, who in 175 B. c.

usurped the throne of Syria, figures in the perspective of history *as* the unintentional savior of Judaism, for he delivered it by his attacks from the " foes of its own household," and awakened it to new life and activity. lu the eyes of his Jewish subjects, he was a fierce, merciless persecutor, delighting only in deeds of treachery and bloodshed (Dan. viii. 23; xi. 21). According to the Greek historians, he was a restless, energetic, arrogant, ill-balanced man, driven by ambition and caprice to undertake tasks beyond his power to accomplish. He took a childish delight in show and pomp. Moderation was unknown to him. So strange was his action at times, that by many he was regarded as insane. He was an ardent champion of everything Greek. Under his rule Antioch was greatly beautified, and made a centre of Hellenic learning. Public buildings reared by him in Athens and many other Greek cities testified to his love of personal display and of art. The desire to extend the influence of Greece throughout all his kingdom was natural; and his fury, when confronted by opposition, was what might be expected from a passionate, undisciplined ruler, reared, as he was at Rome, side by side with the dissolute sons of the nobles who dominated the world. Surrounded by flatterers and intriguers, and not gifted with the power of understanding the peoples under him, he was destined to commit a series of fatal blunders. 302. The treachery of certain of the Jews precipitated the calamities which overtook their race. At the accession of Antiochus Epiphanes, the high priest Onias III. was in Antioch to answer the charge made by the perfidious Simon of having saved the temple treasure by deceiving Heliodorus, the royal messenger (sect. 280). At the instigation of the Hellenistic party at Jerusalem, which was led by the family of Joseph the tax-collector, the faithful Onias was deposed, and his brother Jason, who promised to pay into the Syrian treasury a much larger tribute than he in return for the high priesthood, and the privilege of farming the taxes of Judea, was appointed by Antiochus, in his place (II. Mac. iv. 3-8).

By these means the Hellenistic faction gained control of the temple, for Jason was in sympathy with the most radical innovators. Counting upon the support of Antiochus, and to win his favor, they built a gymnasium in Jerusalem and introduced Greek games. Young Jews flocked to the places of public amusement; even the priests, following the example of their official head, neglected their duties in the temple for the games of the palaestra (II. Mac. iv. 9-15). A passion for Greek costumes, Greek customs, and Greek names seized the people. Large numbers were enrolled as citizens of Antioch. Many even endeavored to conceal the fact that they had been circumcised. To the horror of the faithful, Hellenism seemed to be carrying all before it. Jehovah and his commands were being completely forgotten, and the INTRIGUES OF THE JEWISH HIGH PRIESTS 325 end of Judaism appeared to be at hand. To demonstrate that he had left all the traditions of his race behind, Jason sent a rich present for sacrifices in connection with the great festival at Tyre in honor of the god Hercules. The messengers, not being so far paganized as their master, paid over the money to the fund for the royal navy (II. Mac. iv. 18-20). 303. In 171 B. c., Jason was succeeded by a still more unprincipled renegade. A certain Menelaus was sent by the high priest to Antioch to represent him in the court. Menelaus improved the opportunity to bid a larger sum for the high priesthood, and accordingly was appointed by Antiochus. The family of Joseph supported the new appointee, who came from their ranks; but the majority of the Jews preferred Jason. At last, with the aid of Syrian soldiers, Menelaus drove his rival into exile, and then began to plunder the temple treasure in order to redeem his promise of tribute to Antiochus. The aged ex-priest, Onias III., who dared to condemn this impiety, was treacherously assassinated in his place of refuge near Antioch by an agent of Menelaus (II. Mac. iv. 23-38). In Jerusalem, the Jews, goaded to madness by his repeated robberies of the temple, arose and killed Lysimachus, the representative of Menelaus. They then despatched a deputation to prefer charges before Antiochus at Tyre against their shameless high priest. Again bribes saved Menelaus, and brought upon the suitors for justice the death-penalty (II. Mac. iv. 43-50). Fortunately for Judaism, by such acts as these the popular passion for Hellenism was being rapidly cooled, and in its stead there grew up an intense hatred for Antiochus and his tool, Menelaus. 304. In 170 B. c., the Syrian king invaded Egypt and vanquished the army of the reigning Ptolemy (Dan. xi. 25). While there, the report came that Antiochus was dead. The former high priest Jason improved the opportunity, with a small army of one thousand men, to seize Jerusalem, and to shut up his rival JVIenelaus in the citadel. Instead, however, of winning the favor of the Jews by acts of clemency, to satisfy his inhuman thirst for revenge, he put many of them to death. Finding no real support within the city, and learning that Antiochus was returning from Egypt, Jason again fled, and after long wanderings died miserably (II. Mac. v. 1-10). This unfortunate insurrection gave Antiochus an excuse for venting his anger upon the Jews. Marching directly to Jerusalem, he turned the city over to his bloody soldiery with commands to slay and spoil. No attempt appears to have been made to distinguish between the innocent and guilty. No mercy was shown to women and children. Many were slain in the streets and in their homes. Many more were dragged off to supply the already crowded slave markets of the Mediterranean cities (II. Mac. v. 11-15). Upon the unresisting people was heaped still greater ignominy. Led by the vile Menelaus, Antiochus entered the holy temple and plundered its treasury, bearing away (according to II. Mac. v. 21) eighteen hundred talents of silver. The temple was also stripped of its golden altar and candlestick, of its sacred vessels and ornamentation. Jerusalem was left in sackcloth and ashes (Dan. xi. 28; I. Mac. i. 20-28). 305. Henceforth the relations between Antiochus and his Jewish subjects partook of the nature of a personal feud. Their internal dissensions, their weak- THE ATTEMPT TO HELLENIZE THE JEWS 327 ness, and their complete isolation from the rest of the world alone restrained the Jews from open rebellion. Antiochus, well aware of their secret hatred, regarded their refusal to abandon their religion and to become completely Hellenized, like the rest of his subjects, as an act of rebellion. The existence of a large Greek party at Jerusalem, and the misleading testimony of Menelaus, who recognized that his only hope of maintaining his position lay in the destruction of the loyal Jewish party, encouraged Antiochus to believe that he might yet succeed in exterminating the Jehovah cult. His constant need of money also led him to improve every opportunity to rob his subjects. Accordingly, when, in 198 B. c., he returned from his second Egyptian campaign, completely baffled by the intervention of the Romans, he visited his discontent upon the Jews (Dan. xi. 29, 30). In his attempt to Hellenize them, he had the sympathy of the heathen world. Tacitus states that " Antiochus endeavored to root out the Jewish superstition, but was hindered by a Parthian war from reforming this vilest of people " (Hist. v. 8). Antiochus was also encouraged and advised by the malicious suggestions " of those who had forsaken the holy covenant." A Syrian garrison, composed in part of renegade Jews, under a barbarous Phrygian by the name of Philip, was already established at Jerusalem (II. Mac. v. 22). Antiochus also sent Apollonius with a large army to put an end to the worship of Jehovah by exterminating all who remained faithful to it, and by recolonizing Judea with Hellenized subjects. Professing peace, Apollonius fell upon the unresisting inhabitants of Jerusalem, and slaughtered them without pity (I. Mac. 29, 30; II. Mac. v. 24-26). When the men who had escaped by flight had been slain, the women and children were led away as slaves, and the wealth of the city confiscated. While the houses and walls of Jerusalem were torn down, the citadel of Acra, which overlooked the temple, was strongly fortified and garrisoned with Syrians and apostate Jews. It was also well supplied with arms and provisions so as to endure a long seige. Henceforth, until it was captured by the Jews in 141 B. c., it was the stronghold of Hellenism, and a constant menace to the worship of Jehovah (I. Mac. i. 31-36). 306. The commands of Antiochus were executed with a grim thoroughness and system. Having gained control of the centre of Judaism, the temple was dismantled and desecrated (Dan. xi. 31). With the blood of Jewish victims was mingled that of unclean animals sacrificed in despite of the Jewish law. On the site of the great altar of Jehovah was set up, in December, 168 B. c.," the abomination of desolation,"— an altar to Olympian Zeus. Ten days later, sacrifices were instituted upon it in which all the remaining inhabitants of Jerusalem were obliged to participate. Within the sacred precincts were soon practised all the immoral customs so often associated in that degenerate age with a heathen shrine (I. Mac. i. 37, 54, 59; II. Mac. vi. 2-5). Even Jehovah's sanctuary on Mount Gerizim was transformed into a temple of Zeus (I. Mac. i. 46; II. Mac. vi. 2). All sacrifice to Jehovah of course ceased. By royal decree, the observation of the Sabbath or of the sacred feasts, and practising the rite of circumcision, were absolutely forbidden under penalty of death. All copies of the law were destroyed. Heathen altars and temples were erected throughout EFFECTS OF THE PERSECUTIONS OF ANTIOCHUS 329 Judea, and every Jew was compelled in public to sacrifice to idols, swine's flesh or that of some other unclean beast, and to present conclusive evidence that he had ceased to observe the laws of his fathers (I. Mac. i. 47-49). On the occasion of the feast of Dionysus, every one was obliged to participate, marching in procession crowned with wreaths of ivy (II. Mac. vi. 7).

307. At first the policy of Antiochus seemed to have succeeded. By fire and the sword, he converted Jerusalem into a heathen city. To his standard resorted hundreds of Jews who were bound to him body and soul, for having once proved traitors to their religion and race, they could never hope to be received again within the ranks of the faithful. Henceforth, they devoted themselves to betraying those who defied the decrees of the king. Many more, terrified by the prospect of torture and death, bowed before their persecutors. Thousands fled to Egypt and the surrounding countries, or else sought refuge in the many caves and deserted regions in and about Judah (II. Mac. v. 27), preferring to endure the most awful privations rather than give up their religion. Instead of crushing Judaism, Antiochus soon discovered that his persecutions, like an electric shock, had awakened a slumbering giant. Hellenism had conquered all else, but now it was confronted by an insignificant people whose spirit no human power could break. Furious because of this unexpected opposition, Antiochus redoubled his persecutions. Rather than admit his defeat, he was ready to make Judea one vast cemetery. The example of the martyrs for the law encouraged others to follow in their footsteps; while the taste of their blood transformed their persecutors into beasts. It was a brutal, heartless age, and many if not all of the traditions preserved in I. and II. Maccabees may be regarded as true (compare Dan. xi. 33-35). Women who had circumcised their children were led about the city with their babies hanging to their breasts, and were then cast headlong from the wall (I. Mac. i. 60, 61; II. Mac. vi. 10). Others, betrayed while observing the Sabbath in their places of refuge, were burned to death. Men, like the aged scribe Eleazer, calmly met a martyr's death by scourging, rather than save themselves by seeming to be unfaithful to the commands of the ceremonial law I (II. Mac. vi. 11-31). Women, whom the ancient Orient ordinarily treated contemptuously, were given high places in the list of immortals. A long story is told of a mother who, forced to witness in succession the death by the most horrible tortures of her seven sons, exhorted them to the last not to apostatize, and then unflinchingly went to her own death. The heroes of the faith realized in part the ideal of service presented by the great prophet of the exile, for by their voluntary self-sacrifice they inspired the survivors to remain true to the law. The fact that some of them, like the contemporary son of Sirach, had no fixed faith in a personal immortality awaiting them, only magnifies the greatness of their devotion.

THE GREAT VICTORY OF JUDAISM 308. At every crisis in the history of Israel, a prophet arose to interpret its meaning, to encourage the people, and to point out the way of duty; but now for a century or more the idea had been current that the voice of the prophets had ceased (Ps. lxxiv. 9; Zech. xiii. 3-5). The extreme needs of the hour influenced the author of the Book of Daniel to break the long silence. He did not, however, have the courage to speak in his own name. Although his message was clad in strange and mysterious form (sect. 261), it brought to the hearts of his fellow-sufferers, who were familiar with the apocalyptic type of thought, the much needed comfort and inspiration. The book contains two distinct elements: personal narratives respecting the prophet Daniel, and predictions placed in his mouth; but the same practical, immediate application is apparent in each. To men confronted by the choice between a horrible death, or apostasy to the law, the hortatory significance of such thrilling stories as that of Daniel and his comrades, who defied powerful heathen monarchs in order not to defile themselves by eating food ceremonially unclean (i.), or to worship idols (iii.), or to omit the daily prayer (vi.), is obvious. Their miraculous deliverance by Jehovah, as well as their steadfastness, enforced the truths which the prophet wished to teach. The fate which overtook the arrogant persecutors of the faithful in the past (v. 20-31) was doubtless intended to assure the afflicted that Antiochus Epiphanes would ultimately meet his just deserts at the hand of Jehovah. 309. The predictions vary greatly in form, but their messages are the same. Each presents a sublime philosophy of history. They teach that every experience of mankind, the rise and fall of nations, and the misfortunes which had befallen the Jewish race, were no mere accidents, but all in accord with Jehovah's eternal and unchanging purpose, which was thus revealed to man. Now that the dominance of the powers of evil had reached their height, the prophet felt that the time when Jehovah would interfere and vindicate his promises, by the destruction of his enemies and by the exaltation of his faithful people, was near at hand. The burning question was, How long before deliverance will come? Jeremiah's prophecy that the Jews would be restored within seventy years furnishes the author of the Book of Daniel his definite data (Dan. ix. 2). Since seventy actual years had not brought its fulfilment, he reasons that seventy weeks of years (490) must have been intended (ix. 24). According to this reckoning, the deposition, or else the murder of the last lawful high priest Onias III., " the anointed one" (sects. 300, 301), marks the end of the sixty-ninth (7+62+1) and the beginning of the seventieth or last week of years (ix. 26). The abolition of the daily sacrifice came at the middle of this last week of years, so that three years and a half were to elapse before the " end of the breaking in pieces of the power THE MESSAGES OF THE BOOK OF DANIEL 333 of the holy people" (xii. 7,11; vii. 25). With less chronological detail, he reiterates in a series of visions the inspiring message that the great heathen powers — the Babylonian, Median, Persian, and, last of all, the Greek — have had their day, and will speedily be succeeded by the universal and everlasting kingdom of the saints of the Most High (ii.; vii.). Then, " many of them that sleep in the dust of the earth shall awake; some to everlasting life, and some to everlasting shame and contempt. And the teachers shall shine as the brightness of the firmament, and they that have led many to righteousness as the stars forever and ever " (xii. 2, 3). 310. It requires little imagination to understand how great was the influence of these prophecies during the supreme crisis of Judaism. The fact that the different sections repeat the same general teachings, and that each consti-

tutes a complete unit, independent of the others, suggests that they may have been issued at different times and finally combined. In the form of tracts, they probably circulated secretly among the hunted fugitives. From the first, they appear to have been eagerly accepted by the people as authoritative (compare I. Mac. ii. 59, 60). Therein they found plainly and unhesitatingly stated what they hoped, but hardly dared believe. Although immediately succeeding years did not bring the complete fulfilment of its detailed predictions, the essential teachings of the marvellous book — the proclamation that God is working in and through all history, that the right will ultimately triumph and faithful service be rewarded — became foundation stones in the faith of later Judaism and Christianity. 311. The realm of religious ideas in which the author of the Book of Daniel lived, and the hopes which comforted the hearts of the martyrs, are also clearly presented in chapters i. to xxxvi. and lxxxiii. to xc. of the Book of Enoch. The history of the world from the creation to the Maccabean uprising is traced in the form of a vision put in the mouth of Enoch, and clad in the same mysterious symbolism as is found in the Book of Daniel (lxxxix.; xc.). Here again the period of the uprising receives the chief attention. After the final victory of Judas Maccabaeus, Jehovah himself is to appear to condemn the wicked to punishment in Gehenna, and to establish the new Jerusalem (xc. 20-29). Then the scattered Jews and the righteous dead are to be gathered to share in the kingdom of God (xc. 31-36). If not a belief in personal immortality, at least the hope in a bodily resurrection, and in the speedy establishment on earth of Jehovah's kingdom (compare Enoch xxii.; xxv.), was a possession of many of the noble martyrs who defied the rage of Antiochus (II. Mac. vii. 9,11, 14, 23, 29, 36). 312. The merciless policy of Antiochus left no way of escape for the faithful but by taking up the sword. Their delay in so doing is only explained by their habit of submission, which had been forming for centuries, and by the apparently absolute

hopelessness of successfully defying, with a disorganized handful of men, the still powerful Syrian empire. At last, however, in the language of the Book of Enoch, " horns grew upon the lambs," and they turned against the birds of prey that attacked them (xc. 9-19). The little town of Modein, among the limestone hills on the western edge of the central plateau of Palestine, THE REVOLT LED BY MATTATHIAS 335 near the narrow valley which leads from Bethhoron on the heights to Lydda on the plain of Sharon below, furnished the leader of the inevitable revolt. Here dwelt in seclusion an aged priest of the order of Joarib, by name Mattathias. He and his five stalwart sons felt most keenly the wrongs and indignities which had been heaped upon their race and religion. When the Syrian officials visited the town of Modein, and endeavored by promises of royal favor to influence him to set the example by publicly presenting a heathen sacrifice, the stern old priest bade defiance to the king's command, and declared that even if they alone of all their race remained faithful, he and his family would never forsake " the law and the ordinances " (I. Mac. ii. 1-22). The sight of an apostate Jew advancing to sacrifice on the heathen altar aroused his hot indignation. Fired with zeal for the law, he slew both the traitor and the royal officer, and then pulled down the hated altar, calling upon all who were loyal to the covenant to follow him. With his sons, he fled into the mountains. Profiting by the awful experience of a large body of fugitives who, because they refused to defend themselves on the Sabbath, had been remorselessly massacred by the Syrians, Mattathias and his followers determined to fight whenever attacked (I. Mac. ii. 23-41). 313. His energy and wisdom at once attracted to his standard the pious (Chasids or Hasideans), " the mighty men of Israel, every one who offered himself willingly for the law " (I. Mac. H. 42). The party of the pious, which figure in later history as the Pharisees, came into existence during the years of Syrian persecution, and represented an intensely conservative reaction against the prevalent Hellenizing influence which was upheld by the secular party, known in later time as the Sadducean. The aim of the pious was to preserve unchanged the law and traditions of their race. In this respect they were the successors of the earlier Puritans (sect. 293). In contrast to their opponents, they also cherished in modified form the Messianic hopes of their race. To these they added the new belief in the resurrection. Thus, while they were the conservatives and the zealots, they were also in faith the progressives within Judaism. The scribes were the natural leaders of the party of the pious; but the persecutions of Antiochus forced into its ranks all who were zealous for the law: priests, Levites, and laymen. It appears to have been organized before Mattathias headed the revolt (I. Mac. ii. 42; iii. 13; vii. 13). In all probability, he belonged to the new party, for he and his sons were at first in perfect sympathy with its aims, and in Mattathias and Judas the pious found ideal leaders. 314. Their heroic struggle for religious liberty is a familiar chapter of human history. At first only outlaws hunted from place to place, Mattathias and his followers devoted themselves to putting to death all apostates whom they captured, to tearing down heathen altars, and to instituting by force the rite of circumcision, whenever it had been neglected. In time, as they increased in numbers and experience, they were able to strike open blows against the persecutors of their race (II. Mac. viii. 1-7). The effect upon the wavering Jews was most salutary, for with many hope took the place of despair; while others remained loyal to the law, because of fear of the swords in JewTHE VICTORIES OP JUDAS 337 ish hands (I. Mac. ii. 44-48). Within a few months, the aged Mattathias died (in 167 B. c.); but he was succeeded by his son Judas, who was called Maccabaeus, " the Hammerer," and from whom came the name by which his family are popularly designated. He inherited the courage and the devotion to the law which had animated his father, and in addition was possessed of an indomitable energy, a rare ability to com-

mand, and skill as a strategist which has secured for him a first place among the generals of the past. 315. The difficulties which confronted him were seemingly overwhelming, but he soon had a fearless little army at his command; while his foes were only paid mercenaries, well equipped with arms, but not with courage nor with determination. The physical contour of Judea was also favorable to the Jewish cause. While the Syrian general Apollonius was leading his force from Samaria to put down the rebellion, he was suddenly attacked by Judas and slain. His followers who did not escape by flight, shared the same fate (I. Mac. iii. 3-12). Henceforth, Judas wielded the captured sword of Apollonius, and his men armed themselves with the weapons of the slain. Another larger Syrian host under Seron, " the commander of the army of Syria," was soon after attacked by Judas near his home at Modein, as they were advancing into Judea through the narrow pass of Bethhoron, and completely vanquished (I. Mac. iii. 13-24). 316. Fortunately for the Jews, the Syrian treasury was depleted. To secure new resources, Antiochus entered at this time (166 B. c.) upon the disastrous Parthian war in which he ultimately lost his life. He left the task of suppressing the Jewish revolt to his vice-regent Lysias. Instructed by previous disasters, the most elaborate preparations were made to exterminate completely the rebellious race (I. Mac. iii. 27-37). An army of forty-seven thousand was despatched under the command of three experienced generals, — Ptolemy, Nicanor, and Gorgias. Anticipating certain victory, a host of slave merchants accompanied the Syrian army to be present at the great sale of Jewish captives. While the Syrians were encamped at Emmaus, on the plain at the entrance of the hill country, Judas gathered his followers at the historic stronghold of Mizpah, a few miles northwest of Jerusalem. He had at his command a small but fairly well armed and organized army, inspired by deep religious faith and filled with desperate courage, begotten by the knowledge that defeat would be worse than death.

All who might quail at the critical moment were allowed to depart. With marvellous skill, Judas marshalled his forces. Learning that Gorgias, one of the Syrian generals, was advancing with a strong detachment to attack him by night at Mizpah, he advanced by another route directly against the main body of the Syrian army at Emmaus. Appealing to their faith and patriotism and enthusiasm, he led his men in a sudden fierce onset which put the entire hostile army to flight, and left him in possession of the Syrian camp. Recalling his men from the pursuit, Judas stood ready to meet the detachment under Gorgias, as it returned from its futile pursuit of the Jews. The sight of their burning camp, and of the victorious army of Judas, unnerved the Syrians, and they joined in the general rout (I. Mac. iii. 38 to iv. 25; II. Mac. viii. 8-29). The spoil which fell into the hands of the Jews was enormous, and enabled them to equip THE REDEDICATION OF THE TEMPLE 339 themselves for the next great danger which threatened them. In the autumn of 165 B. c., Lysias himself led a new and still larger army against the Jews. Avoiding the fatal northern passes, he invaded Judea from southern Canaan, which was held by the Edomites (sect. 22). At Bethzur, on the road from Hebron to Jerusalem, a great battle was fought in which the small army under Judas won another crowning victory, which compelled Lysias to retire and leave the Jews for a time unmolested (I. Mac. iv. 28-35). 317. After two years of almost constant fighting, Judas and his associates, by their courage and zealous devotion, had won the religious freedom for which they had sacrificed all else. With mingled feelings of sadness and joy, they turned to the sacred city to restore the interrupted service of the temple. Renegade Jews and hated Syrians still insulted them from the frowning battlements of the citadel of Acra, which Judas was unable to capture. While his soldiers guarded against attack from the Syrian garrison, and the assembled people lamented over the desolation of the sanctuary, '' blameless priests cleansed the holy place and bore out the stones of defilement" (I. Mac. iv. 42, 43). The desecrated stones of the great altar they laid aside " in a convenient place until there should come a prophet to give an answer concerning them" (I. Mac. iv. 46). Then a new altar was built, the temple repaired and furnished anew. On the twenty-fifth day of the ninth month, December, 165 B. c., just three years after it had been defiled by Antiochus, the temple was rededicated, and its service reinstated. Universal joy filled all hearts, and found expression in solemn sacrifices and loud songs of praise. For eight days, they celebrated the great event, and decreed that ever after it should be commemorated by a yearly feast (I. Mac. iv. 47-59). The occasion was a memorable one in human history, for it represented the triumph of religious faith and devotion over material interests and brute force, and declared to the heathen world that there was something in the religion of Jehovah which distinguished it from all others. For the Jews, it marked the close of a long period of suppression and persecution, and inaugurated another filled with national hopes and victories. The four centuries between Zedekiah and Judas opened with the destruction of the temple and the annihilation and enslavement of the Hebrew nation. It ended appropriately with the rededication of the temple, the reunion of the Jewish people, and a foretaste of national independence. During the intervening years, Judaism was born, developed, tested, and not found wanting. APPENDICES APPENDIX I THE NABONIDUS INSCRIPTION DESCKIBING THE

DESTRUCTION OF THE ASSYRIAN EMPIRE Recent excavations have unearthed an important inscription coming from the reign of Nabonidus, which contains the first monumental account, thus far discovered, of the overthrow of the Assyrian empire (in 606-5 B. c.) by the combined attack of the northern hordes and the Babylonians. It also records the first advent of the Umman-Manda as an organized, united people.

The inscription has been published by Messerschmidt in the Mitteilungen der Vorderasiatischen Gesellschaft, 1896, I., 25. For convenient reference a translation is herewith given:

He gave to him (Nabopolassar) a helper,
He furnished for him a confederate.
The king of the Umman-Manda,
Who had no equal,
5 He made subject
To his command,
He appointed for his aid.
Above and below,
Right and left
10 He overthrew, like the storm flood,
He took vengeance
For Babylon,
He increased the retribution (?).
The king of the Umman-Manda,
The fearless,
Destroyed
The temples
Of the gods of Assyria
All together, 20 And the cities in the territory
Of Akkad,
Which to the king of
Akkud
Had been hostile
And to his help
Had not come. 25 He destroyed
Their sanctuaries,
Left nothing remaining,
Laid waste
Their cities, 30 Increased (the desolation),
Like the devastating hurricane.
Of that which belonged to the king of Babylon
Through the work of Marduk,
Whose revenge (?) 35 Is plundering,
He took no share.
To the sanctuaries
Of all the gods
He turned graciously. 40 He did not on a bed of rest
Lay himself down.

APPENDIX II
THE JERUSALEM OF NEHEMIAH
The minute description of the building of the walls by Nehemiah contained in the third chapter of his memoirs, furnishes the most complete data extant respecting the location and general characteristics of Jerusalem. These data are further confirmed and supplemented by the detailed account of the dedication of the walls (Neb. xii. 31, 37-40). The facts are doubly valuable because the walls which Nehemiah restored were those of pre-exilic Jerusalem. Thanks to the extensive excavations which have been carried on under the direction of the Palestine Exploration Fund, the exact location of the southern wall has been determined. The southern halves of the western and eastern walls have been traced; while their northern courses are established with comparative certainty by the contour of the hills on which Jerusalem stands. Only in regard to the exact course of the northern wall is it necessary to resort at certain points to conjecture.

Josephus states that in his day there were three walls on the north. The oldest, which was probably the one built in the days of Solomon, extended almost due east from the present Jaffa gate (following the David street) until it reached the temple mount, where it turned a right angle to the north so as to include the sacred hill. The second began at " the gate which they called Gennath" (probably the Ephraim gate on the map opposite page 172) which belonged to the first wall; it only encircled the northern quarter of the city and reached as far as the tower of Antonia (Wars v. 4, 2). The third, which was built by Agrippa, started from the tower Hippicus (near the modern Jaffa gate) and followed the line of the present northern wall.

The second northern wall was without much doubt the one restored by Nehemiah, for there is no record of another wall being built after his time until the third was reared by Agrippa. On the other hand, it is suggested by various Old Testament authorities that the ancient city of Solomon was extended to the north by the later Jewish kings, and that the new addition was called " the second quarter " (II. Chrs. xxxiii. 14; II. Kings xv. 35; xxii. 14 - Zeph. i. 10). It appears to have included the upper Tyro-po3on valley, which, because of its peculiar shape, was called "the mortar" (Zeph. i. 11).

The order followed in the description of the rebuilding of the walls by Nehemiah (iii.) is the reverse of that followed by the second procession at the time of their dedication (xii. 38, 39). It begins with the sheep gate, which was north of the temple, and approached from the Kidron valley on the east through the deep ravine which originally formed the northern boundary of the sacred area. This valley is described by Josephus (Ant. xiv. 4, 2; Wars i. 1, 3) and has been partially excavated (Pal. Ex. Fund, Jerusalem Memoirs, 122-141); but to-day it is almost entirely filled up with *debris* so that it is marked only by a slight depression in which is located the pool of Israel. The sheep gate was undoubtedly so named because at this point the people brought in their victims for the temple sacrifice. Its reconstruction was appropriately undertaken by the high priest and his associates, and after its completion it was consecrated by them. At the upper end of this ravine, where the temple mount was connected with its northern continuation, was one of the most exposed points about the city. Here stood the strong tower APPENDIX II 347 of Hammeah ("the hundred ") and its twin the tower of Hauanel. Without much doubt they stood on the site of the Roman tower of Antonia and of the modern Turkish barracks. Excavations to the north and south of this point have revealed no traces of an ancient wall, while in the foundations of the tower of Antonia are the rock cuttings and antique masonry of what may have been the original wall (P.E.F., Jer. Mems. 127).

Descending the western slope of the temple hill, the wall extended to the fish gate down in the upper Tyropoeon valley. This was the market quarter of the city (Zeph. i. 10), and the gate in all probability was so named because it was near the booths of the fish-mongers, who, as in Roman times, brought in from the sea of Galilee and Joppa their attractive delicacies. Like the modern Damascus gate, it represented the northern exit of the important street, which, following within the city the Tyropoeon valley from south to north, became without the walls the direct highway leading to Samaria and Galilee.

Whether the wall described a curve or a straight line between the fish gate and the gate of the old (city or wall) can not be determined because the land being comparatively level admitted of either, and excavation here has been impossible owing to the fact that the city at this point is thickly settled. The proportionately large number of workmen assigned by Nehemiah to this section of the wall indicates its strategic importance, for it was flanked by no deep valleys, and therefore was a favorable point of attack. The gate of the old (city or wall) was in all probability the corner gate. This, according to the chronicler, was provided by King Uzziah with a protecting tower (II. Chrs. xxvi. 9). Possibly it was spoken of as the gate of the old because it marked the end of the old and the beginning of the shorter new wall, which, according to the natural translation of the Hebrew text of Nehemiah iii. 8" (supported by the Septuagint and Vulgate), was then built between this point and the Ephraim gate, so that here part of the territory included within pre-exilic Jerusalem was left out. If, as is claimed by many, the last section of the thirty-first chapter of Jeremiah is post-exilic, the thirty-eighth and thirty-ninth verses corroborate the general reconstruction suggested on the map (opposite page 172): "The city shall be built to the Lord from the tower of Hananel unto the gate of the corner. And the measuring line shall yet go out straight onwards unto the hill Gareb and shall turn about unto Goah." If the passage is exilic, its testimony is still valuable, for it affirms that the city which then lay in ruins would all of it again " be holy to the Lord." The suggested reconstruction of the wall also conforms to the physical contour of the native rock at this point, which has been deeply buried by later deposits (P.E.E. , Jer. Mems. 285-292). This brings the wall to the Ephraim gate, which was located in the northwestern branch of the Tyropoeon valley.

South of the Ephraim gate, where the city was exposed to attack from the west, it was protected by a double wall The remainder of the western wall has

been traced along the brow of the hill. The references in Nehemiah suggest that the tower of the furnaces was found on the southwestern corner of the city near the gate which has recently been disclosed by the excavations. The furnaces or ovens which gave the name to the tower located there, whose foundations had been unearthed, were in all probability those used by the potters in baking their wares. That their shops were located at this point down in the valley of Hinnom just outsicle the gate, which from the fact was earlier called the gate of the potsherds, is clearly indicated by the references in Jeremiah xviii. 2-4= and xix. 1-6. Without much doubt, the tower was the one which the chronicler states was built by Uzziah at the valley APPENDIX H 349 gate when he fortified the corners of the city (II. Chrs. xxvi. 9).

That the valley gate is identical with the one discovered by Doctor Bliss at the southwestern corner of the ancient city, and not with the one near the modern Jaffa gate, as he suggests, is reasonably certain. The name itself is much more appropriate for a gate situated far down in the valley of Hinnom than for one up on the heights; and the names of the gates of Jerusalem were derived from their use or from something near them. The minute descriptions in Nehemiah are satisfied only by the first identification. At the dedication of the temple, the two bands started from the valley gate at the corner of the city opposite the temple. The one band went to the right, along the southern and eastern wall, while the other went to the left, along the western and northern wall. The latter went first *above* the tower of the furnaces (which must therefore have been located in the valley), then, after passing along the broad wall, and then *above* the gate of Ephraim (which must have been located in the slight depression made by the northwestern branch of the Tyro-poson valley), went by the gate of the old wall and the fish gate to the sheep gate. Also on the occasion of his midnight ride Nehemiah " went out by the valley gate toward the dragon's well and to the dung gate " and the fountain gate (ii. 13,14).

Furthermore, if Doctor Bliss's identification of the gate in the valley of Hinnom with the dung gate be accepted, Nehemiah made no provisions for the repair of the nineteen hundred feet of wall between that and the fountain gate (iii. 14, 15); but if it be identified with the valley gate the one thousand cubits of wall restored by the inhabitants of Zanoah between the valley gate and the dung gate (verse 13) conforms closely to the results of the actual measurement of the distance between the southwestera gate and the little gate discovered only a few feet west of the fountain gate. The fact that no especial group of workmen was assigned to the wall between these gates finds its complete explanation in the fact that they were so near to each other. Of the identity of the fountain gate as the chief exit at the southern end of the city, there can be no doubt; while the object of the little gate, which was only four feet ten inches in width, and too near the large fountain gate, where the streets converged, to be of use to the general public, is satisfactorily explained by the name, " dung gate." The execution of the strict sanitary laws of the Pentateuch appears to have made necessary a special gate through which refuse of the city could be carried out. It is also interesting to note that it occupied precisely the same position relative to the ancient city as does the present dung gate to modern Jerusalem.

Its position on the sloping side hill, and the fact that it was in part cut out of the native rock, explain how one gang of workmen sufficed to repair most of the southern wall. The excavations have also given us a vivid conception of its character. On the southwest corner has been found a tower base measuring about forty-five feet each way, and rising twenty feet from an outer ledge of rock (Bliss-Excavations at Jerusalem, 2-4). Between this and the valley gate, there are numerous cuttings in the rock which indicate that once it was the base of formidable fortifications. In places the natural rock has been so cut that it rises to a sheer height of forty feet, with

a shallower cutting within. It thus constituted in itself an almost impregnable wall. On the west side of the valley gate was found the base of another tower, forty-three feet in length on its face, and running back for a long distance.

The width of the ancient valley gate was only eight feet ten inches on the outside, and somewhat greater on the inAPPENDIX II 351 side. The thickness of the wall on the east of the gate was nine feet. The lower sockets of the gate are still in position (Bliss-E.J., 16-20). The worn pavement of the ancient street which led to the fountain gate and the usual drain beneath have also been uncovered.

Along the southern wall were found several buttressing towers of different sizes and of unequal distances from each other. The fountain gate — nine feet six inches in width — was also guarded by towers.

Where the ancient wall crossed the lower TyropO3on valley from the fountain gate to the ascent of Ophel, it was flanked on the outside with six buttresses, resting 011 a base wall about twenty feet thick (Bliss-E.J., 97). Along most of its course from the southwestern corner of the temple area to the fountain gate, the main street, which ran along the bottom of the Tyropceon valley, has been traced. Its width varied from twenty-five to fifty feet. It was paved and provided with a curb. Where the ground ascended, there were broad, low, rock-cut steps constructed like some of the modern Jerusalem streets, so that they could be used by beast as well as by foot-passengers. Beneath the street was the great drain, which probably followed it through its entire length from the fish gate to the fountain gate. One street was found branching to the west toward the Ephraim gate, but none to the east. On the east side of the pool of Siloam, rock-cut steps were found leading down to it and joining the main street. The southern slope of Ophel between the Tyropoaon street and the eastern wall was occupied by the palace and public buildings. About the great pool within the walls, and just north of the fountain gate, were found the king's

garden (Jer. xxxix. 4; Neh. iii. 15). Close to the wall were the stairs which led up to Ophel (Neh. iii. 15; xii. 37) of which the recent excavations appear to have uncovered traces (Bliss-E.J. 176). If the surface immediately north of the king's garden had been carefully excavated, we might know the exact location of the sepulchres of David and of the public building situated there. The absence of any trace of a gate between this tower and the fountain gate is in perfect harmony with the descriptions of Nehemiah.

The water gate was just above this tower (Neh. iii. 26), and was the most important eastern entrance to the city. It was probably so named because from it the road led down to Jerusalem's one perennial spring, — the present Virgin's fount. It opened into the official quarter of the city. In front of it, within the city, as before the Ephraim gate and the modern Jaffa gate, was an open space where the people assembled on public occasions (Neh. viii. 1,16). The horse gate was a short distance further north. The reference in II. Kings xi. 16 indicates, as does its name, that it was originally built as " the horses' entry to the king's house." It marked the northern limit of the royal buildings and the beginning of those which belonged to the temple and the priests (Neh. iii. 27; Jer. xxxi. 40).

The gate of Hammiphkad was near the northeast cor» ner of the city, east of the temple, and without much doubt identical with the gate of the guard, where one of the companies who took part in the dedication of the walls paused before the sanctuary (Neh. xii. 39; compare II. Kings xi. 6). The shafts sunk by the Palestine Exploration Fund uncovered a massive masonry wall forty-six feet to the east of the present sanctuary wall, running from the south to the north, and turning to the northwest at the northern angle of the golden gate (P.E.F., Jer. Mems. 144). That this is the northeastern angle of the ancient wall is confirmed by the configuration of the natural rock, which descends suddenly at this point into the ravine to the north, which leads up from the Kidron valley.

Inside the gate of the guard were found the bazaars at APPENDIX U 353 'which the people coming from a distance could purchase those things which were needful for their offerings; and here also dwelt a group of the Nethinim, who perhaps took charge of the animals which were brought in for sacrifice.

Combining the testimony of the biblical references with the results of modern excavation, we are thus able to gain a very definite conception of ancient Jerusalem. Although it did not extend as far north, it reached so much farther down into the valley to the south that its total area was the same as that which is inclosed within the walls of the modern town. Compared with our western cities, Jerusalem was very small, for its greatest width was less than three-quarters of a mile; but, measured by Oriental standards, the city of Nehemiah was described as " wide and large " (Neh. vii. 4).

APPENDIX III

BOOKS OF REFERENCE UPON JEWISH HISTORY

The new interest and importance now associated with the exilic and post-exilic periods have already called forth a number of monographs and articles which have made it necessary at certain points to modify the conception of the course of events presented in the histories of Ewald, Stanley, Renan, Stade, and even in the more recent brief sketches by Wellhausen, Klostermann, and Cornill. The pioneer work has been done by the Dutch scholars. In 1890 Van Hoonacker in his *Nehemie et Esdras* first maintained that while Nehemiah's activity was during the reign of Artaxerxes L, that of Ezra was under the rule of Artaxerxes II. This conclusion he has reasserted in his later works: *Nehemie en Van 20 d'Artax. J., Esdras en Fan 7 d'Artax. II.,* 1892; *Zorobabel et le Second Temple,* 1892; and *Etudes sur la Bestauration Juive apres VExil de Babylone,* 1896. Kuenen in *De Chronologie van het Perzische Tijdvak,* 1890 (translated in *Gesammelte Abhandlungen,* 1894), replied, defending the commonly accepted date of Ezra's expedition (458 B. c., before the appear-

ance of Nehemiah in Judah). While he practically proved that Nehemiah must have gone to Jerusalem during the reign of Artaxerxes I., his arguments in regard to the date of Ezra are not so conclusive.

In 1893 appeared the *Herstel van Israel in het Perzische Tijdvak* (translated by Basedow, *Die Wiederherstellung Israels,* 1895) from the pen of the late lamented Professor Kosters of Leiden in which, after carefully analyzing the APPENDIX III 355

Books of Ezra and Nehemiah, he presented an array of evidence supporting the conclusion that the true order of the three great events in the Persian period were: (1) the rebuilding of the walls of Jerusalem by Nehemiah, (2) the work of Ezra, and (3) the general return of Jews to Judah from Babylon; while the temple was rebuilt about 520 B.c., by the Jews who had been left behind in Palestine.

Although this thesis, which is strongly supported by its intrinsic reasonableness, as well as by the testimony of the earliest sources, has since been subjected to the most searching criticism, it has been only slightly modified. In his reply to Kosters *(Die Biickkehr der Juden aus dem babylonischen Exil in Nachrichten d. Konigl. Gesellsch. d. Wissenschaftun zu Gottingen* 1895, p. 166-186), and in his latest writings, Wellhausen, although nominally maintaining— with not a little dogmatism— the current view, is forced to make so great concessions that he practically admits the claim of the Leiden scholar that there was no considerable return in 537 B. c. He also suggests that the " seventh year " in Ezra vii. 8 read originally the " thirty-seventh" (the " thirty" having been omitted by some copyist), so that Ezra's expedition followed the rebuilding of the walls by Nehemiah.

The famous historian, Eduard Meyer, issued in 1896 his *Entstehung des Judenthums,* in which he throws much new light upon the life and development of the Jewish community during the Persian period. He skilfully arrays all the arguments in favor of a slightly modified form of the older view concerning the order of events; but in some

cases he ignores and in others he fails to explain away the facts, which call for a new reconstruction. Although in the main supporting his earlier positions, the book was the object of a bitter attack by Professor Wellhausen (*Gottingische Gelehrte Anzeigen,* 1897, p. 8997), which elicited a counter-reply from Professor Meyer *(Julius Wellhausen und meine Schrift: Die Entstehung des Judenthums,* 1897). Unfortunately the personal and dogmatic elements in these articles are so prominent that little new light is shed upon the subjects under consideration. Dr. Torrey gave a new turn to the discussion in his monograph, *The Composition and Historical Value of Ezra-Nehemiah,* 1896; for, after a scholarly critical analysis of Ezra-Nehemiah, he comes in all seriousness to the surprising conclusion "that, aside from the greater part of Nehemiah 1-6, the book has no value whatever as history," and that " the work of the chronicler, whatever else may be said of it, certainly throws no light on the history of the Jews in the Persian period" (p. 65). Dr. Torrey's methods are purely those of literary criticism, and in the thorough application of them he has made a definite contribution to the knowledge of the origin of Ezra-Nehemiah. Accepting his data, however, the historical student must fundamentally question his conclusions, because they involve the unwarranted and improbable assumption that later traditions, and especially those in regard to the post-exilic period with which the chronicler and his first readers were familiar, were absolutely untrustworthy.

While a few of the recent writers, like George Adam Smith in *The Book of the Twelve Prophets,* 1898 (Vol. II. p. 204-215). Piepenbring in his *Jfistoire du Peuple d'Israel,* 1898, and Klostermann in his *Geschichte des Volkes Israel,* 1896, continue to hold to the older view of a general return of Jews to Palestine from Babylon about 537 B. c., a growing number accept that of Kosters. Thus, Sellin in his *Serubbabel,* 1898, Marquart in his *Fundamente Israelitischer und Jildischer Geschichte,* 1896, (p. 28-68), and Cheyne in his *Jewish Religious*

Life after the Exile, 1898, adopt the new view as the basis of their treatment of the history.

Appendix in 357

In addition to the standard work by Driver, *Introduction to the Literature of the Old Testament* (6th edition), 1898, English readers will welcome the translation, under the author's direction, of Kautzsch's *Outline of the History of the Literature of the Old Testament,* 1898.

The critical analysis of the closing chapters of the Book of Isaiah has been greatly advanced within recent years by the fundamental work of Duhm in *Das Buch Jesaia,* 1892, and by Cheyne in his *Introduction to the Book of Isaiah,* 1896. The results of Ley, presented in his *Historische Erkldrung des zweiten Theils des Jesaia,* 1893, are suggestive but will not command general acceptance. Of great interpretative value is George Adam Smith's *The Book of Isaiah,* Vol. II., 1890. The same is true of his second volume of *The Book of the Twelve Prophets,* 1898, which treats of the post-exilic prophets, presenting admirable introductions to each. The commentaries of Bevan and Farrar on *The Book of Daniel* are the most useful. The recent book by Streane, *The Age of the Maccabees,* 1898, besides having much excellent material bearing on the literature of the Greek and Maccabean period, contains an appendix (C) which presents in a very complete form the conservative refutation of the argument against the late date of Daniel.

Although our concept of the historical background is somewhat different, the epoch-making works of Wellhausen, *Prolegomena to the History of Israel,* 1885, and of Kuenen, *The Hexateuch,* 1886, and the more recent work of Addis, *The Documents of the Hexateuch* I., II., 1893-1898, are valuable guides for the analysis of the books which contain the Priestly Code which was the constitution of Judaism. *The Book of Enoch* has been rendered easily accessible to the English student by an admirable translation, prefaced with concise introductions and supplied with notes, by Charles. The edition of the text of Herodotus, with notes and in-troductions by Sayce in his *Ancient Empires of the East,* 1883, is very useful.

The Babylonian and Persian inscriptions have been made accessible to the public in the *Records of the Past,* 1892, and in the more carefully prepared *Keilinschriftliche Bibliothek,* 1889-1896, edited by Schrader. Chiefly of value because of his insight into the social and religious life of the Jewish people is the recent *Histoire du Peuple d'Israel,* 1898, by Piepenbring. Hunter's *After the Exile,* I., II., 1890, is a vivid, popular sketch of the century of Jewish history following the conquest of Babylon by Cyrus. The old view of the order of events of course is the one followed. The first volume of Schurer's *The Jewish People in the Time of Jesus Christ,* 1890, contains a reliable summary of events during the latter part of the Greek period. A revised and reconstructed edition of this monumental work is now appearing in Germany.

A vital question in the history of Judaism is thoroughly treated by Bertholet in *Die Stellung der Israeliten und der Juden zu den Fremden,* 1896. In his *Origines Judai-cae,* 1895, Cobb presents in attractive form many interesting facts and theories respecting the origin of Jewish institutions. The articles in Hastings's *Dictionary of the Bible,* 1898, in Benzinger's *Hebrdische Archaologie,* 1894, and in Nowack's *Lehrbuch der Hebraischen Archaologie,* 1894, are concise and reliable.

The religious development of later Judaism is treated from a broad point of view by Toy in his *Judaism and Christianity,* 1890. The memorable work of Kuenen, *The Religion of Israel,* 1883, is still full of suggestion, especially in the treatment of the Persian and Greek periods. Professor Cheyne has introduced a wealth of material respecting the religious development of Judaism into his *Origin and Religious Contents of the Psalter,* 1889. APPENDIX III 359

His latest book, *Jewish Religious Life after the Exile,* 1898, is in many ways the most important which has yet been written upon the period, for it presents in popular form the results of a ripe scholarship, and is based upon the new historical reconstruction. *The Religion of the Ancient Hebrews,* 1893, by Montefiore is a brilliant and scholarly treatment of the origin and growth of the Jehovah religion from the point of view of modern progressive Judaism.

New light has been shed upon contemporary Jewish history by the *Untersuchungen zur altorientalischen Geschichte,* 1889, by Winckler and 1897 by Kost. Mahaffy's *Greek Life and Thought,* 1887, and *The Empire of the Ptolemies,* 1895, and Droysen's *History of Hellenism* give realistic pictures of the background of Judaism in the Greek period.

The results of the recent important excavations of the Palestine Exploration Fund are presented to the public in the carefully prepared volume by Dr. Bliss on *Excavations at Jerusalem,* 1898.

At last the chronology of the Babylonian, Persian, and Greek periods appears to have been definitely determined through the thorough investigations of Mahler, presented in *Der Schaltcyclus der Babylonier* (in *Zeitschrift fur Assyriologie,* ix. p. 42-61) and in the *Denksvhriften der kaiserlichen Akademie der Wissensohuften,* 1895, Ixii. p. 641-664. They are confirmed alike by the historical data and by the testimony of astronomy. Detailed questions of chronology are treated by Kuenen (*Gesammelte Abhand-lungen,* 1894, p. 212 ft'.) and by Oppert (in *Zeitschrift der Deutschen Morgenldndischen Gesellschaft,* lii. 259-270, compare Mahler in the same, p. 227-246).

BOOKS OF REFERENCE LITERATURE Abbreviations.

DrLOT.... Driver — Introduction to the Literature of the Old Testament (6th edition), 1898.

SmOTJC... W. R. Smith — The Old Testament in the
Jewish Church, 1892.

EnB Encyclopaedia Britannica.

CornEAT... Cornill — Einleitung in das Alte Testament (2te Aufl.), 1892.

ReussGAT... Reuss — Geschichte des Alten Testaments, 1890. KostWI....
Rosters — Wiederherstellung Israels in der persischen Periode, 1895. MeyEJ....

Meyer — Entstehung des Judenthums, 1896.

HISTORY

EwHI.... Ewald — History of Israel, V. (Eng. transl.

1885). RePI Renan — History of the People of Israel, III., IV., 1895. CornHPI. .. Cornill — History of the People of Israel, 1898.

GrHJ.... Graetz —History of the Jews, I. , 1891. SchJPTC... Schiirer—The Jewish People in the Time of

Jesus Christ, Div. I. I., II., Div. II.

I.-IIL, 1890. StGVI.... Stade— Geschichte des Volkes Israel, II., 1888. PiepHPI... Piepenbring — Histoire du Peuple d'Israel, 1898. TieleBAG... Tiele — Babylonische-Assyrisclie Geschichte, II., 1888.

BOOKS OF REFERENCE 361 PROPHECY Abbreviation.

SmBI G. A. Smith — The Book of Isaiah, II., 1890.

SmBTP.... G. A. Smith — The Book of the Twelve

Prophets, II., 1898.

CheynelBI... Cheyne — Introduction to the Book of

Isaiah, 1895.

CornPI.... Cornill — The Prophets of Israel, 1895.

RELIGION

CheyneJRL... Cheyne—Jewish Religious Life after the

Exile, 1898. KuRI Kuenen — The Religion of Israel, II., III., 1883. MontRAH... Montefiore — The Religion of the Ancient

Hebrews, 1892. SchultzOTT.. Schultz —Old Testament Theology, I., IL (Eng. transl. 1892).

REFERENCES

Part L —THE BABYLONIAN PERIOD OF JEWISH HISTORY

THE HISTORICAL SOURCES AND LITERATURE OF THE PERIOD II. Kgs. xxiv., xxv; Isa. xiii. to xiv. 23; xl. to Iv.; Jer. xxiv.; xix.; xlvi.; l. 2 to li. 58; Ezekiel; Obadiah; Lamentations; Psalm cxxxvii. ; Daniel; History of Susanna; Bel and the Dragon; Book of Baruch; DrLOT" 219-223, 236-246, 266-298, 318-321, 456-465; EnB viii. 828-30; xiii. 379-384, 751, 752; CheynelBL 67-78,121-128, 204-211, 237-310, 412-431; CornEAT 138-155, 169-171, 178-180, 244-248.

II THE DISPERSION OP THE JEWS

KuRI II. 174-182; RePI III. 282-308; GrHJ 313-316; MontRAH 207-209; ReussGAT 422, 423.

m THE CHARACTER AND CONDITION OP THE JEWS IN PALESTINE AND EGYPT

SmBTP II. 177-184; GrHJ 317-328.

IV

THE JEWISH EXILES IN BABYLON

SmBI II. 48-68; CornHPI 145-148; KuRI II. 98-105; RePI III. 309-322; EwHI V. 1-19; GrHJ 329-332; MontRAH REFERENCES 363 222-230; TieleBAG II. 424-457, 485-610; StGVI II. 3-15; ReussGAT 429, 430; PiepHPI 438-444.

V PERSONALITY AND WORK OF THE PRIEST-PROPHET EZEKIEL

SmOTJC 374-382; CornPI 115-124; KuRI II. 105-118;

GrHJ 332-334; RePI III. 323-360; MontRAH 238-259;

StGVI II. 15-18, 24-63; ReussGAT 431-440; PiepHPI 445-466.

VI THE LITERARY ACTIVITY OF THE EXILE

KuRI II. 147-173; RePI III. 361-367; MontRAH 231-236; ComEAT 131-133; StGVI II. 19-24; 63-67; ReussGAT 440-445; PiepHPI 467-510.

VII THE CLOSING YEARS OF THE BABYLONIAN RULE

KuRI II. 119-120; EwHI V. 33-41; CornPI 125-130; EnB vi. 752-753; xiii. 417; xviii. 564-566; RePI III. 368-373; GrHJ 342-344; CornHPI 148-150; MontRAH 260-263; TieleBAG II. 457-472.

VIII THE MESSAGE OF THE GREAT PROPHET Or THE EXILE

SmBI 71-407; CornPI 131-144; KuRI II. 121-141; EwHI V. 41-47; RePI III. 390-422; GrHJ 344-349; SchultzOTT I. 311-320; MoutRAH 264-280; StGVI II. 68-94.

Part II. —THE PERSIAN PERIOD OF JEWISH

HISTORY

THE HISTORICAL SOURCES AND LITERATURE OF THE PERIOD

Ezra; Nehemiah; Ruth; Haggai; Zechariah; Isa. xxiv. to xxvii.; Ivi. to Ixvi.; Malachi; Joel; Jonah; DrLOT 1-69, 126-159, 307-313, 321-325, 343-346, 355-391, 408-435, 453-456;

EnB viii. 831,832; xi. 270, 271, 756-759; xiii. 704-706; xv.

313, 314; xx. 29-34; xxiv. 773, 774; SmOTJC 188-225;

CornEAT 174-176, 193-218, 229-237, 242, 243. 262-270;

MeyEJ 1-71.

n

THE CONQUEST OF BABYLON AND THE POLICY OF CYRUS

KuRI II. 141-147, 202-208; EnB xiii. 417; CornPI 145-149;

EwHI V. 47-52; GrHJ 349-353; RePI III. 373-389;

TieleBAGII. 472-484.

m

THE REVIVAL OF THE JEWISH COMMUNITY IN PALESTINE

CheyneJRL 5-12; MontRAH 286-296; SmBTP II. 198-220;

StGVI II. 98-112; KostWI 29-42; PiepHPI 511-521.

IV

THE REBUILDING OF THE TEMPLE AND THE SERMONS OF HAGGAI

SmBTP II. 225-252; KuRI II. 205-210: CornHPI 152-154;

EnB vi. 825, 826; xviii. 566-571; StGVI II. 113-123;

KostWI 1-29; MeyEJ 79-89; ReussGAT 467-470.

REFERENCES 365

THE HOPES AND DISCOURAGEMENTS OP THE TEMPLE BUILDERS

SmBTP II. 255-328; KuRI II. 210-215; RePI IV. 30-44;

CheyneJRL 12-24; StGVI II. 123-128; ReussGAT 471, 472;

PiepHPI 522-528.

VI

THE SEVENTY YEAR3 OF SILENCE FOLLOWING THE BUILDING OP THE TEMPLE

SmBTP II. 331-372; KuR II. 215-218; MontRAH 302-304;

StGVI II. 128-138; MeyEJ 105-130; ReussGAT 478-482;

PiepHPI 529-535.

VII

THE REBUILDING OP THE WALLS UNDER NEHEMIAH

KuRI II. 224-231, 234-239; EwHI V.

Lightning Source UK Ltd.
Milton Keynes UK
UKOW021810261012

201275UK00009B/42/P